best **Food**
WRITING
2009

best *Food* WRITING 2009

Edited by

HOLLY HUGHES

Da Capo
LIFE LONG

A Member of the Perseus Books Group

Set in 11 point Bembo by the Perseus Books Group

Cataloging-in-Publication data for this book is available from the Library of Congress.

First Da Capo Press edition 2009
ISBN 978-0-7382-1369-9

Published by Da Capo Press
A Member of the Perseus Books Group
www.dacapopress.com

Da Capo Press books are available at special discounts for bulk purchases in the U.S. by corporations, institutions, and other organizations. For more information, please contact the Special Markets Department at the Perseus Books Group, 2300 Chestnut Street, Suite 200, Philadelphia, PA, 19103, or call (800) 810-4145, ext. 5000, or e-mail special.markets@perseusbooks.com.

2 3 4 5 6 7 8 9

CONTENTS

THE MEAT OF THE MATTER

HOME COOKING

SOMEONE'S IN THE KITCHEN

DINING AROUND

THE FAMILY TABLE

INTRODUCTION

by Holly Hughes

This summer, I got the itch to eat my way across America. I'd recently wrapped up months of working on a travel guide—*Frommer's 500 Places for Food and Wine Lovers*—on top of my usual routine of poring over stacks of magazines, newspapers, books, and food blogs to select candidates for this tenth anniversary edition of *Best Food Writing*. I had food on my mind more than ever, and I had a yen to visit some of those restaurants I'd written about. But it wasn't the temples of haute cuisine I yearned for, the Alineas, French Laundries, Fat Ducks, and El Bullis of this world. No, I wanted to eat fresh crab cakes at a waterside shack in Maryland, or pulled pork at a North Carolina roadside barbecue joint; I wanted to sample chicken-fried steak in Texas and fish tacos in San Diego. If being a locavore (the hot buzz word from last year's edition) was so desirable, how much better to be a locavore in a string of different localities?

Just before I left, I got another kick of inspiration by attending two nights of events honoring Craig Claibourne, organized here in New York City by the New School and the Southern Foodways Alliance. Hearing about how Claibourne had "democratized" food writing in his years at the *New York Times* by covering obscure little eateries as well as high-end restaurants, I was eager to go out and score some finds of my own.

Well, you know what they say about best-laid plans. My cross-country odyssey was a family vacation and instead of following a gastronomic trail we ended up choosing a route that took us to as many baseball stadiums as possible. Still, even though half the time we were eating ballpark food, along the way I worked in a few of the regional specialties I'd been longing for. There was the lake trout I savored at a restaurant we discovered by chance in Morgantown, West Virginia, and the memorable homemade chicken noodle soup at the only joint still open when we pulled into Silverton, Colorado. I made a point of dragging the family—even the non-meat eater—to experience Arthur Bryant's delectable barbecue in Kansas City. And who'd have expected that a Hampton Inn on the Navajo tribal lands near Monument Valley would serve a green chile stew I'm still dreaming about? Even the ballpark food had its highlights, like the Skyline Chili coney at the Great American Ballpark in Cincinnati and the Fatburger at Chase Field in Phoenix. Yes, the trip was a success.

Why does food always taste so good on vacation? I suspect it's because it's such a pleasure to eat a meal I haven't had to cook myself. The pleasures of cooking are easily lost in the scramble of daily life, especially with three teenagers' crazy schedules and weird food moods to account for. Many days, I feel less like a cook than a juggler, just trying to lay something on the table that's edible and marginally nutritious. It's especially frustrating when I'm in the middle of editing each year's *Best Food Writing* anthology. Here I am, immersed all day in reading about wonderful food—like Eric LeMay's lush French cheeses (p. 48), Kathleen Purvis's succulent Carolina country hams (p. 125), Robb Walsh's gleaming oysters on the half shell (p. 242), John DeLucie's melt-in-your-mouth mac 'n' cheese (p. 194), or Raphael Kadushin's divine chocolate chip cookies (p. 179) (one of several loving odes to the chocolate chip cookie that tempted me this year)—and all I could look forward to was another evening of hastily grilled turkey burgers and cello-pack salad. The way I was going, I was even salivating over Katie Liesener's celebration of Marshmallow Fluff (p. 67) and Rachel Hutton's feature on Spam (p. 76); a perfectly soft-boiled egg (Margaret McArthur, p. 170, and Francine Prose, p. 335) seemed a very welcome alternative.

Ironically, I kept discovering wonderful essays by various food writers about the shared food memories that bound their families together—from Steven Shaw's riff on grape cravings (p. 296) to Francis Lam's quest for his grandfather's food legacy (p. 319) to the tender eulogies to their fathers written by Molly Wizenberg (p. 325) and Todd Kliman (p. 330). All I can do is hope that someday my family's meals together—those few precious moments carved out of everyone's hectic day—will mean as much to my kids. And luckily, I've got the comfort of knowing that Pete Wells (p. 314) and Matthew Amster-Burton (p. 303) get as stressed out over feeding their children as I do.

Adding to the stress of modern family life are all the food issues that continue to register as hot-button topics on the national media radar. You can scarcely put a bite in your mouth these days without wondering, as my mother would have said, "Where has that been?" It used to be that when I told people I edited a food writing anthology, they would ask me for trophy restaurant recommendations. Now, they want to talk U.S. food policy, debate the virtues of organic farming, and discuss how to keep *E. coli* out of our lettuce. Ten years ago, when the first book in this series, *Best Food Writing 2000,* was published, I didn't need to have a section entitled "Food Fights." In the last few years, it's become a regular feature of the book. This year's section includes less hard-hitting investigative journalism and more testy reactions from professional eaters—like Timothy Taylor's skeptical take on precious foodie-ism (p. 2), Tim Hayward's rant on oversized portions (p. 8), and Lessley Anderson's cautious foray into the divided world of raw-foodists (p. 11). Perhaps, though, with a new administration, the time for political change has come—or so hope Jim Hinch (p. 17), with his profile of a new breed of farmers, and Jane Black (p. 30), with her portrait of the gingerly coalescing lobby of food activists in Washington, D.C.

It's a natural segue from there into the "Stocking the Pantry" section, with its different views of street markets—Rick Nichols' concern for the floundering Italian Market in Philadelphia (p. 36) contrasting with Tim Starks' account of peddling heirloom vegetables at a chic farmer's market in New York (p. 41). And Peter Jamison (p. 81) describes food suppliers that go beyond heirloom vegetables by foraging wild greens and mushrooms to satisfy San Francisco restaurateurs' endless quest for trendy new ingredients.

Even in the "Meat of the Matter" section—another category that 10 years ago wasn't on the horizon—food politics raises its head, informing Betty Fussell's masterful overview of American steaks (p. 98), Monica Eng's determination to qualify as an "ethical meat eater" (p. 137), and Bethany Jean Clement's nuanced account of a pig slaughter (p. 149).

This year it seemed time to retire another section that had long been a *Best Food Writing* staple, "Personal Tastes," what with the first-person perspective becoming more and more the norm in food writing. It runs through all the sections now—Michelle Wildgen's story on making her own mozzarella (p. 165), Joe Yonan's on cooking authentic chicken-fried steak (p. 176), Jason Sheehan's defense of the old-school steakhouse (p. 106), Charles Montgomery's ramble around Mexico City taquerias (p. 208), Mark Caro's not-entirely-impartial reporting on the foie gras wars (p. 267), Josh Ozersky's reminiscence of the restaurants of his Atlantic City boyhood (p. 254), and Ruth Reichl's nostalgic Parisian dine-around (p. 234). That powerful connection between memory and taste is just one of the things that makes food writing so tempting, even for those who don't regularly write about food for a living.

With all that reading so fresh in my mind, I was determined to make our Great Coast-to-Coast Drive of 2009 a food memory as well. Intent on powering across the continent, getting off the interstate for a bite to eat always posed a choice: Should we opt for the fast-food chain or take a chance on a hometown diner? (Remember, there were teenagers in the car—you can guess which option usually won. But at least they *thought* about it.) Watching the tidy farmlands of Ohio and Indiana and Illinois dissolve into the even bigger spreads of Missouri and Kansas, seeing dairy herds replaced by beef cattle, being startled by unnatural patches of irrigated green corn rows in the deserts of Colorado and Arizona—I made sure they didn't miss the opportunity to ponder how America feeds itself. I doubt that many of their friends have had that experience, and I'm hoping it will stand my kids in good stead in the years to come, as their generation tries to forge a new food America. After ten years of reading so much brilliant food writing, I certainly know my agenda has changed. Can food writing save the world? Well, why not?

Food Fights

THE CRANKY CONNOISSEUR

By Timothy Taylor

From *enRoute*

Vancouver novelist Timothy Taylor channeled his own
culinary curiosity into a 2001 novel, *Stanley Park*, which
immersed readers in the life of a restaurant chef. Here we
accompany him on a gastronomic tour of London, pondering
whether our culture's food obsession has gone too far.

Is a world where we can consume whatever we want,
whenever we want and wherever we want it, a happier
world?

I nearly got punched out by a cockney produce vendor in London's Borough Market recently. All I did was ask if the asparagus
was from England or Spain.

I should have known the answer. Borough Market, like a lot of
markets in the foodie West, has become in recent years a temple to
local ingredients. Mid Devon fallow deer. Wild Lakeland rabbit.
Beef and pork identified by breed and farm, just as a wine might
be by a variety and appellation. Over the fishmongers' slab, a sign
reads "Inshore Whitby Dayboat Monkfish." Species, sea of origin,
point of departure and time of day. Surely, all the information required by even the most demanding locavore.

So, there's a good chance the asparagus would be English. But
still, I asked the question, infected as I was by the spirit of the
place, the amped-up awareness, the agitated need for reassurance
that one was buying what was in greatest demand. "Where's it
from?" (My brow no doubt creased into an anxious wrinkle.) "Is it
from Gloucestershire?"

My cockney vendor had apparently been answering the same question every three minutes since opening. She reddened slightly and said, "It's English, yeah? It's all English. The lettuce. The rhubarb. Or not, not the . . . Where's the rhubarb from, Jack? And the carrots. I mean, okay, the carrots are Scottish. And the broccoli. But it doesn't really matter where the broccoli comes from, does it? Because the broccoli is like the strawberries, and they all come in a Dutch box!"

Wow, I found myself thinking, this business of connoisseurship is making us all very cranky. And not just in England, clearly. Who in the Western world isn't a foodie now? Just think of your own social scene. Beyond the oenophiles, who seem to have been around and cranky forever, all these new categories of taste refinement seem suddenly to be blossoming. The guy who swears by a $40 bottle of fruit vinegar or the $15 pound of butter. The woman with the artisanal goats-milk yogurt habit or that couple with the kid who's slurping Malpeques at the age of five.

Maybe you're thinking, Hey, these people are just being picky, not cranky. But I'm starting to think that one leads to the other. And you might agree if you'd been on rustic Saltspring Island last year watching an American tourist, who was provisioning his evening barbecue, eschew a beautiful organic chicken because it wasn't from the island but from Duncan, barely 10 kilometres away.

Even the icons of food connoisseurship in our culture seem to have taken this turn, moving from the pleasantly diverted to the fanatically opinionated. Consider *Observer* food critic Jay Rayner's new book *The Man Who Ate the World*, which describes his apparently lifelong quest for the perfect dinner, including a seven-day gorge through Michelin-starred Paris, which—of course, like there was ever any doubt—leaves him as insatiate as when he began.

Perhaps all this is merely the product of what high-brow food magazine *Gastronomica* calls "the acute culinary sensibility of the moment." But that doesn't explain the restless, dissatisfied spirit that seems to characterize the experience of connoisseurship in our day, as if our investment in refinement were no longer producing the same returns in pleasure. As if, in the words of University of Calgary sociologist John Manzo, taste itself might be better understood as "the burden of being disappointed all the time."

Ten years ago, it would have been no social dishonour if you couldn't distinguish a grain of basmati from jasmine, flank steak from onglet, tap water from Bling H_2O. More likely, you would have been considered a bit of a freak to grow irritable in the pursuit of one over the other. Which begs the question: What drives this process? If it isn't pleasure, pure and simple, what else is motivating the Cranky Connoisseur?

St. John Bar and Restaurant wouldn't necessarily seem like the best place to answer this question. Established in 1994 around the corner from the Smithfield meat market, the restaurant has an undecorated white dining room with simple wooden tables and chairs. But despite the distinct lack of foodie vibe, the place has a serious reputation. It was ranked 16th on S. Pellegrino's 2008 list of 50 best restaurants in the world. It was also named by Anthony Bourdain as the place at which he'd rather eat than anywhere else on earth.

"Nose-to-tail" eating is what St. John is all about, an approach that involves making use of the whole animal: head, feet, innards, etc. The St. John menu reflects this in studiously anti-pretentious language: Ox Tongue and Beetroot. Deep-fried Tripe and Chips. Or in the restaurant's signature dish: Roast Bone Marrow and Parsley Salad.

Chef and co-owner Fergus Henderson describes this approach as just "common sense and being polite," a matter of respect for the animals we slaughter. But it's also about finding pleasure beyond the tenderloin. "I mean," he tells me, gesticulating as he speaks, "the head alone has cheeks and little tongues and unctuous snouts, and then you have trotters and hearts! Hearts are the essence of the animal when it comes to taste."

Fourteen years ago, all this throwback meatiness, this hands-on farmer friendliness was highly eccentric. ("Yes," he muses, "you would be safe saying there was no tripe on London menus in 1994.") Since then, however, and in only slightly modified form, it's become ubiquitous. You find brawn, trotters, sweetbreads, cheeks on literally all the hottest new menus in the city. St. John didn't invent them. But there's no doubt that a rare breed, the middle-class diner with a taste for this kind of thing, has replicated to the extent that it is now a genuinely popular phenomenon.

Replication is the key here. It's what Jeremy Strong was writing about in *Gastronomica* in an article titled "The Modern Offal Eaters" when he described how offal and related ingredients had become "largely the preserve of an affluent culinary cognoscenti whose cooking and eating habits are significantly determined by what they see and read." A cognoscenti whose desires, in other words, are copied from the observed world around them.

It's not a new idea. French psychoanalyst Jacques Lacan argued that all desire was fundamentally the desire of "the Other's" desire. Retired Stanford philosopher René Girard wrote in a similar vein: "All fads and fashions operate dynamically because they operate mimetically."

Girard, interestingly, was writing about the strange social contagion of eating disorders. But the comment speaks to the broader reality of appetites, tastes and the project of self-refinement that is connoisseurship. All of us are involved in these pursuits, but none of us arrives at our desires by acting on an objective standard, not for fruit vinegars or bottled water or old-school cuts of meat. Neither do our desires reflect qualities within us that are innate.

Instead, we copy our desires from each other. Girard called this "mimetic desire," which exists only because of the model by which it was inspired and which then transfers from person to person like a gene (or, if you prefer, a virus). In which case, you might say London is now teeming with the evidence of St. John's influence and the fecundity of its ideas.

There's Hix Oyster & Chop House, just around the corner from St. John, where you'll find beef flank, oyster pie, ox cheek and grilled kidneys. There's 32 Great Queen Street, where the walls are adorned with pictures of cows and the menu tends toward large joints of meat intended for table sharing. Here you'll find rabbit brawn and sweetbread terrine, cured mackerel with cucumber and Middlewhite Ploughman.

You even find evidence of this mimetic replication in posh places like Tom Aikens' casual joint in Chelsea, Tom's Kitchen, where the décor might evoke a pub as rendered by Ralph Lauren but where this new haute carnivorism forms the heart of the menu: pork belly, charcuterie, pig's knuckles and pea soup, all served up under the gaze of enormous pig photographs. Pigs stacked or hanging on hooks. A pig's head split in two. Or one in which a man wears a pig's head as if it were his own.

These foodie Mapplethorpes may not be interested in "common sense and being polite." And yes, in the details, each of these rooms may boast their distinguishing demographic features: tattooed hipster staff at 32 Great Queen Street, City types hanging at Hix sipping Cava. But they each ape the esthetic, if not the ethnic, that made St. John (and Fergus Henderson) so eccentric in 1994. And in doing so, they reveal the mimetic process that made St. John magnetic to foodies, who then became magnetic themselves to other foodies (and then to the population at large), ideas and enthusiasms and desires spreading until today, when a striking resemblance may now be found between the hottest new dining rooms of the city.

"It's a pig," the 20-year-old waitress at 32 Great Queen Street tells me when I ask what's in the Middlewhite Ploughman. "A pig from Essex." And at the next table (I couldn't make this up, honest), a couple is talking, excitedly, about St. John. "They use the whole animal," the man is telling his date. And I can tell from his accent that he's from Germany.

"FLAVOURS ARE EMBEDDED in the fabric of the time and space they occupy . . . and cannot simply be wrenched from them," writes Jay Rayner in *The Man Who Ate the World* before proceeding to illustrate how right—and wrong—he is.

Eating at a restaurant he frequented as a young man, he is dismally disappointed, noting that "There were no famous faces to look at." Dining at a fancy-schmancy place in Mayfair with his wife some years later, the same hovering gloom. Looking around the room, she asks, "Can you see a single person that you want to know?" Stripped of people whose desires he might once have cared to copy, these rooms now leave Rayner adrift, wrenched free of the "time and space" that had lent those flavours their brilliance.

But Rayner is also wrong about the rigidity of time and space, and in those passages, the magic may be found. At another bistro, eating the classic food he used to eat with his father, his original model for the gourmand life, he sits opposite the old man, dipping bread in the outmoded garlic butter, and has a wonderful meal.

The model in place, and the desirability of Rayner's desires confirmed. The Gordian knot of connoisseurship is at least temporarily cut. The rampant, agitated quest through the time and space of fashion set aside, rendered irrelevant.

It's a parallel feeling to the one I had eating at Tom Aikens' flagship restaurant and St. John. At the first, the original concept of which, Aikens tells me, was to earn the approval of Michelin, I find a room with a hushed and reverential air. And after seven courses and a cheese tray, they serve you two desserts and then petits fours, a course consisting of a dozen obscurely inventive sweets plus a bank of test tubes with straws and a little rack of shot glasses full of flavoured jelly. If you desire the desire of Michelin, this place will be for you. If not, you may leave craving a plate of brown rice and lentils. Feeling perhaps a little bit cranky.

The next night, however, I went to St. John, which Henderson founded with little culinary experience other than that which he'd inherited from his mother—recipes that included, at one point, something called Boiled Egg and a Carrot. Copied, yes, indeed. But of blood, not rivalry.

Raised on the nasty bits myself, I left feeling full and fortunate. Not particularly refined, but happier for it.

TOO MUCH OF A MOUTHFUL

By Tim Hayward

From *Word of Mouth*

Broadcaster-food writer-photographer Hayward blogs
regularly for the *Guardian/Observer Food Monthly*, parsing the
ins and outs of the U.K. food scene—like the current mania for
outsized portions.

I'm a pretty big bloke: big body, big appetites and a great big mouth. I'm also keen on street food. I like to pick up my lunch and launch into it with a vulgar gusto involving as much of the upper body as possible. I've been this way ever since I first blossomed from an underfed, etiolated teenager into the man of substance I became. But these days I'm beginning to feel less comfortable. Not with the size of my body . . . oh dear God, no . . . my problem is with the size of the food.

Last week I walked past a fashionable butcher's in Knightsbridge. It was approaching lunchtime and, as I paused to browse a display of offal, I noticed a section of the counter serving sandwiches. These weren't, you understand, those depressing triangular plastic pods containing bread-wool, mayonnaise and a thin stratum of morose charcuterie; these were the kind of sandwiches an earl would duel to call his own. Each contained a good 250g of prime cooked meats, tomatoes that screamed flavour and a healthy subcanopy of foliage, all encased in a hunk of fresh-cooked baguette the thickness of a human thigh. That, I thought, looks like lunch, and in moments we were united. Like long-separated lovers, we hurried to a nearby park bench to indulge and it was there, to my abiding shame, that my body failed me. Try as I might, I couldn't get the bloody thing into my mouth. I tried nibbling at the sides, only for my teeth to skid off the armoured crust—I must have looked like a rat gnawing a torpedo. I tried it end-on, stretching my mouth to its fullest but, without the extensible jaw of an anaconda there was simply no physical way I could get any kind of dental purchase on the thing.

I was damned if I was going to sit in full public view, picking my lunch apart like some irritable-bowelled receptionist and so I hacked at it with a clasp-knife, swearing cathartically until passers-by began to stare. Finally, with half the sandwich consumed, a small but bloody gash in my right thigh and a jaw that felt like I'd been chewing a tyre, I wrapped the other half neatly and handed it to a nearby panhandler. If he didn't want to eat the thing he could probably hollow it out and sleep in it.

Why? Why this mad arms race to create ever more stupendously gargantuan foods?

Since man first found a dead mammoth and decided it might do for tea, human food preparation has been as much about managing size as managing heat. It's not cooking that turns a cow into a steak, a sheep into mutton or a pig into pork chops: it's the cutting, the act of reducing it to a manageable and eatable size.

The greatest triumphs of our culinary development as a species, from Odysseus's lamb kebabs through Catherine di Medici's ravioli to the chicken McNugget, have involved the reduction of ingredients into bite-sized chunks. Japanese cuisine, arguably the most refined and advanced on the planet, is so committed to delivering food that's easy to pop in the mouth that they don't use knives in the dining room.

There are places, of course, where big food makes sense. Some of the sandwiches at the legendary Carnegie Deli in New York feature around a pound of charcuterie—but there the excess is the whole point. You're not supposed to eat it all . . . even the most dedicated fresser is supposed to be stunned by it, take it apart, reassemble it into manageable sections and ask for a doggy bag.

Perhaps the most irritating manifestation of oversized food is the 'gourmet' burger. Say what you like about a compressed mince patty in a cotton-wool bun but at least it squashes down nice and thin and fits in the hole at the bottom of your face. A near spherical lump of char-grilled, traceable, organic, grass-fed Wagyu in a hand-finished, artisanal, ancient-grain mini-loaf might make your mouth water but it won't go past your teeth—not without completely non-ironic deconstruction, ideally with a power saw.

Perhaps the best illustration of the phenomenon comes from Comptoir Gascon, the 'fast' manifestation of one of London's most exciting French restaurants. They serve a gourmet duck burger—rare, pink and pristine, topped with a creamy slice of foie gras and served in a fresh crisp brioche roll with a friable, razor-edged crust that makes any kind of assault from the human mouth a technical impossibility. Am I missing the point? Am I overlooking the chef's exquisite jeu d'esprit in the meal's intellectual narrative? A culinary torture: perfection so tantalisingly close yet enclosed by a baked cage of chastity. They might as well wrap it in an eight-inch ball of barbed wire.

But it's been today's lunch that's been the last straw. I bought a beautiful, hand-raised pie. You know the kind of thing; rich meaty filling in a robust pastry crust, designed to be eaten by simple rustics in a short break from threshing. But now I can't simply eat it: I have to plan how I'm going to get into it. Preliminary reconnaissance has revealed a line of weakness in the lower crust which might reward attrition. But if I go in from that angle—like Luke Skywalker seeking the vulnerabilities on the underside of the Death Star—I'm going to end up with gravy running down my neck.

Any cook worth his Maldon salt, be he three-star chef, sandwich slinger or piemaker, will have thought long and hard about every aspect of a dish he's created. By the time he's given it a final wipe with the rag and sent it out to delight me he will have used all of his knowledge, skill, experience and training to ensure that it is properly sourced and prepped; perfectly cooked, seasoned, rested and sauced. Is it really too much to ask then, that it should also fit in my mouth?

THE RAW DEAL

By Lessley Anderson

From chow.com

As the raw food movement teeters on the brink between
fringe status and mainstream acceptance, award-winning
journalist Lessley Anderson—senior features editor for this
wide-ranging foodist Web site—deftly chronicles the looming
schism between purists and popularizers.

On a recent weeknight, two San Francisco omnivores
went on what they proudly referred to as a "healthy
date" to Café Gratitude. A raw vegan restaurant, Café Gratitude
serves, with a few exceptions, nothing that has been heated to over
118 degrees Fahrenheit, to keep the food's vitamins, minerals, and
enzymes intact.

The man had "nacho cheese" made of cashews, and the woman
had "pizza," also with nut cheese, and raw vegetables, piled on top
of what looked like a big Wasa cracker. For dessert they had a slice
of banana cream pie, whose creaminess was the result of coconut
milk and coconut butter, sweetened with agave nectar, with a
crust made of coconut and dates. There was no doubt in their
minds that they were giving their bodies the temple treatment.
Imagine their surprise if they were to have learned that, in the
eyes of some raw foodists, they were nearly eating the equivalent
of McDonald's.

Raw food has become glamorous. Restaurants like Café Gratitude are opening up around the country—from Present Moment
Café in St. Augustine, Florida, to Maggie's Mercantile in Pittsburgh,

Pennsylvania—and lines of raw packaged foods are hitting the shelves of Whole Foods. You can get raw takeout, like at Pure Food and Wine in New York City, or have it delivered to you from catering companies like Los Angeles's RAWvolution.

But this commercial success has led to a schism in the raw foods community. A school of purists thinks "gourmet" restaurants like Gratitude are seducing mainstream diners with secretly unhealthy food. These traditionalists eat very little refined oil, few processed foods, or things like nut pâtés (an avocado or the occasional handful of nuts is about as caloric as it gets). Dinner, they believe, should be salad, or maybe tomatoes puréed with mango. In their eyes, the gourmet trend is potentially destructive to the raw foods movement because its aim is sales, not maximum health. Some of them feel that diners like the couple at Gratitude are getting hoodwinked into thinking they're being healthy, when in fact they're eating a lot of excess fat and calories.

"It's an unfortunate twist to expose people to what we're saying is something different, and the world's most nutritious foods, then giving them raw pizza and raw lasagne," says Douglas Graham, a raw foods author and endurance athlete. "We miss the opportunity to make use of raw foods for what they *are,* rather than turn them into a poor excuse of mimicry of something that was never truly, if you will, nutritious in the first place."

The gourmet raw foodists counter that their pies and pizzas are gateway dishes to eating more raw fruits and vegetables.

"For people who really need comfort foods, they would not be able to start out eating simply," says Cherie Soria, founder of the Living Light Culinary Arts Institute in Fort Bragg, California, a gourmet raw foods cooking school.

And those in the gourmet camp point out that nut pâté and banana cream pie are still a big step up from trans-fatty fries and hormone-laden burgers. At the raw restaurant Quintessence in New York City, you can get the Big Moc: two "burger" patties with lettuce, tomato, and special sauce.

What both camps share is an almost religious worship of raw fruits and vegetables, and a belief that people should be eating them as much as possible, all day long. It's the groups' methods that differ: the pop-lite megachurch version of gourmet raw versus the messianic approach of purists like Graham. The megachurch may get more members, but they may not be well schooled in the particulars.

Let There Be Cheese

At a conference at the Living Light Culinary Arts Institute last August, in a small room on the top floor, raw foods author and chiropractor Leslie van Romer shared a traumatic childhood memory. Her voice trembling with anger, the lanky van Romer spoke of being forced to eat roasted chicken and chocolate chip cookies at the family dinner table.

"Is it *any wonder* we're physically addicted to sugar, salt, caffeine, oils, and flavors, and we've been physically addicted since birth?!" she spat. One must be "vigilant," and stave off cravings, van Romer said. She advocated a diet of 10 kinds of fruits and 10 kinds of vegetables a day—what she calls her "10/10" diet. The philosophy is that procuring so many types of produce won't leave you much time, head space, or stomach capacity to eat much else. "There are things being served here at Living Light," van Romer said, conspiratorially, "that aren't necessarily good for you."

Yes, in fact a few rooms down, raw foods chef Nomi Shannon demonstrated how to make whipped cream out of blended cashews, dates, and agave nectar. The audience of about 50 raw foods enthusiasts scribbled notes, and when the grayish-white paste was passed around in Dixie Cups, the attendees greedily scraped the bottoms of the cups with their spoons. Downstairs, a couple of hippies were selling raw, "spiritual" chocolates, according to their sign.

Fifteen years ago, the idea of a raw foodist eating whipped cream might have been the opening line of a joke. The movement started in the second half of the 20th century, when a handful of raw food health activists emerged, the most prominent being Herbert Shelton and Ann Wigmore, an intense woman with giant glasses, a pageboy haircut, and shiny shirts.

The diet was hard-core. Cherie Soria attended a Wigmore retreat in the early 1990s, before starting the Living Light Culinary Arts Institute, and found that the food was all blended into a bland green soup. "Once a week we had a salad we could chew, but there was something like soup *over* it." The point of the diet was optimum health, not enjoyment.

After being served a fermented sunflower pâté that seemed like a bad version of raw vegan cheese, Soria started experimenting to find out if she could make a really good version. Turned out that soaked, ground, fermented almonds had the same texture as feta. Cashew cheese "was so much like Philly Cream Cheese you could hardly tell the difference," and she could make Parmesan from pine nuts in a dehydrator with salt.

Raw, the first (and now defunct) raw foods restaurant in the world, as far as anybody can remember, opened in San Francisco around that same time, in 1993. Juliano (one word, like Madonna) discovered how to make raw crackers, the base for gourmet raw mainstays like sandwiches and pizza, when a jar of buckwheat he'd been sprouting became "oversprouted, slimy, and gross." Immobilized by a foot injury, he couldn't attend to it and it became "totally dried out" into a kind of tasty crust.

By 1997, people had figured out how to make raw versions of things like enchiladas, pizza, and lasagne, and Soria had opened the Living Light Culinary Arts Institute. Today, the school has trained more than 2,000 chefs, including Roxanne Klein of the now-closed Roxanne's Restaurant in Marin County, California, and probably the most famous raw foods chef. Klein is friends with raw foodist and actor Woody Harrelson, and she coauthored a "cookbook," *Raw*, with chef Charlie Trotter. In large part thanks to her, raw foods broke free of their fringy-hippie vibe and became associated with Hollywood and celebrity. Eating raw no longer meant having to eat green mush served by somebody with a pageboy haircut. But it also meant you were no longer eating for optimum health.

Weird Science

Raw foodists talk about how they don't need sleep. They feel light. They glow. They heal themselves from fatal illnesses. Ann Wigmore wrote about successfully treating her colon cancer by eating weeds she'd foraged in a vacant lot.

Unlike vegetarianism or even veganism, raw foodism has a halo effect that often feels divorced from a scientific understanding of nutrition. Sarma Melngailis, who owns New York's Pure Food and Wine, described the feeling of going raw on her blog as "like being on E."

Raw foodists claim that when plants are cooked, their enzymes are broken down so that the body must use its own enzymes to digest the food. This, raw foodists say, overtaxes the body. But scientists have not found this to be true.

"This is nonsense," says David A. Levinsky, professor of nutritional sciences and psychology at Cornell University. "One of the first things our body does when a particular food is ingested is break the proteins down anyway, so we can absorb them." The body produces more than enough enzymes, say scientists, to digest food without the help of the plants' enzymes.

Though some vitamins and minerals—folic acid, for instance—are sensitive to heat and can be destroyed by cooking, studies have shown that letting vegetables sit for a week or two in your fridge before eating them will cause them to lose more nutritional value than steaming or lightly sautéing them.

"If you boil vegetables to death, you'll lose some of the vitamins, but most people don't do it this way," says Bruce N. Ames, professor of biochemistry and molecular biology at the University of California–Berkeley.

However, the persistence of this belief about cooking and enzymes serves the gourmet raw foods movement well. Like the label *organic,* the term *raw* has begun to stretch to include not just caloric restaurant food but also packaged energy bars, granola, candy, and other questionably healthy items.

The same old rules apply to raw foods as they do to any kind of diet: Fats, sugars, and even protein should be consumed in extreme moderation, and one should eat as many water- and fiber-rich fruits and vegetables as possible. But the consumer can justify eating a candy bar, and even think it's healthy, because it hasn't been cooked and therefore contains magical, life-giving enzymes.

Rick Dina, a Northern California chiropractor and raw foods educator who teaches at Living Light, has an office close to where Roxanne's restaurant was. "My wife and I would meet [fans of the restaurant] who said, 'I went on a raw food diet, and I gained weight!'" says Dina. "Well, they went on a *gourmet* raw food diet, which is rich, creamy, and dehydrated. They kind of defeated the purpose."

Dina is one of the purists: For breakfast he has a few cantaloupes; for lunch, salad; for dinner, salad. But he thinks eating lots of vegetables, even if you're also eating cooked grains and the occasional piece of meat, is better than eating a bunch of sweet, processed foods that just happen to be raw. He jokingly calls people who go raw, only to eat packaged foods and restaurant dishes, productarians.

Purist Douglas Graham authored a book called *The 80/10/10 Diet*, which refers to the percentage of carbohydrates to fat to protein he believes should comprise one's daily caloric intake. A typical breakfast consists of eight peaches. Lunch or dinner might be a bowl of soup made from three tomatoes blended up with two cucumbers.

"So far, at least in the last 20 years that I have been talking about 80/10/10, nobody has wanted to follow suit," says Graham, referring to the world of raw foods cookbook authors, chefs, and entrepreneurs. "There's no product associated with it. Nothing to sell. People can do it on their own."

And therein lies the conundrum for the raw foods movement. How do you commercialize vegetable matter in its natural state? How do you sell a diet that's founded on the idea that you can do nothing better for your health than picking and eating weeds from a vacant lot? The answer is, you can't.

MEDIUM-SIZE ME

By Jim Hinch

From *Gastronomica*

Despite the gloom-and-doom predictions of Michael Pollan
and other critics, there may still be hope for America's food
chain—hope embodied in a new wave of mid-sized farmers like
these upstate New Yorkers profiled by Jim Hinch, an award-
winning Californian reporter now living in Manhattan.

The village of Penn Yan, New York, doesn't look much
like a crucible of American agriculture. Home to the
two-hundred-ten-year-old Birckett Mills buckwheat grinding
plant ("Buckwheat is Best," a row of peeling yellow grain silos in-
forms visitors crossing a bridge to Main Street) and marked only
occasionally by the defensive nostalgia of American's spurned rural
heartland—Victoriana, flags hung gamely on sagging porches—
the town, which straddles the north shore of one of New York's
Finger Lakes, mostly appears to be abandoning farming altogether.
Bolted to one four-story wall of the Birckett mill is a twenty-
eight-foot-high iron pancake griddle, black, flat, and taller than the
bookstore across the street. A sign painted below explains, "This is
the original griddle used to make the WORLD RECORD PAN-
CAKE" at the annual Buckwheat Harvest Festival—twenty-eight
feet and one inch in diameter. But that was in 1987.

When I visited the village one autumn day in 2006, a National
4-H Week banner that was strung across Main Street looked forlorn and out of place. A new video game hall was opening below
it. The books displayed behind the plate glass window at Long's
Office Supplies carried urban titles such as *Understanding Iraq* and

Take This Job and Ship It: How Corporate Greed and Brain Dead Politics Are Selling Out America. Farmers I talked to complained of having to hire illegal immigrants from Mexico to harvest their crops—local youths were deserting the fields. When I walked into Lloyd's Pub my first night in the village—down Main Street from the Birckett mill—I saw where the young people had gone. Students from nearby Finger Lakes Community College were packed inside, squeezing their way to the bar and flitting from table to table with the exuberance of teenagers eager to break the bonds of rural life. "She keeps puking and forgetting what she did," one girl said to another above the din. A boy in a backward-facing baseball cap and precariously sagging jeans approached two girls beneath an inflatable bottle of Guinness beer suspended from the ceiling. "Are you just walking around and eating?" one of the girls asked, reaching out to finger the boy's shirt. "Yeah," he said. "It's good times. Good times." The rain, which had been gentle when I drove into the village, intensified, and a few of the students ran out into it, standing in the street with their arms extended, sweatshirts spotting, then soaking with water.

And yet. Though only 1.7 percent of Penn Yan's 5,219 residents marked "farming, fishing and forestry" as their occupation in the most recent census, farming is on the rise here. And not just any farming. The farmers of Penn Yan—stolid, tractor-cap-wearing, churchgoing men and women who actually send their kids to events like National 4-H Week—are quietly living out what may be the last, best hope for America's tortured relationship with its own food. Dotted throughout the rolling hills and winding, tree-lined valleys of surrounding Yates County are about fifteen organic farms, many spreading over hundreds of acres and producing sizable yields of commodity crops—corn, wheat, soy, and hay—more often associated with the Midwest and Great Plains. Most of those crops are processed at Lakeview Organic Grain, a local mill started by a Penn Yan farming couple in 2001, which has become the hub of a functioning, medium-scale agricultural economy that manages to balance the sustainable imperatives of organic farming with the relentless pressures of America's capitalist food system. Lakeview, New York's only entirely organic grain mill, grinds more than two hundred tons of grain per week and sells it to organic dairies and livestock farms in New York, Pennsylvania, and Ohio. Its operations are big, but not too big. Each winter, when fields lie cold and fallow, Klaas and Mary-Howell Martens, who own Lakeview and farm fourteen hundred organic acres of their own, convene about one hundred organic farmers in the nearby city of Geneva for monthly meetings to swap expertise, introduce newcomers to organic regulations, and foster what has become a luxury on most of America's mechanized, corporate, and subsidy-driven farms—community.

Much has been written recently about the supreme difficulty of reforming the American diet. Not just exposés such as Eric Schlosser's *Fast Food Nation*, but more nuanced studies by writers as varied as New York University nutrition professor Marion Nestle and journalist Michael Pollan, both of whom detail the seemingly intractable compromises built into every stage of the process by which America grows, buys, and eats its food. Pollan's recent *The Omnivore's Dilemma: A Natural History of Four Meals* even outs organic farming, that supposedly wholesome and countercultural alternative to America's rural apocalypse, as agribusiness as usual, with its new spokesman Gene Kahn, founder of the Cascadian Farm organic fruit company, who sold out to General Mills and now drives a Lexus with license plates reading "ORGANIC."

In Penn Yan, however, the picture is a little different—and a little more hopeful. None of the farmers I met there drove a Lexus. They were too busy charting a middle way between what Harvard professor Steven Shapin, writing last year in *The New Yorker*, called the "counterculture" of organic farming's origins and the "bean-counter culture" of its present-day incarnation. That middle way is nothing more complicated than a dialing back of America's agricultural clock to a time about seventy years ago when most American farms had adopted simple mechanization but not the engineered fertilizers, genetically modified seeds, and chemical pesticides that characterize modern agribusiness—not to mention flash-frozen jet transport across the country. In line with federal surveys showing that medium-sized farms are, in fact, more efficient than their larger industrial counterparts, Mary-Howell Martens, speaking from behind the dusty counter of Lakeview Organic Grain, told me that Penn Yan's agricultural experiment has, so far, succeeded brilliantly. Before local farmers went organic about a decade ago, Penn Yan was "a town with a bombed-out center," she said. "Now it's a thriving village."

More to the point, farmer Larry Lewis, a friend of the Martens with whom I spent the better part of a day touring his roughly six hundred acres of organic corn, soy, wheat, and hay a few miles from Penn Yan, told me that *he* was thriving. In 1996, when Klaas Martens persuaded him, against his better judgment, to try thirty acres of organic red kidney beans, Lewis said he was "pounding my head against the wall" as a conventional farmer—this from a man with farming "in my blood" who told me he began baling hay on his grandfather's dairy the day he was old enough to grasp a pitchfork. The mounting costs of chemical fertilizers, clothes reeking of pesticides, seesawing commodities markets, Cargill and other agribusiness brokers abandoning smaller, less efficient farms—Lewis said the pressures facing most American family farmers threatened to drive him from his calling.

Then that first crop of beans came up. Organic produce, Lewis discovered, can sell for more than twice its conventional equivalent—and prices, free from government crop-supports and intentional competition, remain stable. The soil science Lewis had learned in college came roaring back as he gauged nutrient levels and contrived natural acidity adjustments. The competitiveness of conventional farming—farmers hungry for land keeping an acquisitive eye on struggling neighbors—evaporated, replaced by the Martens and their family-run mill. A life ruled by chemicals gave way to a life ruled by land. "If there are no weeds, it's because you got out in time and set the cultivator right," Lewis said. It felt like childhood again, that "beautiful country farm," as he called it, of his grandfather's. The day I met Lewis, we stood shortly before sunset on a hillside where he keeps his tractors and other equipment. Golden light bathed the slope below—the area surrounding Penn Yan undulates across a fan-like pattern of glacier-carved ridgelines and valleys. Lewis surveyed some rows of corn, which, unlike conventional fields bare of all but their designated crop, bobbed with ragweed and goldenrod. Once, he said, he would have regarded those weeds with a mercenary eye. "Now I see the beauty of goldenrod," he said. "I'm doing what I want to do."

Pollan doesn't profile many farmers like Lewis in *The Omnivore's Dilemma*. Neither does Shapin, whose *New Yorker* essay, titled "Paradise Sold," concludes morosely that the cottage-gardener image of organic agriculture is a sham concealing a madcap grab at organics' fourteen-billion-dollar-per-year market. The finger-pointing is understandable. America's relationship to its food is weirder and more contradictory than ever, with gourmet chefs on television and Cheetos going all-natural even as Americans get fatter, farms grow bigger, and agribusiness's hold on government food policies tightens. And, of course, writers like Pollan and Shapin write, ultimately, from the perspective of their readers, people like them, middle-class professionals who interact with food at restaurants, in their kitchens, and on their plates—not on farms. Pollan's book, after all, is a natural history of four *meals*.

But if America is to change its eating habits—and Pollan is excellent at documenting the urgent need for such change—it is farmers, not writers, who will have to lead the way. And so it is towns like Penn Yan that are the real crucibles of American agriculture—places where farmers are figuring out how to grow food without selling their souls or jumping off the grid. In a *New York Times Magazine* article titled "Unhappy Meals," Pollan offered some practical suggestions for bringing down the agribusiness empire—if not to its foundations, then at least down to earth: "Don't eat anything your great-great-grandmother wouldn't recognize as food. . . . Get out of the supermarket whenever possible. . . . Pay more, eat less." It's good advice. But what Pollan doesn't address is how to make Americans *want* to dial their dietary lives back seventy years. Current approaches—mostly warnings of imminent bodily or environmental catastrophe—aren't working. And so perhaps it is time to let the farmers try. Most Americans don't know farmers, but they like them in the abstract. And maybe, if they heard about Penn Yan and learned that its future depended on what they ate, they would pay a little more attention when they go to the grocery store. Who knows? It may be that what Americans really need to eat more sensibly is an introduction to Larry Lewis.

Lewis is a stolid man of medium height with a face at once cherubic and canny. The day I met him, he was wearing jeans, a flannel shirt, and a tractor cap emblazoned with the Lakeview Organic

Grain logo. His boots, black, crumpled, and muddy, sat beside the door of the log house he and his girlfriend, Annie Niver, built by hand about five years ago. The house, at the end of a dirt drive, was decorated—crammed, really—with the couple's collection of antique farm gear and carnival paraphernalia. Egg baskets, glass milk bottles, toy tractors, tricycles, a jukebox, a mechanical swing, Borax tins, speed-limit signs, and Howdy Doody dolls lined walls and shelves and hung from honey-stained ceiling rafters.

Lewis offered me a seat—draped with a folded American flag—at the kitchen table and showed me his morning reading: agricultural newspapers with names like *The Natural Farmer* and *Country Folks*. The papers, he said, ran useful stories about field techniques, and classified ads with good equipment bargains. The phone rang, and Lewis's face darkened as he talked. The call concerned his mother, who has dementia. Lewis was trying to get her into a twelve-room facility in Geneva—another expense. Annie works full time as a sheriff's dispatcher in Penn Yan, and Lewis said it was only when he was officially certified organic in 1999—three years after that first crop of kidney beans, the amount of chemical-free time required for federal organic certification—that he began making a living as reliable as hers. "We're separate as far as income," he said. "The farm is pretty much self-sustaining."

Lewis shuddered as he recalled his pre-organic days. Growing up in the 1950s in southwestern New York, he had acquired, seemingly from birth, a passionate love for working land. His father was a rural mail carrier, his mother a teacher. But Lewis had gravitated to his grandfather's dairy farm eight miles away as soon as he was old enough to take the bus there. The dairy, four hundred acres of rolling pasture and hay crops, was called High Up, and Lewis spoke of it reverentially. "I loved being out there," he said. "I got to do tractor work, driving the tractor at age nine or ten, baling hay, then handling the bales." When Lewis was in high school, his grandfather, slowed by heart trouble, invited him to move to the farm on weekdays, and he readily agreed, giving up his paper route and squeezing homework into breaks between chores. "I got up early and found [my grandfather] already weeding the garden before milking the cows," he said. "I saw his love for that, and it came to me."

After graduating from Cornell in 1973 with a degree in agronomy—where he learned soil science, pesticides, and artificial fertilizers, and studied with a professor who analyzed moon rocks—Lewis worked on farms until he had assembled enough capital to buy his own land. By the mid-1990s he owned about six hundred acres planted with a typical array of Midwestern crops: corn, soybeans, winter wheat, and various grasses used to make hay. It should have been the realization of his childhood dreams. But conventional farming, he found, was like a treadmill. Every year, prices offered by commercial processors lowered, even as costs for spray, fertilizer, and equipment rose. Most farmers responded to such pressure by buying more land, thinking to generate more revenue. But more land meant higher input costs, which in turn meant more debt and the need for even more land and revenue. Farmers waited for neighbors to fail, and if anyone found a high-paying customer or a low-priced source of seed or equipment, he kept it to himself. Lewis's two older boys drifted away from farming into town careers, and he feared he'd lose his third, Matthew, before long.

When, in 1996, his friend Klaas Martens suggested going organic, Lewis thought he was joking. "It used to be you had to be crazy or a hippie [to go] organic," Lewis said. But Klaas, who had become something of an organic proselytizer after suffering temporary paralysis in a pesticide accident, "kept at me," Lewis said, and he finally agreed to try. The result was a revolution—not simply in crops, but in Lewis's entire life as a farmer. After enduring a few seasons of teasing—"what exactly are you growing on those strips?" skeptical neighbors asked when they saw weeds poking through Lewis's fields—Lewis found himself unexpectedly reliving his hallowed youth. "We do what our grandfathers did before innovations in the 1940s and 1950s," he said of himself and the other organic farmers he began meeting. "You try to use those management practices, rotation to break weed cycles. . . . If the plant is healthy, pests and bugs don't compete with it. . . . The key is balancing. We take soil samples, balance things. That's where the agricultural expertise comes in. Like most everything else, it's hands-on that really does it."

Lewis took me to Lakeview Organic Grain and talked of his pleasure in selling crops to the Martens, a family whose kids were enrolled in Future Farmers of America—not the sharp-eyed bargain hunters from Cargill. He used words like "phenomenal" and "exciting" to describe his sudden ability to sell buckwheat for eight dollars a bushel—Birckett Mills, which buys only conventional grain, paid at most three dollars. He described his relief at no longer having to handle ominously sweet-smelling pesticides and artificial fertilizers that literally burn soil away, leaving only a pure chemical substrate. And he spoke with wonder of the Martens's monthly meetings, the novelty of farmers sharing ideas and pooling resources instead of impatiently eyeing each other's acreage. "You get to become part of a community," he said.

But, mostly, Lewis came back again and again to that idea of recapturing life on his grandfather's farm. "Farming is sort of a simple way of life, a sustainable way of life," he said. Or, at least, it can be for organic farmers. "Conventional farming doesn't require as much thinking or work," he told me as we drove back roads on a tour of his various fields. "You do a lot from your pickup truck. Now, with organics, you have to see weeds when they're tiny. So you have to be in the crop, one step ahead." Lewis mused that the real cost of the so-called Green Revolution (the introduction, in the early twentieth century, of technologically advanced farming methods that dramatically increased world food production) was not only the health risks posed by chemicals, but the loss of generations' worth of knowledge about soils, weeds, crop rotation, natural fertilizer—all the techniques passed down through farming families for growing food in cooperation, not competition, with the land.

Lewis was not describing some communal hippie paradise. The Dairyman's Diner, where he and I ate lunch with his friend, dairy farmer Guy Christianson, featured a ticking John Deere clock and silent, round farmers hunched over plates of decidedly nonorganic ham sandwiches on white bread. Lewis made vague references to his Republican political leanings and fretted about his retirement money. What he meant was that, as an organic farmer, he could again feel proud of, in control of, and, perhaps most important, interested in his work. After showing me the crumbling wooden barn where he keeps his equipment—various rusting weeders, cultivators, hay balers, and a thirty-year-old blue Ford 5000 tractor with five-foot-tall rubber tires—he marched me to a row of corn, where dry stalks rustled in a late-afternoon breeze. Grabbing a few heads of ragweed—a pesky invader that grows wherever corn isn't thick enough to shade it out—he launched into a detailed explanation of soil nitrogen, principally how much the ragweed could leach away before seriously damaging the corn. His voice quickening, he pointed to a patch of dandelion and said it signaled a lack of potassium in the ground. "I might need to change the soil composition," he said, alluding to various natural additives organic farmers are allowed to use—gypsum for calcium, limestone to lower acidity. Then he pulled a few kernels from a cob of corn, handed one to me and told me to bite it. "That's how I tell when it's dry enough to harvest," he said.

When Lewis is ready to sell his grain, he takes it to Lakeview, which occupies a long, low-slung mill building beside a stretch of railroad tracks a few hundred yards from Main Street in Penn Yan. There, trucks back up to a loading dock and exchange bushels of corn, wheat, and soybeans for bags of ground grain and organic seeds. Inside, a wooden ceiling vaults over four rows of grain bags stacked about twenty feet high. On the day I visited, the small staff was working without much conversation. Mary-Howell Martens stood behind a counter in the office, answering the phone and fielding questions from arriving truck drivers. A seed specialist named Chuck Richtmyer inspected bags in one corner, while the foreman, Daniel Hoover, a local Mennonite, drove a forklift. Coating virtually every surface was a fine, diaphanous layer of flour.

The company began almost by accident, Mary-Howell told me. In the 1990s, when she and Klaas were just getting their bearings as organic farmers, three dairies approached them with a problem. To qualify as organic, dairies must feed their cows either organically grown grain or pasture grass. "They said, 'You have grain. Could you make organic feed for us?' We said okay." Five years later, in 2001, the Martens had one hundred fifty customers, and decided to use their accumulated capital to buy a conventional grain mill that had recently gone bankrupt—a victim of consolidation and price fluctuation. The Martens, eager to avoid that fate, vowed to run Lakeview "like a co-op," Mary-Howell said. "Because we're farmers, I know what it's like to be jerked around and not treated right." That means the Martens form personal relationships with customers, give fair and equal prices to the farmers they buy from, and aim, whenever possible, to keep their product local. "I feel like a born-again farmer," Mary-Howell said.

The only flaw in this beatific scene is its future. With demand for organic produce rising 20 percent a year, and national chains such as Wal-Mart and Whole Foods Market squeezing ever more efficiency out of organic growers, medium-sized rural economies such as Penn Yan's face pressure to join the "bean-counter culture" of large-scale organic production. So far, said Mary-Howell, Lakeview farmers have gotten along and found a refuge in their new calling because "the pie (of steadily rising sales) is big enough"— the market for organic produce has been growing 20 percent per year. Agribusiness giants, however, are never far away. Cargill, via one of its subsidiaries, entered the organic grain milling business on the East Coast in 2007, said Mary-Howell in a recent phone interview. So far, they have poached only a few of Lakeview's customers—apparently "they didn't find there was enough margin" in a business still dominated by family owners. (A Cargill spokeswoman declined to comment.) Still, the presence of big players, likely to increase as commodity prices skyrocket (organic corn alone more than doubled in the past year), is unsettling. "I'm seeing a tremendous amount of agitation among existing organic farmers," Mary-Howell said at Lakeview. "The big guys are a potential danger. How we'll deal with that I don't entirely know."

A few months before visiting Penn Yan, I saw firsthand why Mary-Howell is so afraid. Reporting a magazine story on the aftermath of a tornado, I visited conventional farmer Phil Hamburger, who, along with his wife, Barb, two of his four nearly grown children, his brother, Elmer, and his parents, Harvey and Irene, farm ten thousand acres of corn, wheat, and soy on a desolate expanse of South Dakota prairie. Though the Hamburgers work as a family, their farm more resembles a medium-sized industry. The sprawling complex they call their "farm yard" features dozens of silos—some as tall as thirty-five feet—a pair of two-story galvanized-metal storage sheds, a seed-making plant, semi-truck garages, and a workshop for repairing equipment. Phil told me it costs him nearly two million dollars to put each year's crop in the ground. (Larry Lewis spends seventy thousand.) That figure includes seed, pesticide, fertilizer, fuel, grain hauling, and land rental. Barb spends much of her time in an office in the house, sorting through changes to subsidy laws and keeping track of taxes and bank records on the computer. A five-foot-tall bookshelf outside the office is lined with binders labeled "Crop Protection Reference" and "P and B Hamburger Farm—Finance." Phil and his brother drive two green harvesters the size of dump trucks, which cost three hundred fifty thousand dollars apiece and feature computer controls, air conditioning, and a glassed-in cab where Phil listens to Christian audio-books while grinding up corn rows.

An enterprise so capital-intensive leaves no margin for error, Phil said. "We used to be able to make double our input costs," he told me as we drank coffee at the dining room table and looked out a sliding glass door toward the farm yard. "With six hundred acres we could make a living. Now, to be feasible, we need six thousand acres to make a living. The margins are slimmer. You need bigger equipment to get the work done. You can't find good help. . . . If anything unexpected comes, it wipes you out. So you have to get bigger. Then, getting bigger, you still need government money. . . . And so you keep growing. Older farmers quit. There aren't near as many young farmers. You can't get in and get started."

Even with his large family, Phil said that at peak planting, spraying, and harvest times—spring to late fall—he works one-hundred-hour weeks, up to eighteen hours a day. It's a lonely life, said his father, who sat with us reminiscing about the bustling community he encountered when he arrived in South Dakota in 1959. Now, as farms die and consolidate, the land around the Hamburgers' home is nearly empty. The family drives twenty-five miles to the nearest town, Gettysburg, to attend church. Their next-door neighbor is a mile away. When visitors approach, the plume of dust rising from the road can be seen long before the engine is heard. While visiting, I stayed at a bed and breakfast near Gettysburg. When I arrived late on a cold March night, I found a group of insurance adjusters from Arkansas wandering the lawn in camouflage, firing rifles into the air. They were on vacation after a hectic fall and winter sorting

Hurricane Katrina claims, and had come to South Dakota to hunt pheasants on land rented only by a nearby farmer—another bid for financial survival.

Over dinner, I asked Phil's kids whether they planned to stay on the farm. Melody, who is twenty and was on spring vacation from college in Iowa, said she was leaning toward a career in education. Rachel, who is eighteen, talked of wanting to be a missionary. Charles, the youngest at seventeen, said that until recently everyone had assumed he would take over the farm. He is a large, quiet boy who works hard and has mastered most of the equipment. But lately, he said, he has been dreaming of "doing other things. Playing football. Or driving a truck of frozen food."

I would like to think that America's agricultural future looks more like Penn Yan than Gettysburg, South Dakota. The numbers aren't encouraging—90 percent of organic produce (which itself comprises less than half of 1 percent of all U.S. farmland) is bought by national wholesalers and supermarket chains, suggesting that even food cognoscenti remain stubbornly addicted to the summer-all-year, distance is-no-object abundance of industrial agriculture. I wonder, though, what would happen if those shoppers knew more intimately the effects their food choices have on farmers—not on some hypothetical health or environmental equilibrium, but on a real, live person, a neighbor. If American consumers knew the power they held over Larry Lewis or over Mary-Howell Martens's three kids, ages ten to seventeen, who all plan to stick with farming, would they buy that weird stuff their great-great-grandmother wouldn't recognize? Would they pay lip service to words such as "locally grown"? Would they, in short, think of food primarily as a *meal*?

Hard to say. What I do know is that, near the end of my day with Lewis, we drove to the farm of one of his neighbors, a Mennonite named Eddie Horst. Eddie, his wife, and eight kids milk forty-eight cows and raise the organic grain to feed them on one hundred eighty acres they own and rent. When Lewis and I arrived, Eddie and one of his older sons were repairing a barn. They put down their hammers, and we chatted in the westering sun. "All the kids do their bit," Eddie said, as a few youngsters in traditional black and white suits and dresses scampered out of the farmhouse. Even "the little ones gather eggs. My oldest son is sixteen. He keeps the others out of mischief." Eddie told the familiar story of tiring of chemicals (most Mennonite and Amish farmers, though forbidden certain technological advances, do use both chemical pesticides and artificial fertilizers) and realizing he could make more money as an organic farmer. "It's a more pleasant way of farming," he said. "Less tractor work. Less stressful. . . . The cattle are in the field. You walk out, take the kids, there's no farm machinery, no danger."

The mention of children prompted Lewis to talk about his own youngest son, Matthew, who had appeared to be on his way out of farming a few years previously when he took a job with a local sporting-goods manufacturer. Now, though, Matthew "is as crazy [about farming] as I am," said Lewis. The two have begun working together, and Matthew has gone part-time at the sporting-goods factory. "He'll stick with it," Lewis said. "I want to make it so he can." We got back in the car and wound through Penn Yan's rippling countryside to Lewis's log house. We passed the shed where Lewis stores his seed, and he joked that, forbidden by organic regulations to use even chemical rat poison, he had to trust his cats to keep the seed from being eaten. As we parted, he was deep into an explanation of how a six-inch snow cover in March is perfect for insulating young roots that would otherwise be stressed by the freezing and thawing of oscillating spring weather. He recalled friends from college who had taken office jobs. "They're complaining about having to go to work," he said. "Every day, I'm looking forward to getting up and getting things done."

Go Slow, Foodies, It's the Way To Win

By Jane Black

From the *Washington Post*

As one of the top reporters at the *Washington Post*'s food
section, Jane Black is in a prime position to critique the new
Obama administration's impact on the nation's capital—and
how that may shape the food policy of the country as a whole.

Can the combination of Barack Obama and a $500-a-
plate meal of grass-fed beef in a rustic guajillo chili
sauce and a warm tart of local apples and pears change the world?
Or at least the way America eats?

Alice Waters, the renowned chef behind Berkeley's Chez Panisse
and the doyenne of the local foods movement, sure hopes so. That's
why she and a group of fellow food activists invited a passel of
prominent Washingtonians to a series of homey charity dinners
during last week's inaugural festivities. There was D.C. Schools
Chancellor Michelle Rhee, sipping an aperitif near a table of heirloom country ham at the glitzy event at the Phillips Collection. At
another locale, Daniel Boulud, probably the country's top French
chef, served crab salad with green apple gelée and celery root re-
moulade under the charming misimpression that this counts as
"homey."

The aim of it all? To ignite a conversation about food policy.
With Obama, a man who actually knows the price of arugula, at
the country's helm, these activists think they finally see their

chance to recast the national debate about food. It's not about organic fruits and vegetables for sunchoke-munching yuppies and elite big-city chefs, they say. It's about healthier food in schools, programs to help food-stamp recipients buy nutritious fruits and vegetables and tax breaks for small family farmers. "Good food is not for snooty elitists," declared Ayelet Waldman, a novelist and Obama fundraiser who helped organize the dinners. "It's an issue for everybody. And now we have control of the dialogue."

To which one can only raise a glass of Champagne and say, "Bonne chance."

Because it's not that food is unimportant, even in the midst of two wars and, as we are endlessly reminded, the worst economy since the Great Depression. Nor does the Obamas' decision to retain the current White House chef, Cristeta Comerford, prove that the new president isn't interested in food. (She's a good chef. And it's essentially a banqueting job that no celebrity chef would seriously consider.) And it's not even because a pricey charity dinner—even one that raised $100,000 for local anti-hunger and farmers market organizations—is a curious way to send a message of inclusiveness. The problem for the food folks is the message itself.

"They don't have a central, core message," James Thurber, an expert on lobbying and the director of American University's Center on Congressional and Presidential Studies, told me. That, or they're not getting it out. "Is this about reducing obesity in schools?" he asks. "Is it about pesticides on the farms? It's a wonderful thing to try to change policy, but what policy are they trying to change?"

Well, they're trying to change them all. And why not, they say. After all, there's no one policy for improving food in America. To bring real change, policymakers need to look at the system more holistically—because everything, as foodies see it, is connected. Federal subsidies of grain and corn make it cheap to produce meat. Industrial meat production, which takes advantage of cheap feed, is responsible for about one-fifth of the world's greenhouse gases. Eating too much meat and too many processed foods made with corn products such as high fructose corn syrup has contributed to the sharp spike in obesity over the past 30 years.

Michael Pollan, the author of the bestselling *The Omnivore's Dilemma* and the spiritual leader of American foodies, summed it up in an open letter to the new president in the *New York Times Magazine* last October. He urged Obama to make "reform of the entire food system one of the highest priorities of your administration: unless you do, you will not be able to make significant progress on the health care crisis, energy independence or climate change."

That's laudably nuanced thinking, in my opinion. But is it too fuzzy for lawmakers to handle? Would it be better to follow other lobbying groups' lead? Whether you're Detroit, which just won $25 billion in bailout money, or the International Sleep Products Association, which is currently asking Congress to add a $5,000 tax credit for consumers to buy furniture to the new stimulus bill, the key to success is focus. By contrast, the sustainable food movement is asking for a fundamental overhaul of the entire U.S. food system—and everybody has their own ideas of how to begin. Waters wants to see an organic garden on the White House lawn and at schools across the country. Washington chef Jose Andres's top priorities are a secretary of food and mandating that gastronomy be taught in every classroom. Bravo's *Top Chef* co-host, Tom Colicchio, wants mandatory disclosure on all genetically modified food. And those are just three of the chefs who cooked last weekend.

The movement's diversity does have its benefits. It has successfully raised awareness among a broad mass of supporters. About 85,000 people descended on San Francisco last August for Slow Food Nation, the first national food conference. Many chefs—and not only chefs such as Waters, who's famous for her obsession with fresh, local ingredients—now believe that their job is about more than simply serving good food. It's about standing up for local farming and working against agribusiness. There's not a week that goes by that someone I'm talking to doesn't start a sentence with the words: "It all changed after I read *The Omnivore's Dilemma*.

But raising awareness is only the first step. The second, crucial one is to call for specific action. Too often, says Thurber, activists focus too much on tactics instead of strategy. He points to the Darfur campaign. Everybody saw the posters and agreed that the situation was tragic. But the campaign never proposed any remedies, so it never achieved any real change. Without concrete follow-up, it will be the same for Waters's inaugural meals. "The tactic here is having a dinner," says Thurber. "It gets attention, but then what?"

Chefs could take a page from their own playbook. In 1998, 27 high-profile chefs joined an environmental campaign called "Give Swordfish a Break" and agreed to take the endangered North Atlantic swordfish off their menus to reduce demand. Within six months, more than 100 chefs had joined, and President Bill Clinton called for a ban on the sale and import of smaller fish. International quotas were adopted in 1999. By 2002, a scientific report declared that the swordfish population had reached 94 percent recovery. A similar campaign against the dangerously trendy Chilean sea bass also successfully allowed ocean stocks to be replenished.

We've come a long way since Waters first pestered a first-term Bill Clinton for a White House garden and compost heap. Obama's agenda may be packed. But thanks in part to Waters and others, the word is out that food matters. And it's time for the food lobby to start making specific demands.

A food czar, which comes up on many activists' lists, might be a good rallying point. A Cabinet-level official who sees the world through a broad food lens could help disparate agencies work together to promote organic foods, diversify American farms and support local growers.

Better yet: Advocate for radical change this year when Congress renews the Child Nutrition and WIC Reauthorization Act, which includes $21 billion annually for programs including school breakfast and lunch. Currently, cash-strapped schools are forced to rely on government surplus and sales of soda and other junk foods, a combination that results in millions of French fry-centric meals. Stricter school nutrition standards and increased funding for fruits and vegetables could change that. Secretary of Agriculture Tom Vilsack indicated in his confirmation hearing this month that he sees better nutrition as a tool for defeating childhood hunger.

Choosing one issue doesn't mean that food activists have to abandon their broader agenda or leave anyone behind. When it comes to food, chefs know that it's a mistake to crowd too many flavors onto a plate. All they need to do is apply the same principle to food politics.

Stocking the Pantry

Seeking Market Freshness

By Rick Nichols

From the *Philadelphia Inquirer*

In an age of trendy gourmet markets and farmstand chic, the decline of an old-school Philly institution like the Ninth Street Italian Market concerns columnist Rick Nichols, a seasoned commentator on the cultural implications of his city's culinary happenings.

If you linger on South Ninth Street long enough, it can come to have the feel of a boulevard of broken dreams—and not just because trash bags are heaped on occasion at the very base of the "Italian Market" signpost.

A sausage-maker tried to get a merchants' Web site going. Nobody wanted to chip in, he says. SEPTA bus service got cut back, you'll hear, after stall owners complained their canopies were getting clipped.

Every two hours, workers at Superior Pasta have to run out to move their cars to another meter or risk a ticket: The fine can be half a day's pay.

And so on. It's not just trash-phobic suburbanites who dump on the Ninth Street Market. The locals do a pretty good number themselves: They're in perpetual fret over its identity (Is it going too "Mexican"?) and its viability (Whole Foods is barely two blocks north, and weekly farm markets have popped up like chanterelles).

The question of its very relevance—after 100 years of ebb and flow—is not beyond intense discussion, if you bring it up, over a cappuccino at Anthony's, or next to the walk-ins stacked with romaine on Christian Street.

That Rocky ran here is little comfort. That it is the country's oldest and largest curbside market is no insurance. That it lives for the weekends, clings to the holidays, can be unnerving.

Which is why it is of no small consequence that Emilio "Mee Mee" Mignucci, 41, has chosen this moment to step up. He is the hard-working, third-generation co-owner of Di Bruno Bros, the cheese house (est. 1939) at 930 S. Ninth. And in August he took over as head of the market's moribund and famously fractious—often stalls versus stores—business association.

You can, if you poke around, dredge up mutterings that Di Bruno's itself, by opening a glittering Center City spin-off, is part of the problem: It is one less reason to schlep down to Ninth Street.

But the far larger consensus is that Mignucci, diamond studs in his ears and a hair-trigger hug, is making a heroic stand: "He's basically taking on a second job," said Michael Anastasio, the produce wholesaler.

Mignucci isn't starting off slow. He has a one-year term. And already he has recruited other sons of market pioneers (coffee shop owner Anthony Anastasio, for one, whose own grandfather started a produce stand in 1938), launched committees on lighting and parking and trash, lobbied city councilmen, met with New York developers.

"After 100-plus years," Mignucci wrote of his new troops, "we are young and virile and ready to effect change in 'The Market.'"

Not just to clean it up without Disney-fying it. Not just to find more parking, the eternal quest. But to get tenants for the empty storefronts. To invite new housing. To revive the gritty romance; to make it sing again, somehow louder than the grumbling.

At first blush, it is not unthinkable that this time—given Mignucci's raw energy and track record, and the right aligning of the stars—the market's latest identity crisis could turn out differently, well, than the last half dozen of them.

But there is a good chance that things won't unfold quite the way, or at quite the pace, that Emilio Mignucci envisions.

There are other market conditions in play, far afield of Ninth Street.

IN A DRIZZLE one recent morning, Mignucci cradled a cup of tea and surveyed the stretch of South Ninth that heads north of Montrose.

Directly up the street from Pronto, the prepared-food shop his family owns, their parking lot has been reconfigured as a poor man's piazza, red umbrellas furled at a cluster of cafe tables.

Mignucci said 300 patrons were polled in June and their top request was "more seating." So there, he said: 40 more seats, up for grabs, open to anyone.

One step forward. Except like so much here, there's another part of the story: The back wall of the lot is painted with that towering mural of Frank Rizzo, the late mayor. But it is also the side wall of one more vacant storefront on Ninth, the former butcher shop of one A. Bonuomo, sealed up like a tomb, maintained as a memorial by his widow.

It is hard to get a precise count, but about 10 percent of the storefronts in the core of the market (between Christian Street and Washington Avenue) are empty—some relegated to storage (as are three owned by the Di Bruno interests), others plastered with "Fabulous Store" leasing posters, some (an old bread shop, for instance) scarred by fire and boarded up, others simply dark, most visibly the shuttered Butcher's Cafe at the key corner of Ninth and Christian.

For these Mignucci has plans, too: First, he is closing Pronto itself after the holidays, but just for conversion to a wine and cheese cafe. Then he wants to find someone to bring in a craft-beer emporium like the 500-bottle Foodery that is such a hit in Northern Liberties.

And why not another space filled with a bustling trattoria presided over by a headliner, say, Marc Vetri, the rustic-Italian golden boy? (It's not such a stretch! His father grew up in the 'hood! Vetri's partner, Jeff Benjamin, says if they ever did a deal with anyone, it would be with the Mignucci family.)

And what about the fallow stalls, lined in Astroturf, or home to a ripped mattress, at this northerly end of the market? Mignucci sees a future for them, as well: Get some Lancaster County farmers in there, have curbside join farm market: What's old is new!

A few blocks south, the operating stalls are piled high with soul-food collard greens and second-quality lemons, with croakers and porgies and whiting, immigrant Mexican vendors selling to African American shoppers.

No $19-a-pound Spanish cheeses down here, none of Fante's hammered-copper pots, or Sonny D'Angelo's exquisite game sausage: Here price trumps local, bargain beats organic.

Farther south, across Washington Avenue where the old ice-house once stood, Mignucci (who runs the Di Bruno properties with two other Mignuccis, his brother Billy and cousin Billy) sees something else, in his mind's eye, at least: a row of new retail, with condos above, rising from the demolition site.

Midwood Management, the New York developer, bought the property: "They must know something," Mignucci says.

So that's his wish list—a cleaned-up market, more parking, farm-fresh produce, lights on not just until 7 but until 10 at night, coffee shops open, cafes jumping, his own Pronto reimagined, looking out at that three-story mug of Frank Rizzo.

Maybe then the hip, young crowd that lines up outside Sabrina's Cafe will spend a few bucks after brunch.

ANOTHER FUTURE, though, suddenly seems just as likely as the economic crisis plays out: a back-to-roots scenario in a market born in hard times and, perhaps, soon to be rededicated by hard times.

It's not that the old ways would be replicated, exactly. Demographics have changed in surrounding Bella Vista—Italians front and center, maybe, but young professionals to the left, Mexican immigrants to the right, African Americans towing shopping baskets, Asians with their own markets a few blocks east, brimming with baby bok choy, Thai basil, and lemongrass that hasn't dried out.

Oh, and there's been refrigeration: So the business for 40 (that's correct) butcher shops that sold meat to daily shoppers on Ninth Street in the day isn't coming back; about seven remain.

But "Ninth Street was built on cheap," to quote Michael Anastasio, the produce wholesaler.

And it is that end of the trade—the bins of fish heads and ham hocks, the cheap cuts of chuck and five heads of garlic for a dollar—that could see a revival unbidden by a business association or promotion budget.

That open-air low overhead is why Philadelphia granted the curb market license to poach on a public street in the first place; "to counter," as a local historical marker notes, "the high prices and food shortages after World War I."

From the beginning, the market was a target of anti-immigrant sentiment and harangues about lousy sanitation. But here it still stands, the droopy awnings, the sidewalk chants, the raw commerce little changed in style since 1915—though the product line has a new accent.

Isgro's still stuffs cannolis to order. George's stews its tripe. Di Bruno still celebrates truffle season. But towering Mexican wedding cakes totter in the window at Las Lomas, and there are tamales and pollos rostizados, and at Lupita's Luncheria, workers spoon down steaming bowls of posole.

Yes, you can get most of this stuff—the pots and pans, the gravy-soaked pork sandwiches, the bony fish, the hair-relaxer, the cheeses, the tamales, posole and roast chicken—in other parts of the city these days.

What you can't get, of course, is the Ninth Street Market in all its faded glory—fire barrels showering sparks, peppers by the bagful, skinned rabbits in the windows.

So while the economy's nosedive may sidetrack the higher-concept piece of Emilio Mignucci's rescue, it may—without anyone's lifting a finger—give a second life to the stalls still struggling at the curb.

They may not speak Italian. But they are, still, The Market.

THE MISUNDERSTOOD HABANERO

By Tim Stark

From *Heirloom*

Ironically, Tim Stark first planted an heirloom vegetable
garden only to supplement his meager income as an obscure
writer. But with his unique produce so desired by Manhattan
restaurateurs, he's now a famous full-time farmer—and he
finally landed a book contract to write about it.

I t's one of those days at the farmers market—a bright October sky, tables piled high with late-summer bounty, the
sun so tolerable you can't get enough of it. People are buzzing
around my stand, not buying much, asking too many questions.
People always ask too many questions when they see a hundred
varieties of chile peppers arrayed before them like this.

"Excuse me, which pepper is the hottest?"

"The one in my hand," I answer.

"What is that, a chocolate-covered walnut?"

"It's a hot pepper. A very hot pepper."

"What kind of hot pepper looks like a chocolate-covered walnut?"

"Chocolate habanero. Chocolate Scotch bonnet. Like the one
in Trinidad known as seven-pot pepper." I add the part about
seven-pot pepper as a temptation for these two ladies from Port-
of-Spain, who were lured to my stand by the familiar wrinkled
brown pepper in my hand. But they're not buying yet. Like most
West Indians, they are skeptical about the pungency of my Penn-
sylvania-grown specimens. "Okay, so maybe this one only fires up
five pots," I say, cracking open the chocolate hab so its distinctive

perfume wafts toward the ladies, eliciting the expected smile of recognition.

"I just need something to spice up a tomato sauce," says a red-headed college girl.

"Throw half of this in your sauce," I advise, handing over a weightless, papery-skinned Thai chile. "If it's not hot enough, throw in the other half. That'll be fifteen cents."

She gives me a quarter and says, "Keep the change."

"Which one is the hottest?"

"This one. Chocolate habanero."

"Are those real peppers? They look plastic."

"That's because they're fresh. Picked yesterday."

"Picked yesterday? They lose their heat if you let them sit around, right?"

"Um . . . no."

"That's what I heard. They get milder with age . . . don't they?"

The man who says this has a beard, and he's wearing a shabby tweed coat. He's holding a branch of yellow Thai chiles in one hand, a branch of red Thai chiles in the other. A warning flag goes up at the back of my brain: It's him. By *him*, I mean the philosopher guy, the one who always ties me up in metaphysical knots over some hitherto unexamined property of chile peppers. While my chiles have developed a cult following, and I am deeply grateful for, say, the woman who puts chiles in her socks to keep her feet warm (if anyone would know whether the heat diminishes over time, she would, I suppose) and the sorceress who uses them to ward off evil spirits, the last thing I want to do just now is engage in a lengthy debate with this modern-day Socrates over the staying power of my chiles. All the same, I can't resist falling into his trap: "If anything," I reply firmly, "it should be the other way around. The capsaicin gets more concentrated when the chile dries out. Pound for pound, the chile gets hotter."

"Hmmm. Not what I've been told. You know, I don't like my chiles too hot. Which of these is milder?" He holds up both the yellow and the red Thai chile branches.

"Both of those are scorchers."

"But which is milder?"

"I would not advise you to bite into a yellow or a red Thai if you're expecting something mild."

"You call that yellow?" he says. "It's more orange, isn't it?"

Every one of my answers begets another question. He's just like Socrates, all right. So I'm grateful for the man in a Hawaiian shirt who approaches with a jalapeño in his hand. "Mind if I try this?" he asks in a foreign accent, Germany maybe.

"Sure, go ahead." All eyes turn to the man with the jalapeño, who does more than just try it. He bites off all but the stem, swallowing with expressionless aplomb. "Not hot," he announces before wandering off, putting a damper on the case I've been trying to make to the Trinidadian ladies.

They show up regularly at my stand, these culinary thrill seekers with uncommonly tolerant taste buds. Chile heads. The jalapeños I grow are not the wimpy version piled up in gringo grocery stores, bred by seed companies to conceal a bell-pepper meekness beneath that glossy façade. It's a no-brainer, as any MBA could tell you: Make the peppers mild and your heat fanatics will just have to buy more of them. Dilute the hot sauce with vinegar and your chile heads will dump a whole bottle of it into a vat of stew. So I guess my degree in literature helps explain why I am trying to make a living off a pepper so hot it is reputed to fire up seven pots of grub.

What do I do with all my extra chiles? Luckily, there are some unconventional sales outlets in New York City, where sex appeal lands my chiles in all kinds of supporting roles. I once sold every red chile I had brought to market—eight bushels in all—to a photographer who had Penélope Cruz recline in them for a promo snap for her movie *Woman on Top*. In 2002, my Serrano chiles were strung together into a bikini that Molly Sims wore in the *Sports Illustrated* swimsuit issue. My chiles have definitely been places I can only dream about.

I'm lucky, too, because of New York City's unique ethnic mix—people from remote villages of countries far and wide who break out in unabashed smiles at having chanced upon the unmistakable chile they remember from home. South American ceviche peppers like *ají limón* and *ají panca*; the smoky *mirchas* of northern India; the thick-skinned paprikas of Hungary and the former Yugoslavia. My customers bring me seeds and teach me most of what I know about chiles. They are my mentors and my bread and butter. If I can only get these Trinidadian ladies to try some of my chocolate habs, I know they'll be back. Unfortunately, Beverly and Frieda and all my regulars from the West Indies came first thing in the morning, as usual. They could attest to the "true island heat" of my chocolate habs.

"Excuse me. I want to know which is the absolute hottest pepper you got."

"This one in my hand. Chocolate habanero. Some say *fatalii* is hotter." I hold up a slender triangular yellow chile. "This is an African version of the Scotch bonnet."

"Those grew in Africa?"

"The seed is from Africa. I grew everything in Pennsylvania. *Fatalii* and Scotch bonnet and habanero belong to the same species of chiles. The *chinense* species."

"Chinese? I thought you said these chiles were from Africa?"

"I said *chin-ense*. *Chinense* is one of five domesticated species of chiles." Once the word *chinense* is out of my mouth, I slip into my curator-of-the-chile-pepper-museum routine. "The *chinense* has its origins in the Amazon basin." My hand instinctively reaches for a tiny, canary-yellow chile, about the size of a mung bean. "This one grows wild in Brazil. It's called *cumari*."

From Brazil and Peru, the *chinense* peppers were spread into the West Indies by indigenous people. Since chiles are notoriously promiscuous, taking advantage of every chance for cross-pollination, the varieties spawned vary in color, size, and heat. Every island has its darling. The Scotch bonnets of Jamaica, the Congo pepper of Trinidad, the "goat" pepper of the Bahamas. The first chile of the *chinense* species that I ever grew is one I named Tun-80 (it's a darts term), in honor of Keith, who played on my darts team when I lived in Brooklyn. Keith brought seeds for Tun-80 back from Trinidad, where he had supplied his village with corn, spinach, and passion fruit from the acre and a half he turned with a shovel. In Trinidad, the pepper was simply called hot pepper. Or, on Keith's tongue, "ought peppa." The first time Keith saw all my chiles arrayed at

Union Square, he smiled and spread his arms out and said, "the United Nations of Peppas."

"Excuse me," asks an old lady. "What is that in your hand?"

"A chile pepper."

"It's beautiful. Can I chop it up in a salad?"

"Not unless you want smoke coming out of your ears."

"It's not as hot as a jalapeño, is it?"

"It's fifty times hotter than a jalapeño."

"Fifty times hotter than a jalapeño?" According to the Scoville heart unit scale, the habanero is, indeed, fifty times hotter than a jalapeño. Just how hot is fifty times hotter than a jalapeño? "If you give a ought peppa to a monkey," according to Keith, "the monkey will hate you for life."

The lady who wanted to put my pepper in her salad scoots away in horror. "But it has great flavor," I say in her wake.

"How can a pepper fifty times hotter than a jalapeño have any flavor?" It's Socrates again, with another question.

I reach for a thick-skinned, reddish-orange pepper, about the size of a jalapeño and with a fold at the tip. The pepper, called pimiento in Trinidad, gives off that daunting habanero reek when I take a bite. But it's not hot at all. The Trinidadian pimiento is also called seasoning or flavoring pepper. Most of the islands have their own versions of it. The best known of these is *ají dulce*, which is shaped like a dented spinning top. Grocery stores in Latino neighborhoods carry *ají dulce*, also known as *ajicito*, which has roots in Puerto Rico. At my stand, *ají dulce* once stopped a young lady from Venezuela in her tracks. As I was talking to her, a man who had grown up in Cuba pulled up and explained that he knew the same variety by the name of *chile cachuca*. "We just call that seasonin' peppa," chimed in a Jamaican girl. Only in New York could such an obscure pepper engage four different people in conversation. The seasoning pepper brings a new layer of flavor to anything it touches, according to Beverly Williams, my biggest customer for that pepper. She stir-fries them with vegetables and chops them up into salads. Seasoning peppers are the key ingredient, along with Caribbean *cilantro*, in a classic Trinidadian condiment known as seasonin'.

While Caribbean cuisine also features the eye-watering *chinense* varieties, this does not mean the habanero is off-limits for all but the masochists and the jerk barbecuers. For instance, an unripe Scotch bonnet or habanero is typically dropped whole into a pot of boiling rice, then plucked from the fluffy finished product, thereby imparting a fraction of its heat along with that much-desired aroma. But woe unto the taste buds if the pepper is punctured while the rice boils!

"So which is the milder of these two?" Socrates asks, holding up the red Thai chile branch along with a cluster of Japanese *santaka* chiles. Two fiery cayennes.

"Machs nix," I answer, a Pennsylvania Dutch expression that means "six of one, half a dozen of the other." I shouldn't expect him to understand Pennsylvania Dutch, but I'm getting more than a bit testy. For all my chatter, the past 20 minutes of a fine Indian summer of an afternoon has netted me all of 25 cents. And only 15 of those cents were earned.

"What's that mean? I don't like my peppers too hot, you know."

"Both of those are extremely hot."

"But peppers get milder over time, don't they?"

Out of exasperation, the shark in me finally rises to the surface. "So if they get milder, then by all means buy either pepper and wait a long time before you eat it."

"Hmm." Before Socrates can formulate another question, the guy who ate the jalapeño is back. "There is nothing hot in this whole market," he says, looking at the peppers arrayed on my table. So I hand him a Bulgarian carrot pepper, a few notches above the jalapeño on the Scoville scale. He inhales the pepper, then gives me the thumbs-down.

I give him a serrano: "Nah!"

A cayenne: "That does not do much for me." He is in search of that quasi-religious experience known to all chile heads: the endorphin rush—a euphoric sense of indestructibility achievable only through a sort of crucifixion of the tongue.

I don't like giving peppers away, but I'm in a bind here. The Trinidadians are watching intently. "He says your peppers are not hot," says one. I look at the chocolate habanero in my hand and then at the chile head. But no. I couldn't. Or could I?

I'm beginning to feel a little high. It occurs to me that the pimiento I just ate is doing the endorphin thing to my inner constitution. In a variation on Pavlov's salivating dog, my body, having been alerted by the invasion of habanero perfume, is experiencing a profound sense of relief over the absence of the anticipated pain.

So what the heck! I hand over the hab and Mr. Chile Head gulps it down. For a moment, he doesn't seem the least bit affected. But then he starts making this huffing noise. Huffing and puffing as his eyes open wide. His mouth opens, too, and he tries fanning it with his hand. Then he begins to hop. Hop, hop, hop. "Try milk!" I call after him as he hops away. "Or thumbscrews."

Call me evil. Call me a salesman. I sold five pounds of chocolate habaneros to those ladies from Trinidad.

Illegal Cheese

By Eric LeMay

From *Gastronomica*

For those who love European raw-milk cheeses, the U.S.
ban on importing them can be maddening. LeMay—
a poet, essayist, writing teacher, and cheese-lover based in
Cambridge, Massachusetts—registers this passionate plea
for true *fromage*, an excerpt from his upcoming book
Immortal Milk.

Smugglers shouldn't be users. I knew this narcotics-
trafficking truism from the crime movies I've imbibed
over the years, movies in which an imposing drug lord or cartel *jefe*
has to clean up after some toady who should have delivered three
keys of coke but hasn't because, as the squirming toady eventually
confesses, "I had to has me a taste!" The cleanup usually involves
the toady's skull spattering on a white wall. These scenes always
struck me as forced, even for Hollywood. Surely a real trafficker
would never let his desire so grossly skewer his judgment. Surely
he'd know how it—and he—would end.

Yet, as I walked toward the U.S. Customs Inspectors, with a
huge scarlet "A" (for "Animal Products") scrawled on my declara-
tion form and six shrink-wrapped bundles of illegal cheese stuffed
in my suitcase, I understood the toady. I didn't care about the inspectors glowering at me above their mustaches or the conse-
quences of breaking a federal law. I cared about the cheese. What if
they opened it and spoiled it? What if they took it? Would I have
time to jam any of it into my mouth? I had come too far with it,
waited too long. I had to has me a taste.

How did this happen? How did I devolve into a lawless, heedless, lacto-obsessed cheese smuggler?

The immediate answer is that I was returning from Paris, where cheese isn't caught in the stranglehold of murderous laws. I mean this literally. The Brie or Camembert you buy here has been murdered.

Let me explain. Cheese, as you know, comes from milk, and milk from cows, goats, sheep, and the odd buffalo. Now if this milk isn't extracted by a machine out of the abused udders of animals that are caged in steel stalls, injected with hormones, and fed on bioengineered fodder, but, for example, hand-milked from Alpine or Saanen goats by farmers who have raised them for generations and herded them through the Loire Valley's rich pastures all spring and summer so the goats could munch on lush grass, clover, wildflowers, and herbs, then this milk will have a flavor unlike any other in the world. It will express the whole of its creation—the land on which it's made, the animals from which it's made, and people who make it. In its *terroir*, cheese is like wine, as bound to the land as the vines that yield Sancerre or Saumur-Champigny. Think of goats as big, fluffy grapes.

Here's the problem: the delicacy and nuance of flavor that make cheese a supreme expression of place come from microorganisms that live in the milk, and it's these miniscule flavor-makers that the Food and Drug Administration demands farmers kill. You might not be a fan of bacteria. You might consider Louis Pasteur a hero. But when milk gets pasteurized, the bacteria and enzymes that were in the raw milk die and, with them, much of the milk's flavor.

The FDA would have you believe that raw-milk cheese can cause diseases such as listeriosis or salmonellosis, and if you're pregnant, elderly, or have a bad immune system, this might be true. But in countries such as France, where these microorganisms aren't heated out of existence or left to die over a span of sixty days as U.S. law requires, most of the cases of food poisoning that do involve cheese are the result of pasteurized cheeses. Sure, there are bad bacteria, but cheese makers can avoid them without murdering their milk. They've done so for centuries in the Pyrénées mountains and the hamlets of Provence.

Of course, if you don't care about the rare flavors that milk can create or if you need to ship your milk to a factory, pasteurization is great. Extending milk's shelf life allows you to make cheese en masse, like the monstrous Kraft Foods. (In fact, Kraft makes the pasteurized, processed, cheese-food-but-not-really-cheese product for which we're known: American cheese.) Pasteurization also makes your milk consistent. As the legendary *fromager* Pierre Androuët explains, "All pasteurized-milk cheeses of whatever sort, mild or strong, have one point in common with respect to their flavor: their blandness."

Androuët is kind. More often than not, when artisan cheese makers, mongers, and enthusiasts taste a cheese that's been cleansed of its living, taste-giving microorganisms, they'll say it's "dead."

"This cheese is like—'Fuck off.'"

It's a challenge to describe the flavor of an excellent French cheese. My love and I had come to Paris in search of the mythic cheeses said to thrive an ocean away from the FDA. At longing last, we were in our tiny rental in the Marais, hovered over a single plate, tasting a Langres. This cheese, as it's described in one rather bland guide,

> originates from the high plains of Langres in Champagne. It is shaped like a cylinder and has a deep well on top called a *fontaine*, a kind of basin into which Champagne or *marc* may be poured. This is a pleasant way to eat this cheese, and is characteristic of wine-producing regions.

We didn't have the funds for Champagne on this evening, but we had managed to get tipsy on a serviceable *vin de pays*, which is also a pleasant way to eat a Langres.

"It doesn't play well with others," she continued, the thick smack of *pâté* slowing her speech. "It doesn't respect lesser cheese."

"It's like a road trip through Arizona in an old Buick," I offered.

"It's like Charlus, but early in Proust."

"It has a half-life inside your teeth."

"It has ideas."

"It gradually peels off the skin on the roof of your mouth."

"It attains absolute crustiness and absolute creaminess."

The problem with most descriptions of cheese, the sort you find in guides, is that they're reductive. Officially, the Langres is sticky, wet, shiny, firm, and supple, "melts in the mouth," and has "a complex mixture of aromas." Such descriptions convey, at best, a blueprint of the tasting experience, like a score does a symphony. They're useful, I suppose, in their reliability. Anyone can read that a salt-washed Langres is "salty," then taste its saltiness, but not everyone will taste in it the brilliant and irascible character of Proust's Baron Palamède de Charlus. Yet these more personal descriptions capture the experience of a Langres. It sparks associative leaps, unforeseen flashbacks, inspired flights of poetry and desire. Its riches reveal your own. W. H. Auden once remarked that when you read a book, the book also reads you. The same holds true for cheese: it tastes you.

On the whole, the cheeses we met in Paris found us tolerable. A Signal Savoyard that cracked in our mouth like a mudcake appreciated our humility. It had seen more of the world than we had, and we deferred to it. A Rocamadour saw that, although we were Americans, we could appreciate the fleshier, creamier forms that fill the canvases of Rubens and Fragonard. "It responds like chub," observed my perfectly tummied love. We were plucky enough for a Tomme de Brebis, which tried to toughen us up with sharp punches to the palate. And a floral Pélardon believed that our urban lives hadn't ruined us for country pleasures, that we could still respond to the idyllic. "This," said my love, "is what milkmaid's cheeks should taste like."

Why is cheese so delicious?

You'll find a few answers out there, but none of them are entirely satisfying. There's an appeal to history: since humans first cultivated goats and sheep, about ten thousand years ago (give or take a few millennia), they've made cheese. As evidence, you can cite a Sumerian frieze from around 3000 B.C.E. that refers to cheese, and cheese making is portrayed on a mural in an Egyptian tomb that's roughly the same age. There's also the Cyclops in Homer's *Odyssey*. He has a cave full of homemade cheese and keeps his one eye on the goats and ewes he milks to make it. By the rise of classical Rome, cheese making was an art. In his *Natural History* Pliny catalogs the variety of cheeses that Romans eat, and in *De Re Rustica* Columella describes a process of cheese making not so different from some used today. Cheese has been around a long time.

Still, that doesn't explain why it's good. At best, the history of cheese, as well as its presence throughout much of the world, proves it's a survivor. No dodo of gastronomical Darwinism, cheese thrives in cultures and climes as diverse as Canada and India. It can even come back from extinction, as did the wonderful Spanish Queso de la Garrotxa. Yet cheese has survived in part because it's good; it isn't good because it survived. To say it another way, cheese isn't delicious just because it's *been* delicious.

And it's not delicious because it's nutritious, either. That's another answer that you'll find: cheese has protein, vitamins, calcium, phosphorus, and may even prevent tooth decay. I suppose cheese makers need to woo the huge demographic of Americans watching their saturated fat and waistlines, but ugh. Who'd want to eat with them? Pleasure doesn't matter when you see food only as chemistry, and "deliciousness" doesn't appear under the "Nutritional Facts" on food labels. Let the inch-pinchers and heart healthies know: cheese can't be reduced to mere fact. It teems with too much life.

This liveliness may be the very reason cheese is delicious. Max McCalman, the *maître fromager* at Artisanal, sees the link between cheese and life. Cheese, he says, is "the ancient, venerable method of preserving the precious, sustaining fluid of the mother animal." He's talking about milk, that very first taste which ewes, kids, and calves experience. I'd add us. We're another mothered animal, and for those of us who didn't go straight to some Kraft-like formula, milk is our original flavor, the primordial way we're given life. Milk is what we're fixated on before we can focus, when we're little more than pudgy mouths at the nipple. Indeed, the psychoanalyst (and Frenchman) Jacques Lacan famously claimed that these milky moments, before we're aware of the world beyond ourselves or even that we have selves distinct and tragically cut off from the warm breast that feeds us, are as close as we ever come to paradise. In milk, we taste Eden.

And cheese is *condensed* milk. It's milk in its most concentrated form. (According to McCalman, you need about ten pounds of cow's milk to make one pound of cheese.) When you eat cheese, you mainline the uncut elixir of life.

No wonder I'd break laws for it.

Yet if milk's prelapsarian flavor is an answer, it's only half an answer. The other half lies in a cheese called Livarot, which we discovered when we chanced on perhaps the finest *fromager* in Paris, Pascal Trotte.

The shop is a modest one on the Rue Saint-Antoine, a few blocks west of the Bastille. Outside, a chalkboard describes the current state of the cheeses, which when we arrived were benefiting from the fresh spring grasses. Inside, it's a gauntlet. Rows of cheese flank you, and though there aren't many, each has a place and a placard. The smaller cheeses are piled in pyramids or baskets, and the larger ones subtly glow with more shades of butter and cream than you knew existed. If you linger around, you'll see pictures of the caves where the cheeses are aged, for Pascal Trotte is also an *affineur*, which means he's brought these cheeses to perfection.

But you probably won't linger. The shop's size, about the width of a grocery aisle, forces you onto one of the *fromagers*, who's likely to gaze at you with that blank expectant look Parisians reserve for Americans: "I acknowledge you are human, but that is all I acknowledge."

That, at least, is how we interpreted the look of the striking corvine man in his late forties who may or may not have been Pascal Trotte.

My love is the one of us who has French, so she asked about the cheeses as I looked on with Pavlovian anticipation and feigned indifference. It didn't go well. For the last few years she'd been reading Zola and Balzac, not confronting *fromagers*. After we left, she translated the exchange:

"Hello, sir."

"Hello, mademoiselle."

"I was hoping you might be able to help me. We'd like to buy a cheese, but we don't know very much. Could you please help me to buy a cheese made from the milk of a horse?"

The man remained stony faced. "That does not exist."

"Huh?"

"Perhaps you mean goat?"

Love laughed, "Of course, yes."

The man did not. "What are you looking for? What do you like?"

Love got flustered.

"Perhaps a soft cheese?"

"Yes. Or a hard one."

"Maybe two?"

"That sounds good."

The man selected a cheese and squeezed it.

"Oh," said love.

He selected a second cheese.

"Is that the one different from the other?"

"They're completely different."

They were completely different, but neither was a Livarot.

"Thank you so much. Looks great. Thank you for your help."

At this point, my love went to pay the man who may or may not have been Pascal Trotte and almost set down her purse on his cutting board. This evoked his one facial expression. It wasn't bonhomie. Its deadliness presaged the Livarot.

My love needed a few days. The mortification she felt over asking for horse cheese had to dwindle before she could go back to the shop, and she needed to go alone because, as she explained, my unalloyed Americanness put too much pressure on her French accent. When she finally returned, she had a crinkle in her nose and a Livarot.

Stinky is not the right word for it. *Exhumed* might be. I have never seen a dug-up corpse, but I could now recognize the smell.

"I don't know if I can eat this," said love, sinuses weeping.

Livarot, as far as I can tell, should be eaten in a windy, open field. It's in the shape of a disc, about the size of a clutch purse when it's cut in half, and it has a tacky, hatched skin that's as thick as a wet suit and pale peach in color. Inside the rind, it's globular and buttery. The French have nicknamed it "The Little Colonel" because it comes circled by thin strips of raffia, but after tasting it, we dubbed it "The Gérard Depardieu" because it posed for us an enigma similar to the one surrounding the actor: why do the French find so alluring what strikes us as raunchy, hulking, and nearly grotesque? The cheese tasted rotten, "really wretched." We wondered if we'd gotten it past its prime.

And perhaps we had. Perhaps the man who may or may not have been Pascal Trotte had fobbed off a bad Livarot on an American who strolled into his shop and asked, with what might have struck him as contemptuous ignorance about his life's work, for horse cheese. Still, we doubted ourselves. All our other transactions with the various *fromagers* who may or may not have been Pascal Trotte (we never got up the gumption to ask who was who in the store) resulted in superior cheeses. And even if this time he had—indeed, perhaps because he had—sold us a putrid Livarot, at least we'd learned its secret, which is a secret of all cheese: they taste of life, but they also taste of death.

"Cheese," says McCalman, "is nothing but spoiled milk," and Steven Jenkins, who wrote the massive *Cheese Primer* and helped bring artisan cheese to the U.S. through Dean & DeLuca, agrees with him, summing up the cheese-making process as "controlled spoilage." Cheese, that is, attains its flavor as milk goes from its most lively and life-giving to its inevitable end as rot. Along the way and through the care of its makers, it develops its unique character and, somewhere between its creation and putrefaction, attains its peak. So that stinkiness, that funkiness, that earthy, ashy tang you taste in even slightly aged cheeses, that flavor sends a half-conscious shiver to the deepest part of your being: *memento mori*, remember you will die.

As you savor cheese, Eros and Thanatos dance on your tongue.

And that's why the Livarot loathed us as much as we loathed it.

We were in love, as Americans in Paris should be, and couldn't heed the tragic notes of any cheese, much less the requiem within the Livarot. We were too full of life and spent too much time luxuriating in the Tuileries and kissing on the Pont Neuf to fear the skull smiling at us through the spoiled milk. We courted Eros (and if you've caught the seminal whiff of a Saint-Marcellin or relished the cunnilingual mush of a Rocamadour, you know cheese celebrates Eros in all its meanings). The death-stung Livarot must have found us wretched in its own way, as unserious and airy as Champagne bubbles.

Too airy, in fact, to take U.S. Customs seriously.

At Logan Airport, as I stared at the mustaches in front of me, I tried to fathom how the cheeses in my bag could be illegal. The Comté, the Sainte-Maure, the Brique Ardéchoise—they were more alive than most people I knew. Could they really be confiscated? The thought of it made me hate every whisker before me, then made me snicker.

"French cheeses are an emotional experience," my love had said when we were in the Marais, swooning over a Brie de Melun, and she's right.

In Paris, love is always right.

Wine Scams:
A Counterfeiter Confesses

By Lettie Teague
From *Food & Wine*

Lettie Teague's award-winning Wine Matters columns for
Food & Wine provide a lively guide to the mysteries of
oenophilia. Here is her entertaining account of her own little
winemaking experiment.

Almost every woman I know (including myself) has
knowingly purchased a fake designer handbag at one
time or another. I know it's wrong—that counterfeiting can cost
legitimate companies a great deal of money, and that it can harm
the unwitting purveyors of fakes as well. For example, eBay was recently ordered to pay $60 million to LVMH, owner of the Louis
Vuitton and Christian Dior brands, for selling fakes on its site.

Of course, fancy handbags aren't the only luxury goods considered worth copying these days; as the price of fine wine escalates,
so, too, has the quantity of imposter bottles on the market. The
number has reached into the hundreds of thousands, as in Tuscany,
where Italian authorities found quite a few Brunello producers
making their fancy wine with cheap, non-Brunello grapes. (The
government's fraud-fighting tactics are quintessentially Italian:
They began training policemen as undercover sommeliers.)

Often, wine producers are the victims, not the perpetrators, of
fraud. When 22 lots of Domaine Ponsot *grand cru* Burgundies with

an estimated top value of $600,000 appeared at the Acker Merrall & Condit auction in New York City this past spring, proprietor Laurent Ponsot showed up in person to protest that the bottles were fakes. Indeed, some of them were from vintages in which Domaine Ponsot never made wine. The lots were withdrawn to much debate about how much responsibility the auction house bore. The consigning collector would not address questions about the wines' provenance and, at the time of this writing, his source is still unknown.

The most publicized claim of fake wine (so far) involves billion-aire American wine collector Bill Koch, who has filed four law-suits alleging that he was sold fraudulent wine, including a 1784 Château Lafite reputedly owned by Thomas Jefferson. (Koch's story, and his outrage, have inspired a book, *The Billionaire's Vinegar*, that is soon to be turned into a movie.) Thanks to Koch, suddenly every wine collector I knew was thinking about—or at least talk-ing about—fraud.

Wine fraud has been practiced since Roman times; in fact, the Romans themselves doctored wines with various substances, in-cluding lead, to make them taste sweeter—never mind that drinkers could have ended up dead. More recently, this gambit was nearly the undoing of the entire Austrian wine industry in the mid-1980s, when some unscrupulous producers employed diethyl-ene glycol as a sweetener. (Sweet wines rate higher than dry ones in the Austrian classification system.) Unfortunately, the com-pound they chose is used to make anti-freeze and can kill or cause kidney damage. The ruse was discovered before anyone died, and a chemist, among others, was eventually charged with the crime. But before the plot was uncovered, a treated wine won a gold medal in a European wine fair.

But all of this is amateurish stuff compared to the claims against Hardy Rodenstock, the German wine collector and concert pro-moter accused of faking Koch's Jefferson bottle. Rodenstock (a.k.a. Meinhard Goerke) was famous for holding dinners with wines no one had ever tasted before, like the 1811 Château d'Yquem. When asked how he acquired such bottles, Rodenstock invariably replied that he couldn't reveal their source or exact loca-tion of origin.

According to Rodenstock's detractors, the "location of origin" may have been Rodenstock's own basement. It was a remarkably simple operation for a man who supposedly fooled famous critics like Robert M. Parker, Jr., and experts like Michael Broadbent of the wine department of Christie's London auction house. Rodenstock held numerous parties and large-scale affairs, serving wines many attendees (including the critics) had probably never tasted before.

Five Common Fakes

Brad Goldstein runs a fraud-investigation team on behalf of billionaire wine collector Bill Koch, who was allegedly swindled by Hardy Rodenstock with counterfeit bottles. Although old Bordeaux are the most commonly faked wines, there are more and more fraudulent Burgundies, says Goldstein. Here are five wines he's found to be most frequently faked.

1947 Château Cheval Blanc "I believe that Serena Sutcliffe, the wine director of Sotheby's, once said there are more bottles of '47 Cheval Blanc in the market than were ever produced," Goldstein remarks of this famous wine from St-Émilion.

1811 Château d'Yquem This legendary Sauternes "wasn't in the market until the 1970s. In fact, the 1811 was nonexistent until Rodenstock 'rediscovered' it," says Goldstein.

1924 Château Mouton Rothschild This was the first year that Mouton estate-bottled its wines; any supposedly estate-bottled wines from before this vintage are undeniably fake, says Goldstein.

1921 Château Pétrus Pétrus (especially in a magnum) is a favorite of fraudsters. Goldstein has seen all kinds of fake Pétrus, including bottles with capsules the wrong color and labels made from artificially aged paper.

1952 Domaine de la Romanée-Conti La Tâche "We're seeing more and more fake DRCs," Goldstein says of this great *grand cru* domaine. It's "the favorite Burgundy property" for counterfeiters, he says.

While Rodenstock is said to be a talented taster (with a conveniently large cache of empty old Bordeaux bottles), I found it amazing that he might be able to fake wines like the 1811 Château d'Yquem. On the other hand, maybe faking very old wine is easy; after all, how many people really know what a 200-year-old Sauternes should taste like? It seemed to me that it would be a lot harder to counterfeit something modern and well-known, like a first-growth 1982 Bordeaux. Fooling collectors with a phony version of a wine they had probably tasted many times could be as big as anything Rodenstock reputedly tried to pull off.

And so I began to consider how I might make my own fake, and how easy or hard it might be to fool my own discerning friends. Was the creation of a convincing fake merely a matter of putting on a good show, fitting a bottle with the right label and maybe adding a bit of faux cellar dust? I ruminated in the same way that I imagined Rodenstock might have, considering the various possible candidates for my ruse: Lafite? Latour? Or perhaps 1982 Pétrus, supposedly the most-faked bottle in the world?

I decided on '82 Château Mouton Rothschild, a Parker 100-point wine I've had several times. But I needed a real bottle in order to create a convincing replica.

The '82 Mouton was easy to find, as there were some 25,000 cases produced. I bought a bottle for $1,200 at the Sonoma-based Rare Wine Co. But who would help me create a great fake? After all, unlike Rodenstock, I don't even have a basement. If my experiment was going to succeed, I needed someone with talent, technical know-how and a slightly diabolical sense of humor as well. One name came to mind immediately: Chris Camarda.

Chris produces some of the best Merlots and Cabernets in Washington state under the Andrew Will label; he also makes a highly regarded Bordeaux-style blend, Sorella. "You want me to fake an '82 Mouton?" Chris repeated when I called. "I can do that." (Chris is pretty confident, too.) Could I be there to help? No problem, Chris said.

I had the real Mouton shipped directly to Chris. A week later, I flew out to Seattle, then boarded a ferry to Vashon Island, where Andrew Will is based. Chris was waiting, in dark glasses, in a black car at the far end of the pier. The combination lent our assignation an appropriately covert air, though the truth was a bit more prosaic. "I had to wait here or they'd have given me a ticket," he said.

When we got to the winery, I saw that Chris had already retrieved several older Andrew Will wines from his cellar, mostly Cabernet Sauvignons, Merlots and Cabernet Francs—the main grapes in Mouton. He'd already decanted and tasted them all, as well as the '82 Mouton. "I can do the body, but I'm not sure I can do the aroma," he declared.

The Mouton's austere structure seemed to me like the most difficult aspect to replicate, as well as its minerality, which Chris called its iodine-y quality. The nose would also be hard to capture, with its complex notes of sandalwood and dried cherries. The Mouton itself was a bit more faded than I remembered it from two years before, when I'd last had a bottle. That one had been much more vibrant. Was *this* one a fake? I wondered. What if I was making a fake from a fake? Would that question cross my mind whenever I tasted a great wine in the future? I thought of Bill Koch and his cellar of 40,000 bottles. Did he lie awake at night asking that same question 40,000 times?

Chris and I tried a few crude blending experiments with his Cabs and Merlots. He poured some '95 Merlot into a glass and combined it with an equal amount of his '95 Sorella, a blend of Cabernet and Merlot. Then we tried to match the Mouton with a mix of his wines from various vineyards and vintages. "I don't think the '94 Merlot adds anything," Chris opined as we poured it into an improvised beaker. "But '94 was a big, ripe year in Washington; '95 was more austere," he explained. "More Bordeaux-like," I declared. "Exactly. It was our Mouton year," said Chris.

We kept tasting and retasting. Our fraudulent endeavor was certainly taking a great deal of time; surely Rodenstock could have turned out 10 Pétruses in the time it was taking us to make one Mouton. In the end, Chris and I decided that the 1995 Sorella alone was as close to the '82 Mouton as we could come. "I think this wine has a real Bordeaux quality," Chris said. "In fact, I think you could dump the whole thing into the Mouton bottle." And that was pretty much what we did.

We put the Sorella-Mouton in the real Mouton bottle, and Chris closed it with an Andrew Will cork. (Like Rodenstock, who whisked the corks away after opening his bottles, I'd make sure my friends weren't around when I opened my fake.) As we prepared the wine, Chris mused on the 93-point Parker score he's received for the Sorella. "I'm satisfied that my wine isn't as good as the Mouton, but I think Parker should have given me a couple more points," he complained. And yet, Chris reveled in his fraudster role. "I just know I'm going to get a call from Hardy Rodenstock when he reads this story. He's going to say, 'I've got some bottles signed by Andrew Jackson that I want you to see.'"

The second half of my plan, fooling my friends, turned out to be the much harder part—but not for the reasons I anticipated. I invited The Collector and his Bordeaux-loving friend, The CFO, to a special dinner. I also invited Glenn Vogt, partner and wine director of Crabtree's Kittle House (a top restaurant in Chappaqua, New York, known for its wine list), as well as my friends Nikos Antonakeas and Roberta Morrell of Morrell & Company in New York. Everyone wanted to know what wines to bring. "Your favorite Bordeaux," I replied.

Instead of inviting people to a restaurant, I'd asked my ex-husband, Alan, to host the dinner at his house. I thought it would keep the mood casual and ensure there would be no nosy sommelier around. Of course, I had to let Alan in on my plan. "You know this is as much about your acting ability as the wine," he said. He meant to reassure me, but it made me more nervous instead.

The Collector was the first guest to arrive. I showed him the bottle of faux Mouton, which I'd opened and set down next to the real Mouton cork. "Nice!" he declared, clearly surprised that I had such an impressive wine. The Collector, of course, brought two wines just as good: a 1990 Trimbach Clos Ste.-Hune Riesling—the greatest Riesling from Alsace, if not the world—and the 1989 Château Clinet, another 100-point Bordeaux.

I opened a (real) bottle of 1989 Taittinger Comtes de Champagne to start. "I've never had this wine before," The Collector observed. Then Glenn arrived, carrying two bottles of 1989 Château Haut-Brion, a white and a red. Both are 100-point wines; the latter is one of my favorite Bordeaux of all time. "I can't believe you brought these wines," I exclaimed, feeling a bit sick about my deception. Did my fellow fraudsters, I wondered, ever feel pangs of regret? "It's just so great to see you again," Glenn replied. He is such a warm, kind man, and The Collector is always so generous, I thought, reproaching myself for my duplicity. "It's my pleasure," said Glenn. Then he saw the bottles on the table. "But look at what you have! I haven't had the '82 Mouton in years."

The CFO arrived looking polished as usual, carrying two world-class Bordeaux: the 1990 Château Beauséjour and the 1989 Château Clinet. Nikos and Roberta came in right behind him. They'd brought two fantastic Bordeaux as well, including the 2001 Vieux Château Certan. "I just really like the 2001 vintage," Nikos explained. "Although you should have told us, 'Bring your favorite 100-point wine,'" he added, looking at the array of bottles on the table.

"I think we should serve the Mouton last; maybe we should even decant it," Glenn, the restaurant professional, suggested, recalling how he'd bought bottles of the wine on release for $37 each at a shop in a suburban mall. "I don't think that will be necessary," I hurriedly replied.

I thought about how Rodenstock was said to have forced his guests to swallow rather than spit the wines at his dinners, which got them incredibly drunk. By the time they got to the fanciest wine, their judgment was impaired and, indeed, they were probably lucky to still be sitting upright. I also thought about the special "Rodenstock" glass that Georg Riedel had created in a collaboration with Rodenstock many years before the big scandal broke. Maybe I should have tried to buy a few of those, too?

We started our tastings with the Clos Ste.-Hune. It was spectacular, as good a Riesling as I have ever had; intensely minerally, with a long, persistent finish. At 18 years of age, it was still remarkably young. Everyone crowded around for a glass, and though the Haut-Brion Blanc that followed was quite good, even it was overshadowed by the Clos Ste.-Hune.

"Let's get to more 100-point wines," said The Collector, who decided we should start with The CFO's Beauséjour. "Parker made the reputation of this wine," announced The Collector, holding the bottle. "I bought it accidentally," The CFO confessed. The wine was wonderfully dense and rich. The CFO himself was looking forward to the Mouton, he said. He'd had it many times. "The Mouton will be superior to everything here, but it needs at least 20 more years," he said definitively. I winced, "But how will the nose show?" The CFO continued. "The aroma, after all, is two-thirds of the wine."

My friends debated the order of the remaining wines. Glenn thought the Mouton should be tasted last. "It will be the biggest," he said. We decided the order would be the Clinet, then the Mouton, and last, the Haut-Brion. We quickly dispatched the Clinet: It was lovely, though rather angular after the lush Beauséjour. It was certainly a rapid tasting of some truly great wines, but everyone was eager to get to the Mouton—me most of all.

Nikos tasted it first. "I like the Clinet more than the Mouton. The Mouton is dumb." The Collector disagreed. "I think the Mouton is a step up from anything we've tasted, especially in the nose." Roberta shook her head: "I know Mouton. I like Mouton. But I don't like this wine." Glenn was more generous (he's naturally that kind of guy): "I like it. I think it just needs more time." But The CFO, the man who'd had '82 Mouton more times than anyone else present, declared definitely, "I think it's right up there with the Moutons I've had before." No one said a word about it possibly being a fake.

But there was one more wine to taste: the 1989 red Haut-Brion, the legendary 100-point wine. Would it show up the Mouton for the fraud that it was? I tasted it. The wine had all the characteristic deep, earthy minerality of the bottles I'd tasted and loved in the past. The finish was penetrating and long; it was a truly great wine. "This is my wine of the night," declared Nikos. Holding up his glass, he added, "My comment on the Mouton is: Can I have more Haut-Brion?"

The CFO and The Collector vehemently disagreed. The CFO placed my Mouton ahead of the Haut-Brion and thought it was a very good Mouton. The Collector went one better: "I think the Mouton is the wine of the night," he declared. Wine of the night? This was going along almost too well.

I met Alan in the kitchen when it was time for the last course (banana cream pie, his 100-point dessert). "When are you going to tell them?" Alan asked. "I guess I'd better do it now," I replied, feeling a rush of dread as I headed back to the dining room.

"I have a confession to make," I began. The CFO looked up at me. As a man in charge of corporate finance, he'd probably heard that line many times before. "It's about the '82 Mouton." No one said anything. This was going to be hard. "It's not really a Mouton. It's a fake."

The Collector guffawed. "You have got to be kidding!" He didn't seem angry—or at least, not entirely. Glenn appeared amused, and Nikos seemed to be quite smug. He had known it didn't taste like Mouton, he said. But The CFO looked decidedly unhappy. He was a man who knew Mouton, after all. I told them the whole story: How I'd bought a real bottle, sent it to Seattle and then created a replica with Chris. "I always thought Sorella was a very good wine, and I've always admired Chris Camarda," Glenn said. "But I'm afraid of fraud; it's why I don't like to buy wine at auction." The CFO said nothing but continued to look very cross. Then The Collector, to my amazement, shook his head. "It's still my wine of the night," he said.

In the weeks that followed, I continued to feel guilty about deceiving my friends. They had been so generous and brought such extraordinary wines for all of us to share, and I'd repaid their generosity with a lie. And yet all of them, save for The CFO, seemed to take being taken in stride. Did they simply not care about fraud? Or did they believe that a deception like this could never (really) happen to them (again)?

I think that's how most people feel about fraud; like death, it always happens to someone else. Consider that customers at wine merchant Farr Vintners in London, when given a choice between buying Bordeaux from an unnamed "reputable source" or paying a slight premium to buy the wine shipped directly from the château (thus assuring its provenance), almost always opt for the former. Indeed, Peter Newton, a Farr salesman, said that he recommended the cheaper wine. His customers, he explained, "aren't too fussed" about provenance, though "they do talk about it from time to time."

And maybe talk is all that will happen in response to wine fraud—at least for now. Or until Bill Koch wins his potential millions in court. In the meantime, I've been trying to get The CFO on the phone—he won't take my calls—and I have promised The Collector that I will never, ever serve him another fake wine. He said that maybe, just maybe, he'd trust me again.

MARSHMALLOW FLUFF

By Katie Liesener

From *Gastronomica*

It's sweet, it's sticky, it's dazzlingly white—and if you grew up
with Fluff, it's the quintessential taste of childhood. Dipping
deeper into the jar of Fluff's history, Boston-based writer-
teacher Katie Liesener gives us the skinny on a truly quirky
American foodstuff.

O n an unexceptional day, in the spring of 2006, a third-
grader named Nathaniel went to his Cambridge, Massachusetts, school and for lunch had a sandwich he liked so much
he told his father about it. It was called a fluffernutter, a peanut
butter sandwich billowing with a sweet, sticky, marshmallow cream
called Marshmallow Fluff.

His father, state Senator Jarrett Barrios, was not enthused.

In a State House teeming with fellow Harvard graduates, Barrios stood out as perhaps the most fastidious legislator of them all.
The son of Cuban immigrants, he advocated for poor and immigrant families. An openly gay man, he was an outspoken supporter
of gay marriage. And as chairman of the public safety committee,
he helped take assault weapons out of the hands of criminals.

In June 2006, when Nathaniel ate his fateful lunch, Barrios had
been training his vigilant eye on the childhood obesity crisis. Marshmallow Fluff seemed to him an obvious culprit—nutritionally
hollow, as its name implied, and most damning of all, half sugar.
"I'm not even sure we should be calling it a food," he told the
Boston Globe. So, he aimed to lift fluff from the hands of children, as
he had guns from criminals, and filed an amendment to a school

junk-food bill to restrict servings of fluff in public schools to one per week.

On its face, the move seemed plausible enough—assuming that parents would not want their kids eating sugar sandwiches. But fluff runs deep in this country. "Every time I open the pantry to get it, it's there," said Tali Kwatcher, a homemaker from Dover, Mass. "Nowadays, everyone's so carb and sugar conscious. But I'll bet if you asked them if they have a jar of fluff in their kitchen, they'd say, 'Oh yeah, sure.'"

Not that they would think to mention it.

"I think [Barrios] could have done all the research in the world, and he just couldn't have known what people's reaction would be unless he'd grown up here," said a State House insider.

Outsiders may know New England for its baked beans and chowder. But fluff has been the stuff of people's kitchens for generations, the twentieth-century veneer on their Puritan bones. The ensuing fallout would hound Barrios for the remainder of his career, demonstrating once and for all a people's passion for their marshmallow paste.

IN SUBSTANCE, marshmallow fluff is the whipped culmination of just four ingredients: egg whites, corn syrup, vanillin, and sugar. Its psychological stamp, however, is more complex, forged in the impressionable, high-metabolism era of childhood. It is on this fertile ground that the typical New Englander encounters his first fluff. In his school lunches, it is the soft, white complement to Wonder Bread; on wintry days, the dreamy dollops melting in cocoa; in mom's hands, the saccharine adhesive for frostings, fudge, Rice Krispie treats, and whoopee pies.

Ingestion is just one way that fluff is internalized. The jar itself is as familiar as a favorite scent: its blue-and-white label features a sketched spoonful of fluff, drawn in 1960s-era Dick, Jane, and Spot style. A ruby-red lid dresses the top. "We see the iconic packaging and say 'fluff' without even reading the label," says Michael Costello, an artist raised in Burlington, Mass. "It's so ingrained in our minds."

The consistency—airier than melted marshmallow, gooier than a meringue—obeys its own fluffy physics. Shove a spoon into a jar of fluff, and the disturbance shows the porous vitals of a malleable marshmallow. Open the jar later, and the surface is eerily smooth again.

As with virgin snow, the impulse is to molest it again. Even adults are not immune to the temptation. Jeffrey Davenport, an Alabama native, first encountered fluff as an adult after watching his boss, a surgeon at Children's Hospital in Boston, eat fluffernutters every day for lunch. "I started eating fluff sandwiches five days a week," said Davenport. "Soon I was experimenting with coconut, Oreos, graham crackers, chocolate chips." For Davenport, it wasn't nostalgic appeal; there seemed to be some primordial element in the fluff itself that elevated his meals into third-grade art projects. Obsessed, Davenport decided to visit the factory. If there were something special to fluff, surely its origins would provide some clue.

But he missed his chance. The sole source of fluff is no longer open to visitors. A yellow brick, two-story building tucked into an aging residential neighborhood in Lynn, Massachusetts, the Durkee-Mower factory is something of a mystery. One lucky visitor (who was forbidden to take photos) described it as a "contraptionville" of chutes and conveyor belts. Reporters have returned with stories of vintage beaters a half-century old, little computerization, and a front office of retro pine-paneled walls.

The golden ticket into this time warp is via the company's single phone line—to Don Durkee, eighty-three, the lean, gray-haired president of the company he inherited from his father. A straight-shooting man, no more sentimental about fluff than widgets, he explains his hermitage in plain terms: "We can't do tours anymore due to space limitations and insurance liability." His son, company treasurer Jon Durkee, is more reflective. If you would like to be transferred to Jon, Don Durkee will put down the phone and shout for him.

"We're not publicity hounds," said Jon Durkee, taking the phone. "If we were a younger company, we would be trying to get all the publicity we could. But our name's been made. We like our privacy."

In fact, the twenty-two-employee company has advertised minimally since the 1960s, when it sponsored a radio show featuring the vocal trio The Flufferettes. Nor does Durkee-Mower pay fees to expand into new markets; instead, the company simply waits and sees if enough pent-up demand prompts an invitation. Except for the addition of strawberry and raspberry varieties, fluff has remained its stoic marshmallow self for nearly a century.

Durkee-Mower's business style has remained as innocent as its pure-white product ever since it struck one of the oddest deals in American business. In 1939, the Limpert Brothers Company of Vineland, New Jersey, notified Durkee-Mower that they, too, marketed a product known as Marshmallow Fluff, though it was thicker and used mainly as an ice cream topping. Improbably, the two companies agreed to continue simultaneously marketing their products under the same name—Limpert Brothers for wholesale, Durkee-Mower for individual use only, except in New England.

"So many businesspeople are in trouble with their moral code and ethics," said Pearl Giordano, president of Limpert Brothers. "But this gentlemen's agreement is something that stands the test of time. It represents all that's good in America."

The Durkees, who own the trademark, can afford to act so gentlemanly because their fan base is so loyal. New England and upstate New York account for well over half of all fluff sales. Don Durkee describes fluff's entrenchment in geologic terms: "It's a function of time and exposure."

Consider, for example, lifelong fluff eater Emmett Rauch, eighty-seven, born and raised in Cressona, Pennsylvania, population 1,635, at the perimeter of fluff's regional stronghold. Except for a few days' hospitalization with prostate cancer, Rauch has eaten a fluffernutter on white bread every morning for breakfast since the day he returned home from World War II.

"He was unsatisfied with army food," explains his daughter, Ellen Rauch. "He was determined when he got back he would eat what he wanted." In his determination to stick with what was sweet and good, he also married Ellen's mother, his sweetheart before the war. She has since passed on, but today Rauch, wracked with the pains of age, still starts each morning with a fluffernutter.

If Rauch's experience is any indication, fluff's appeal may be tied up with a peculiarly American sense of homecoming. If so, this held true for the founders of Durkee-Mower—H. Allen Durkee and Fred L. Mower—who stumbled across fluff as young veterans home from World War I. They encountered fluff thanks to a man who had also found refuge here, an immigrant inventor named Archibald Query.

In Somerville, Massachusetts, then a burgeoning commuter's city north of Boston, Query blended with the crowd—softspoken, dark-haired, with the short, wiry frame of a French-Canadian Popeye. Even his wife, a blazing redhead, towered over his five-foot three-inch frame. But the scrappy little man had a talent for candy-making. In 1917 Query whipped up fluff for the first time in his home. According to family legend, he also invented Mary Janes—the peanut butter and molasses candies now made by Necco—and sold that recipe, too, content to work as a candy-company foreman. "He was the kind of guy who went to work when he felt like it, who didn't need money, just a good cigar and a glass of beer," said his grandson, Jack Query.

Archibald Query never told his own grandchildren that he had invented fluff. Consequently, nobody knows what led quiet, perennially content Archibald Query one day to whip four common ingredients into a fluffy frenzy. By the time he died at age ninety, ravaged by dementia, Query himself had likely forgotten why. Or that he had ever invented fluff at all. And so, it seemed, had everyone else.

"It wasn't something they taught in schools," said Evelyn Battinelli, a lifelong Somerville resident and director of the Somerville Museum. "You had to talk to older people in the city to know it."

For decades, conflicting bits of the fluff legend funneled down through the three-decker neighborhoods of Somerville. They appeared in fragments—Battinelli's remarks on city tours, a plaque misstating Query's name and street—and eventually found the ears of Mimi Graney, the director of a nonprofit organization in Somerville. Graney noticed that in the absence of a trumpeted fluff history, people simply supplied their own history with fluff. "Everyone says fluff is from the era of their childhood," she said. "If you grew up in the '70s, you'll say fluff was such a '70s food. If you grew up in the '50s, it was a '50s food."

And you likely assumed that everyone across the country ate fluff, too. By adulthood, fluff so saturated a New Englander's lifespan as to be invisible. Jon Durkee knows the feeling when he walks through the factory he has worked in since his teens. "I can't even smell the vanillin anymore."

IN THE WEE HOURS of Tuesday, June 20, 2006, Kathi-Anne Reinstein had trouble sleeping; she always did when her firefighter husband worked the graveyard shift. Groggily, she shuffled into the living room and turned on the TV. As if in a dream, she saw a news reporter claim that state Senator Jarrett Barrios wanted to cut back fluff in the public schools.

Reinstein couldn't square this seemingly serious news item with the fluff she had always known, which her grandmother had added to her peanut butter and jelly sandwiches when she was a child. Even as an adult, Reinstein initiated every new apartment with a jar of fluff, and she kept fluff on hand for her nieces.

She also knew what Barrios did not: that fluff contains less sugar than jelly. "Any woman who doesn't have the greatest metabolism knows fluff is good," she said. "God, do you want to take on all these women on Weight Watchers? What about all these finicky kids?"

In Reinstein, Barrios had also taken on a legislator in the Massachusetts House of Representatives. She took a walk on the beach to contemplate her next move. Her late father, a notorious jokester and also once a representative from Revere, had always told her, "Take your job seriously, not yourself." So she decided to underscore her outrage with a little mischief. She asked her secretary to send her fellow legislators an e-mail announcing *her* intentions: to file a bill making the fluffernutter the official state sandwich.

The e-mail sparked as much fire as the first revolutionary shot at Lexington.

Local, then national, news services pounced on the story. By nightfall, Jay Leno was lampooning the fluff feud; by morning, Regis and Kelly were. Soon, news outlets from New Zealand and Japan were gobbling up the story as if it were fluff itself.

The sport, of course, lay in catching legislators grapple like toddlers over a sandwich. But nationwide, the flap also confounded the uninitiated (what was this "fluff" that ignited such passions?) and provoked cravings among relocated New Englanders. Over the next week, Durkee-Mower's online sales jumped eightfold, while media requests jammed their single phone line. Don Durkee could not help pointing out that fluff had been invented in Somerville, Barrios's own district.

Reporters could not resist punning and onomatopoeic bravado. (The fluff feud was alternately a "kerfuffle," a "sticky situation," a "food fight," and a "tempest in a baggie.") A local blog issued a color-coded "fluff threat" advisory. And the *Somerville Journal* editor penned a poetic spoof of Dr. Seuss's *Green Eggs and Ham*: "I do not like to eat my Fluff/I just do not, said he in a huff." As the class clowns multiplied, Barrios looked more and more like the out-of-touch principal, having thrown around the kids' slang, ignorant of its meaning.

Flustered, he withdrew the amendment and promised to sign Reinstein's bill, while his spokesman assured the Associated Press that "He loves Fluff as much as the next legislator."

Had Barrios simply been the victim of a slow news week, it might have stopped at that. Instead, he emerged with a reputation as the man who attacked the people's darling. His failure would become embarrassingly vivid three months later. If Reinstein at first thought she was dreaming, Barrios would find himself in a living nightmare. While he was ducking all mention of fluff, Mimi Graney, the nonprofit director in Somerville, had fluff fervently on the brain. She was busy planning the nation's very first fluff festival, "What the Fluff."

The name might have mirrored Barrios's own sentiments.

"I apologized to Jarrett," said Graney, who sympathized with his intent. "People shouldn't be serving fluff in schools. They need healthier options."

But Graney was looking at fluff from quite a different perspective. As director of Union Square Main Streets, her job was to help revitalize Union Square, an eastern Somerville neighborhood once epitomized in the moniker "Slummerville," now an amalgam of ethnic stores and artists' communities. She needed a local angle to draw people back. Well before the political debacle, Graney, in a burst of inspiration, remembered those persistent tales: that Marshmallow Fluff had been invented there. The festival would be an "ironic tribute" to the candied condiment.

"It's about not taking ourselves too seriously," said Graney. "Essentially, the festival was just a bunch of people hanging out in a parking lot. If you went with it, it was the same as the fun you had as a kid—you were maybe just playing with a rock, but it was cool because you were engaging your imagination."

Fluff became a blank canvas for mass interpretation. Area artists paid tribute in gauzy watercolors and neon, Warhol-like reproductions. Science-fair entrants explored whether fluff enhanced athletic performance (unclear); could be tasty with tuna, mustard, and hot sauce (yes); or had particular adhesive qualities (at least seven pounds per psi). The Flufferettes, reincarnated by a local burlesque troupe, celebrated fluff's sensual appeal, strutting and swaying in feathers to *It's a Marshmallow World.*

Fluff was food merely as an afterthought. The cooking contest elicited a fluff volcano, among other entries, and was judged by two eminent chefs and "Fluff Boy"—an eight-year-old clad in a red cape, blond wig, and gobs of white face paint. (Rising to duty, Fluff Boy tasted his way through a dozen entries, puked, then rallied to finish.)

The end result was an orgiastic frenzy of all things fluffy—old-world village celebration meets American kitsch. A wedding party from a nearby bar spilled into the lot to dance with the people, fluff practically hoisted on their collective shoulders in the day's vernacular—"Fluff on," "Very fluffy," "Long live fluff!"

Most surprising, Graney's "ironic" vision turned out to be anything but ironic. Long lines formed for the "tuna fluffers," watercolors of fluff were tagged for thousands of dollars, and people saw a lesson of unleashed imagination in Query's creation.

Mike Katz, an MIT theater professor who impersonated Query in mismatched checkered suit and floppy felt hat, saw a real American tale. He had heard that Query came from Ireland and had changed his name to disguise his undesirable roots. "Here I am, a Jewish boy who grew up speaking Yiddish, playing an Irishman who gave himself a French-Canadian name," said Katz proudly.

Never mind that the story is false. Or that, truth be told, fluff was not invented in Union Square, as lore and the festival's ads would have it. (Query had lived in another Somerville neighborhood the year of fluff's invention.) But now that fluffophilia had openly erupted, the mythologizing was well underway, untainted by political or corporate influence. The Durkees themselves stayed safely at home, sending ten cases of fluff instead. "If I went, the next thing you know, they'd want me to speak," said Jon Durkee, horrified.

The one political presence at the festival was Somerville Mayor Joe Curtatone. Presiding over a sea of red-white-and-blue fluff containers, he squarely intoned his pro-fluff position: "My house always has been, and always will be, stocked with fluff."

Cheers erupted from the populace. Though Barrios was not there to see it, his amendment had helped bring together the 1,500 fluff revelers. "I thought this originated as a rally," said Aaron Warren, a research assistant from Somerville. "You know, save the fluff!"

After Barrios dropped his amendment, Reinstein dropped her bill in deference to a fourth-grade class that hoped to file its own. Today, fluff's only State House presence is the jars stocked in Reinstein's office, where legislators sneak down for a dollop on their peanut butter sandwiches.

Though Barrios and Reinstein were invited to participate in the festival's highlight—a tug-of-war over a kiddie pool full of fluff—neither was able to attend. Instead, the fluff wars fell to the kids. Winners and losers alike jumped in the pool, and fluff was restored to its proper place, where perhaps it should always belong, smeared on the faces of children.

Spam: It's not just for inboxes anymore

By Rachel Hutton

From *City Pages*

Take a news hook, mix in a local angle, and then serve it with
first-person chattiness and irreverent wit—and you've got the
recipe for Rachel Hutton's "Dish" column in this lively Twin
Cities alternative newsweekly.

The other day, I did something I hadn't done in years. I
pulled a square blue can out of the back of the cup-
board, lifted the ring, and punctured its vacuum seal. The can released a primal scent—salty, sweaty, animal—a smell you'd know
anywhere, even if you hadn't encountered it since the last time
your father cooked you breakfast nearly two decades ago. I peeled
back the metal top, flipped the can over, and squeezed it like I was
trying to shimmy frozen orange juice out of its cardboard tube.

Nothing happened. I whacked the can against the countertop.
Again, nothing. I slipped a knife into the can and pried it around
the edges. Still nothing. Finally, I gave the base of the can a firm
slap, and out slid a soft, speckled brick of pink, porcine flesh. It
didn't look entirely edible.

The economy is down, which means Spam sales are up and the
Hormel plant in Austin, Minnesota, is running two shifts, seven
days a week for the foreseeable future. Spam retails at about $3.50 a
pound, a price comparable to other penny-pinching meats such as
ground beef and braising and stewing cuts. But with Spam, there's
no need to hassle with refrigerating, freezing, defrosting, or even

cooking the meat. It's ready to eat, straight from the can. Yes, people really do eat it that way. If you've already sworn off lattes, canceled the gym membership, and started knitting all your holiday gifts, you may soon be eating Spam, too.

In recent years, people have related to Spam less as a foodstuff than as a celebrity. The meat has its own poetry (Spam-ku, none of which needs to be repeated here), merchandise (neckties, fishing bobbers, onesies), and musical group (the Spam-ettes, famous for performing such tunes as "Mr. Spam-man"). There are Spam festivals (Spam Jam in Waikiki, for example; Hawaii tops the nation in Spam consumption, followed by Alaska) and Spam-carving contests (pigs and hot dogs are popular subjects). Hell, a man once proposed to his girlfriend with a Spam-can ring. (They were artists. She said yes.)

Spam may have a place in the Smithsonian, but it also has its own museum, on Spam Boulevard in Austin, Minnesota, just a few blocks from the Hormel plant. Inside, tour guides with Fargo accents (mine was wearing a Spam belt) direct visitors to an introductory video that plays a clip from *The Tonight Show*. "A can of Spam is consumed every 3.6 seconds," Jay Leno says. "It's sold in 99 percent of the world's grocery stores." In the background, Weird Al Yankovic covers a classic REM tune: "Spam in the place where I live . . . (ham and pork) . . . Think about nutrition, wonder what's inside it now." And during the next 15 minutes, Spam makes its way to Everest and Antarctica, Governor Pawlenty sports a Spam T-shirt in Iraq, and a can-shaped Spam-mobile drives off into the sunset.

Museum visitors learn the story of how Spam was invented in 1937 by Jay Hormel, son of company founder George Hormel (the name was originally pronounced to rhyme with "normal," though except for some Austin old-timers, most people tend to emphasize the second syllable). Spam isn't the "mystery meat" everyone assumes it to be—no snouts, tongues, feet, or hearts (though those parts are used in headcheese and scrapple). Spam is, in fact, a simple combination of pork shoulder, ham (the pig's rear thigh), salt, sugar, and sodium nitrite, which gives it its blushing color. The ground meat mixture is squirted into cans, sealed, and cooked, and, while actual plant tours are hard to come by, the museum contains an interactive station where visitors can try their hand at "making" Spam. As you stuff little pink beanbags into square tins, a timer counts out the hundreds of cans produced by the plant in the same time period.

During the Second World War, 90 percent of all Hormel canned goods were sent to military or lend-lease programs—troops sometimes ate Spam three times a day. While the war may have reduced America's appetite for Spam, it introduced the product to international markets, with particular success in the Asian Pacific. (Today, South Koreans give cans of Spam as gifts, just as Americans might give wine or chocolate.) After the war, Jay Hormel tried to improve the product's image with the Hormel Girls, a musical group that toured the country in a caravan of white Chevrolets, giving performances and conducting in-store promotions. But Spam's wartime overdose wasn't to be forgotten that quickly. Monty Python memorialized the meat in a 1970 sketch involving a cafe that served limitless permutations of Spam. (The actors repeat the word so many times that it clogs up any other dialogue, which inspired the term for junk e-mail.)

Unsurprisingly, the Hormel-funded museum doesn't mention the months-long strike that tore the town apart in the mid-1980s. The strike was so nasty that when the plant reopened, local bars were divided pro- or anti-Hormel, depending on the owners' views. At one Catholic church, some parishioners refused to shake hands and "pass the peace" with others in the same pew.

Another point the museum misses is an explanation of exactly how and when Spam transitioned from pure caloric energy to cultural kitsch, or pop food. And how a generation of young people will clad itself in ironic Spam flip-flops, yet won't dare let the stuff touch their lips.

After I finished touring the museum, I bought every type of Spam the gift shop sold and invited a few friends over for dinner. A few people responded enthusiastically ("Call me Caucasian garbage if you want, but I actually like Spam. I used to eat it all the time as a kid"), but most shamefully admitted they'd never tried the product ("I feel like a bad Minnesotan for asking this, but has anybody ever actually eaten Spam?"). One friend flat-out refused to attend. "It tastes like arm," he said.

Those who were familiar with the holy trinity of salt, fat, and sugar knew that it's best prepared simply: sliced and fried, served on buttered toast. But hundreds of Spam recipes have been developed over the years, some as cheap and easy as cubed Spam tossed in macaroni and cheese, others as sophisticated and spendy as Spam lobster thermidor. The Spam Web site contains the largest recipe clearinghouse, though none are listed under the categories for vegetarian, dessert, or beverages. *The Book of Spam* even provides beer and wine pairings, suggesting American pale ales or sweet, fruity Rieslings.

That night we feasted on Spam sushi, Spamburgers, Spam stir fry, and Spam spread, pureed with mayonnaise and sweet-pickle relish. A Spam casserole—baked beans, canned pineapple, brown sugar, and Spam—was the evening's surprise hit: a mushy, salty-sweet comfort. When all was said and done—when the recycling bin was full of Spam cans and the leftovers packed up in doggie bags—here's what we learned about cooking with Spam.

- The gel is gone! The clear, fatty gel that once encased each block of Spam was eliminated in 2001, when Hormel added potato starch to the mix to absorb the gelatinous grease. The only Spam buyers who miss the gel are those who apparently liked using it—believe it or not—as furniture polish.

- You can actually eat Spam straight from the can. Seriously. It's not bad; it's a lot like bologna. Still, the preferred preparation is seared for a few minutes on both sides so that it's caramel-crisp on the outside and squishy in the middle.

- If you slice Spam very thin and cook it until it almost starts to blacken, you can make what we called "Spam crackers," or alternately, "Spackers." They taste a lot like bacon, though Spam already tastes like bacon. And if it's not bacon-y enough for you, there's always Spam with Bacon.

- Don't buy Garlic Spam. It smells like a mix of sweaty feet and vomit, and doesn't taste a whole lot better.

- Spam Lite might seem like an oxymoron, but it's for real. Compared to Spam Classic, Lite tastes meatier, probably because the salt and fat are toned down enough to allow you to actually taste the main ingredient. Classic has a more pleasing melty, fatty texture, but it's almost too salty to be eaten by itself.

- Despite preconceived notions ("You'd think a Minnesota company would pussyfoot with the spices," my friend remarked), Hot and Spicy Spam lives up to its name, with a pleasant Tabasco burn.

- Spam Golden Honey Grail, packaged in a special Monty Python collector's-edition can, is the most succulent manna—its sweetness like syrup mixing with sausage—and was the top performer in our unscientific taste test. The only downside: The licensing agreement with the Spamalot folks bumped the price up to $5 a can.

When a few guests reached for seconds of my Spam dessert—cubes of chocolate-dipped Spam, a riff on chocolate-covered bacon—I considered the dinner a success. (Unfortunately, I wasn't able to track down a Spam brownie recipe, mentioned by former Congressman Gil Gutknecht in a recent *New York Times* article.) By that time, our table talk had devolved into a discussion about the guys in Wisconsin who dug up a young woman's grave with the intent of having sex with her corpse (they'd seen her obituary photo and apparently found her attractive). One of my friends remarked that perhaps Spam would never shake its lowbrow roots. "This is exactly the kind of conversation you're supposed to have when you're eating Spam," she said.

OUT OF THE WILD

By Peter Jamison

From *SF Weekly*

Farm-fresh? Try forest-fresh edibles, foraged from the nearby wilderness. *SF Weekly* reporter Jamison tags along with one of these modern-day hunter-gatherers, yet another example of the Bay Area being gastronomically way ahead of the curve.

On an unseasonably warm winter afternoon, Iso Rabins stepped out of a silver Subaru Legacy at the intersection of Walnut and Pacific streets, a tony corner of Pacific Heights that abuts the southern edge of the Presidio. Pausing to roll and light a cigarette, he hopped the waist-high stone wall lining the park. Behind him, rows of shingle and brick two-story houses climbed uphill into a bright February sky. As he stepped slowly and deliberately across an overgrown hillside bisected by a dirt walking trail, eyes trained on the ground like a man who had lost his wedding ring, the gentle ping of bats on baseballs rose from fields below. Suddenly Rabins froze, knelt, and began to nibble on a weed.

"This is wild radish," he said absently, eyes scanning the ground as he masticated his find. "I've used it in potato salad, with wild salad greens. There's a subtle flavor to it." A few more steps and Rabins came upon a patch of *Claytonia perfoliata*, or miner's lettuce, so named for the 49ers who grew fond of the plant as a source of Vitamin C during the Gold Rush.

The bounty did not stop. Looking around, Rabins rejoiced at the presence of chickweed (another salad green) and stinging nettle. The latter, once blanched to remove its prickly spines, would be the key ingredient that night for his nettle ravioli supper. "Look at all this!" he said. "This is crazy."

Less intrepid diners treated to the spectacle of this scavenger hunt would probably agree with the crazy part. But in Rabins' world, the weeds that blanket this stretch of the Presidio are of interest to others besides sweater-clad Chihuahuas on the hunt for a latrine. This man is in business, after all, and he was looking at his products—several of them.

Rabins is mounting a first-of-its-kind commercial enterprise, called ForageSF, that would provide the denizens of this food-frenzied urban center with regular access to wild-growing edibles—not just salad, but mushrooms, seafood, and fruit, as well as "wild-crafted" or processed goods such as acorn flour. (The selling of meat from wild game, such as deer, is illegal.) This month, he is launching a "Community Supported Forage" (CSF) box of wild foods. Modeled on Community Supported Agriculture organic-farm boxes, the subscription service will provide clients with a bi-weekly allotment of seasonal foraged products.

"Maybe we're a little spoiled here in the Bay Area, but even the farmers' market has become too pedestrian," says Rebecca Klus, a San Francisco cooking instructor and wild-foods enthusiast.

You can dispute the tastiness of stinging nettles, but there's no contesting the fact that Rabins, like any savvy capitalist, is meeting a demand. Some heavy hitters of Bay Area haute cuisine have joined the wild-food cheerleading section, and chefs at renowned eateries such as Chez Panisse, Pizzaiolo, and Incanto have all done business with Rabins.

"In my cooking, I would love to use more wild food," says Jerome Waag, a chef at Chez Panisse who has worked at the Berkeley restaurant for 15 years and has bought wild mushrooms from Rabins. A native of southern France, Waag describes the appeal of foraged food with continental flair. "It comes directly from the earth and the wind and the rain," he says. "It's sort of a concentration of natural forces, as opposed to something that's been more organized. I think it's for the flavor, but also the whole romantic aspect."

But in Rabins' case, finding an eager and untapped market for his products is the easy part. His is a supply-side problem. In this day and age, hunting and gathering—humans' sole means of feeding ourselves for most of our species' history—is a proposition fraught with ethical, logistical, and legal problems. In the U.S., a gamut of regulations governing food safety and environmental conservation would long ago have rendered any surviving forager societies extinct. And there's no shortage of people who think Rabins' effort to buck the trend of modern agricultural and industrial food production is misguided at best—and dangerous at worst.

San Francisco's chief food inspector, for instance, says a steady stream of unregulated foraged food into the city could bring with it diseases or even death—leptospirosis, a bacterial infection spread through animals' urine, can cause jaundice and kidney failure, and some mushrooms are among nature's most grotesquely effective poisons. There's also the matter of whether wild ecosystems can bear the effects of anything beyond the most modest return to mankind's previous foraging habits. Rabins recently learned that in the Presidio, one of his heretofore steady sources of foraged food, removing his favored salad greens for commercial use is a federal offense subject to a $125 fine.

So far, Rabins' efforts to get ForageSF off the ground raise more questions than they answer. Among the most interesting: How did one of humans' most elemental and ancient activities—finding and eating food in the places we inhabit—become so complicated?

The day before he foraged the Presidio, Rabins had driven down to Santa Cruz to see a guy about the modern era's most valuable and widely consumed foraged food product: mushrooms. As his car chugged along Highway 17, threading the redwood-forested hills south of Silicon Valley, Rabins pulled onto a turnout and hoisted his iPhone from its resting place by the emergency brake.

"Christian," he said. "This is Iso. We're on our way down. Where would be a good place to meet?" After a moment, he hung up and smiled. "They've got me pulling over to make phone calls," he said, shaking his head. "The Man's got his foot on my neck."

At first glance, he seems a less-than-likely target for the Man's subjugation. Rabins is a lean, bearded 27-year-old of middling height, with warm brown eyes and short brown hair. Like some of the foragers with whom he does business, he has led a nomadic existence. He was born in Santa Cruz to parents he affectionately describes as hippies; the product of Russian Jewish forebears, his first name means "shoreline" in Japanese. He lived in different spots as a child—Philadelphia, Vermont—and attended the Buxton School in western Massachusetts, a small boarding school where students split the wood that heated their buildings. He studied film at Emerson College in Boston, traveled in Italy and Mexico, and, like so many other East Coast émigrés, fell in love with San Francisco on a drive up Highway 1. He moved here in the fall of 2007.

Rabins' paying jobs have always been restaurant gigs, and after he moved to the city he started bartending at Fresca, a chain of Peruvian restaurants. While visiting his father a year and a half ago in Willow Creek, an inland hamlet of Humboldt County near the Hoopa Valley Indian Reservation, some family friends brought over a gift of wild, edible mushrooms plucked from the local hills. "I was like, 'No fucking way,'" Rabins recalled. "'Really? You actually forage for wild mushrooms?' It was this amazing moment. I was like, 'You have to teach me this.'"

Soon Rabins was networking with mushroom foragers in Mendocino County, buying in bulk and selling to chefs at famous Bay Area eateries like Chez Panisse. As a mushroom middleman, he began confronting some of the logistical issues faced by any food buyer. At one point, a 100-pound shipment of wild mushrooms worth about $1,500 rotted over the weekend in a UPS shipping warehouse. ("They'd actually started to compost in the middle," Rabins notes dispassionately.)

He also began getting familiar with the eccentric ranks of those who know the woods well enough to find hundreds of pounds of mushrooms in the first place. Rabins remembers in particular a late-night rendezvous with a gentleman in the parking lot of a Burger King in Willits. "I felt so much like a drug dealer, it was insane," he said. "I pulled up and he pulled up in his pickup truck. It was just packed with mushrooms. We spent about an hour weighing them."

ForageSF already offers direct product sales, and this month will launch a small batch of CSF wild-food boxes that will range in price from $40 to $80. Rabins hopes to start with 20 subscribers and build the service over time. He also wants to include an educational component to the business, with foraging tours and talks.

It was to that end that he was headed to Santa Cruz, where he was to meet Christian Schwarz, a budding mycological scholar whom Rabins hoped to bring to San Francisco to offer presentations on mushrooms.

There would be no darkened Burger King parking lots for Schwarz, who requested that Rabins meet him outside a bagel shop downtown. A rail-thin 20-year-old with luxuriant dark hair and a ghostly complexion, Schwarz is an ecology and evolution major at UC Santa Cruz. He became a mushroom enthusiast in his early teens, in the way that other young boys develop obsessions with skateboarding or baseball statistics. But his hometown, San Diego, was not prime fungal territory. Attracted by the Central Coast's moist, forested hills, he came to UCSC.

"My interest in mushrooms is mainly academic," Schwarz said. When talking about mushrooms, he frequently betrays an abstract turn of mind; at one point, discussing the fatal "death cap" mushroom, two ounces of which make a lethal dose, he remarked, "People who have eaten it and survived said it tastes really good."

As he and Rabins drove into the hills of Soquel, where they were to go on a recreational mushroom hunt—the equivalent, in foraging circles, of unfamiliar executives meeting for a round of golf—he expounded upon America's relative dearth of mycological traditions when compared to such countries as Russia or Italy.

"Here in the U.S., we don't have a long foraging history," Schwarz said. In China, he said, citing research by renowned mycologist David Arora, one infamous strain of wild mushrooms provokes an identical hallucination of *xiao ren ren*, or "little people," among all those who eat them. Many do so by accident—for example, after eating the culprit fungus in a dish prepared at a restaurant—and the resulting visions stir no more alarm among Chinese diners than an upset stomach.

The fungal kingdom is a living rebuke to biologists, who still know astonishingly little about mushrooms—how long they live, why and how they spring up when they do (a mushroom can mature in a span of time from several hours to several months), or how they propagate. The mushrooms we eat are the fruiting body of extended, nervelike networks of the organism mycelium, which attaches itself to the roots of trees or to decaying vegetative matter.

The vacuum of hard knowledge surrounding this subterranean entity has invited a plethora of pseudoscientific observations; at least one prominent mycological expert, Paul Stamets, theorizes that the mycelium is a sentient being.

This being was to prove elusive for Rabins and Schwarz, who parked the car and wandered into the woods above Soquel Creek, their shoes crunching over mats of dead fern branches and maroon scrolls of madrone bark. The air was cool. Water from the past week's rains dripped from the boughs of redwood trees. After a time, an excited whistling struck up somewhere in the woods.

It was Schwarz. He had found what would be the day's sole edible mushroom: a black trumpet, or *Craterellus fallax*, an earth-colored bugle of a fungus, typically sautéed, admired for its smoky flavor. After a moment spent admiring the mushroom, Rabins and Schwarz resumed the hunt, with no further luck. Eventually they gave up. Schwarz cast the black trumpet into the woods. "Go," he said softly. "Spread your spores. Please."

On the way back down the trail, Rabins lit a cigarette. Schwarz walked ahead with long strides, whistling "Silver Bells."

The cult of mystery surrounding the mushroom is only enhanced by its aura of danger. Most people know that eating the wrong wild mushrooms can make you see strange things or kill you. What they don't know is just how outlandishly potent some of these naturally occurring poisons are.

Larry Pong, principal food inspector in the San Francisco Department of Public Health, recounts the case of a man who ate a bad mushroom several years ago during a feast at a local winery. "He died a painful death," Pong said, quickly elaborating: "It was painful in the beginning. And then, after his liver disintegrated, he went into a state of euphoria. And then he died." Such cases crop up regularly in mushroom-hunting territory. Between January and November of last year, the California Poison Control System received 721 calls from state residents who had eaten questionable mushrooms, according to Stuart Heard, the agency's executive director. Three of those cases led to serious illness, and one to death.

Mushrooms aren't the only foraged food with which people must take care; hemlock, which killed Socrates, resembles wild parsley and often grows among patches of chickweed. But Rabins says he takes the safety issue seriously. "I know a lot about seven types of mushrooms, and that's all that I ever sell to people," he said. "I wouldn't pick a wild mushroom, look at it in a book, decide it was the same one, and try to sell it to somebody."

For Pong, these assurances don't cut it. Citing the grave risks associated with ingesting wild plants and fungi, he argues that Rabins should be subject to regulations governing other food vendors. Pong says he already knows what his answer will be if an application from ForageSF arrives on his desk: "We would just flat-out tell him, 'You can't do this.'"

But things may not be so simple. Given its novel nature, ForageSF falls into something of a regulatory gray area. Rabins has registered his business with the San Francisco tax collector's department, and says he was told after consulting with city authorities that he did not need special permits to sell wild-food products. His goal, he says, is to run a legal operation open to public scrutiny—but he came away from the permitting process with the impression that government officials weren't quite sure what form that scrutiny should take.

"I just became frustrated with the whole licensing situation," he said. "I feel like I did put in the time trying to make it right, and they didn't know the answers to my questions."

Others fear the ecological toll of Rabins' approach to foraging. Connie Green, a commercial mushroom broker from Napa County, hires nomadic foragers—many of them Laotian and Cambodian immigrants who hunted and gathered in the hills of their native countries—to scour the great morel zones of the Northwest, in places such as Wyoming, Idaho, Oregon, and Washington. While on the hunt, Green sets up camp in the forest with anywhere from six to 14 foragers. Yet even she questions whether putting nature's supply of wild mushrooms on tap for a city in thrall to food fads might not pose new risks of overharvesting. "If people don't have an understanding, be sensitive enough to the life of that plant, they can do real harm, particularly when it's driven by [customer] orders," she said. "You have to be able to say no."

Nature's inability to feed large numbers of people is a simple fact of human history. Various theories of our species' transition to agriculture have been propounded, all turning on the theme that the quantities of food rendered by hunting and gathering were inadequate to sustain a growing population. But our ingenuity in bolstering the food supply came with tradeoffs. Agriculture, for all its improved predictability, delivered a narrower and hence less healthful range of cultivated food staples, as well as the diseases that spread when humans live close to livestock. "The key to agriculture is that it's not necessarily more nutritious," UC Berkeley anthropology professor Kent Lightfoot said. "It's more viable."

An object lesson in the viability of supplying anything beyond a meager clientele with foraged products can be found in the grim fate of humanity's last large-scale source of hunted and gathered food: the commercial fisheries. On a recent Friday morning, Rabins wandered along Pier 45, behind San Francisco's tourist-thronged Fisherman's Wharf. Passing crab pots teeming with seagulls beneath a bright winter sky, he ducked into one loading dock after another. He was looking for a supplier of fresh local fish, which he hoped to include in his CSF box.

One after another, buyers gave him a somewhat astounding answer: Eating fish from San Francisco Bay has become practically impossible because of a dispiriting combination of environmental regulations and economic reality. Salmon season was likely to be cancelled for the second year in a row because the fish had been depleted by poor river conditions, and crab quotas for many fishermen had been met within the first few weeks of the winter. Local sardines were sold to companies operating tuna pens in coastal Mexico. About the only edible fish being pulled out of the bay was herring—and almost nobody eats herring anymore. The fish are stripped for their roe, which is sent to Japan.

Eventually Rabins encountered Ernie Koepf, a tall, shambling herring fisherman sporting a silvery mane of hair and a torn plaid shirt open at the neck. Leaning back against the dock rail above his boat, the *Ursula B*, Koepf offered his own take on the situation: Increasingly zealous regulators had deprived San Franciscans of local seafood.

"It's taken about 15 years, but various interest groups, among them well-meaning, organic, green-thinking folks, have fucked themselves out of having fresh fish," he said. "Now, I can tell you for a fact that there's lots of fish available out there, but I can't get access to them, so the public can't get access to them. That's why those guys over there were all giving you the horse laugh. I'm eating a piece of fish wrapped up in a fucking piece of plastic when the same fish is swimming right out there."

Rabins stood before him in sunglasses, dark blue jeans, and charcoal-colored New Balance shoes, holding a Starbucks cup. "It's wild," he offered. "It is," Koepf said. "It's a perversion. A cultural perversion."

The merits of current state and federal fishing regulations can be argued both ways, but are indicative of a prevalent modern mindset toward wild places that is incompatible with the goals of hunting and gathering. According to this outlook, forests and oceans should be preserved in something approximating a state that predates human civilization—looked at, and not eaten from.

Rabins' hope is that eating wild food can bring people into a more immediate and vital relationship with wilderness. "Right now, we think of the woods more abstractly," he says. "It's out there; we like to walk in it. But we don't value it in that personal way, as a food supply."

He adds, "In a capitalist system, the only way someone's going to care about a resource is if it becomes profitable. I think as interest grows in wild food, it will actually help protect the resource."

Others think the resource is already protected just fine, thank you. Commercial foraging is illegal, for example, in all California state parks. "We have the parks as an inviolate place for plants and animals," says Roy Stearns, spokesman for the state park system. "Parks were not set up to be a commercial enterprise. They were set up to be a preservation of what's there." The same is true of federal parks like the Presidio, which is part of the Golden Gate National Recreation Area.

Rabins said he had been unaware of Park Service regulations governing the Presidio until late last month, and said he plans to cease foraging there. As for the bulk quantities of mushrooms he buys from foragers in far Northern California, he said he trusts that his hunters are prowling private land or other legal spots—but acknowledges there's no knowing for sure. "You really don't know where they're from," he said. "They come from the woods, and someone walks out of the woods and sells them to you. It's sort of a don't-ask, don't-tell situation."

On the evening of Friday, February 27, Rabins showed up at 18 Reasons, the upscale Guerrero Street art gallery and dining room affiliated with Bi-Rite Market, the Mission's renowned gourmet food store. The night's main event was a four-course dinner built around foraged foods, including chickweed salad with Half Moon Bay squid, Portuguese caldo verde soup prepared with nettles, and garganelle pasta with sautéed black trumpet and hedgehog mushrooms. Rabins had brought a sheaf of flyers detailing the final composition and pricing schedule of his foraged-food boxes, ranging from a $40 "Veggie" box of nettles, salad greens, fruit, and mushrooms to an $80 "Pesca-fungitarian" box featuring rock cod and extra 'shrooms. (When it comes to fish, Rabins has been obliged to relax the otherwise regional emphasis of his boxes because of local fishing restrictions. He says he will procure it from locations as distant as Canada when it's not available in California waters.)

After debriefing a small crew of servers on the contents and preparation of each menu item, chef Morgan Maki took a few minutes to offer a reporter his thoughts on ForageSF's financial prospects while dinner guests trickled in. "I think if it were going to succeed anywhere, Northern and Central California would be the place," said Maki, a butcher at Bi-Rite. This isn't just because of the Bay Area's prevailing ethical-food trends. The enterprise of supplying foraged food to consumers is geographically self-limiting. Maki noted that in the wintry landscape of Montana, a state he used to call home, a project like ForageSF would be impossible.

There were 19 guests in all, each paying $40 for the meal. The well-heeled crowd of thirtysomethings gradually took their seats at a long wooden table between walls hung with unframed sketches. Among them was Jennifer Jones, owner of a boutique clothing store around the corner. It was her first foraged meal. "I'm excited to see what it's like," she said.

Halfway through the second course—a bowl of caldo verde, prepared from wild nettles and salt cod, with a vibrant green hue akin to that of wheatgrass juice—she had made up her mind. "It's so overwhelmingly fresh-tasting," she said. "It's so potent. It's not even that the flavors are intense. They are, but that's not it. It's so satisfying to eat something that's so close to the earth."

If people like Jones or Maki don't share the concerns of San Francisco's health inspectors and parks officials, it's not because they're scofflaws, but because they increasingly make culinary decisions based on an antique ethos of food production that today's regulatory apparatus simply is not built to understand. Rabins' big idea depends upon faith in and familiarity with the men and women who procure edible things, not the bureaucratic superstructure that grew up over the past half-century to curb the excesses of industrial-scale food production.

In the world of wild food, says Bi-Rite wine buyer Josh Adler, "there's that element of trust." In other words, consumers must believe their favorite forager knows enough to distinguish an edible mushroom from a poisonous one, or a clean leaf of miner's lettuce from one ridden with bacteria. Rabins hopes his customers will place that extraordinary trust in a film major recently converted to mycological pursuits. Granted they do, it is reasonable to ask where there's room, even in the Bay Area's niche food market, for a forager facing doubts about the safety and environmental toll of his products.

The answer: at 18 Reasons, amid a chatty and affluent crowd. As the meal unfolded, a mirthful din filled the small room. The storefront windows on Guerrero had steamed over. Rabins sat at the head of the table, beaming and fielding questions about wild food, an attractive blond woman at his side. The diners around him conversed avidly, leaning forward on their elbows, sipping wine and unfiltered beer. By the end of the night, three of them signed up for CSF boxes. An eager tension seemed to grip them. The salad course was over; their plates were empty. Like the ill-fated eater in Pong's cautionary tale, these men and women had entered a state of euphoria—but their livers were still intact, and they would live to tell the tale.

Summer's End

By Tamasin Day-Lewis

From *Saveur*

From her weekly column in the *Daily Telegraph* to her
cooking series on the Good Food Channel, Tamasin Day-
Lewis has made her mark as one of the U.K.'s most trusted
food writers, with a special emphasis on traditional British
regional cookery.

September. We begin to batten down the hatches for the
approaching dark, even as we rejoice in the last fling of
abundance the season throws upon us. That is the curious polarity
we face at this time of year, particularly those of us who are country dwellers.

Somerset, where I live, in the southwest of England, is a
county of narrow lanes and high hedges as well as great expanses
of common land with wild ponies, brilliant golden gorse, and
blue moorland bilberries. The poets Samuel Taylor Coleridge and
William Wordsworth drew inspiration from the same landscape
when they lived here at the end of the 18th century. Somerset is
apple-growing country; most small farmers still keep their own
presses and make rough cider, or scrumpy, as it is known locally.
The village of Cheddar, a half hour's drive from my house, gives
its name to what is arguably England's finest hard cheese, and my
neighbor Jamie Montgomery makes the very best version, ma-
tured in giant wheels wrapped in muslin, on his family farm. At
this time of year, blackberries bleed into palms and picking fin-

gers, and walnuts stain skin nicotine—no scrubbing diminishes it—but clawing the wet, knobbled nuts from their green shells is a rite of passage.

My house dates from 1450 and is built of local Quantock sandstone, whose warm, mellow, terra-cotta tones reflect the surrounding red earth. When I bought the house, six years ago, it had a leaky roof, waist-high damp running up the walls, and antiquated heating, plumbing, and wiring. The challenge was to return it to its former glory while making it fit for 21st-century habitation. There was a tumbledown walled garden, in which I planted fruit trees—mulberry, walnut, damson, greengage plum, apple, fig, crab apple, and peach—to create an orchard. I also cultivated the soft fruits our climate suits so well: red and black currants, gooseberries, raspberries, and loganberries.

An ancient bread oven remains inside the great fireplace in the dining room. I have recently restored it to use for baking focaccia, pita bread, and pizzas, and I am experimenting with roasting a whole chicken in the scented embers of oak and apple wood. In my kitchen I cook on a battleship-size, six-oven Aga range, at once the soul of the house and the best roaster, baker, and overnight simmerer of them all. I built my kitchen from scratch, in apple green with a worktable of solid oak. It comes into its own at this cusp of the season, before we dare switch on the heating and admit the winter. We huddle near the Aga for warmth and for every first, fugitive scent of what's cooking.

I taught myself to cook with Elizabeth David's classic books—*French Country Cooking, French Provincial Cooking*, and *A Book of Mediterranean Food*—in one hand and Jane Grigson's *English Food, Vegetable Book*, and *Fruit Book* in the other. Elizabeth David opened up Britain to a new world of food, and to all the glamour and exotica of ingredients, after years of war and rationing. Jane Grigson, the scholar cook, restored great recipes to the canon of British food that bad ingredients, industrialization, and food processing had made us forget. These two writers taught a whole generation of British cooks the meaning of *cuisine du terroir*, cooking with a strong sense of place.

One day my old friend Georgie, who comes for breakfast every morning after she's fed her horse and donkeys, arrives to find me chopping herbs and squeezing lemons. She takes one look at the produce piled on the kitchen table and decides to stay for lunch. Virtually everything has been grown or made within 30 miles of my house: apples from my orchard, blackberries from my hedgerow, crème fraîche from a nearby dairy, eggs from a neighbor's farm. The steak comes from the Wild Beef company, run by a friend on the grassy moors of our sister county Devon.

We turn to red meats and dark-berried cakes at summer's end, wanting something more substantial as the heat ebbs and our appetites grow. Today, I boil and purée floury King Edward potatoes and then whip them along with hot cream and melted unsalted butter to velvety smoothness. I make a dazzlingly red sorbet with raspberries that are still splurting juice and should last until November on the plant. It makes a perfect accompaniment for a blackberry and apple cake flavored with a little cinnamon. I always use wild blackberries; cultivated ones don't have the same sharpness or intensity of flavor.

Once the shooting season starts, I shall have pheasant and partridge. Farmer friends will bring me wild mallards in full plumage, ready to pluck and gut. They will hang in the barn for a week, until they taste properly gamy. At the start of the season I'll roast them; later, when the birds are scrawnier and tougher, I'll casserole them with barley and apple, or with cabbage, salty chorizo, and sweet chestnuts.

This is the time of year when I peer closely at the spiky sloe bushes tucked into the hedgerows along the road. Once the small, purple berries look ripe, I pick them, prick each with a silver pin, and submerge them in sugar and Plymouth gin, my favorite brand, from Devon. In two years' time my sloe gin will make an ideal winter fuel for a hip flask. The damson tree in my garden has just fruited for the first time, and I will turn its plums into sorbet and steep them in gin as I do the sloes. There's just enough fruit this first season for a single jar of damson gin, with its almondy back notes from the plums' cracked kernels. Every so often, when I remember to, I shake the jar and turn it the other way up. Each time, the liquid stains darker, from palest pink to rich ruby, from garnet to purple.

When the apples are ready for harvesting, all the local growers and cider makers celebrate Apple Day. A great crowd of us gathers in the orchard of my neighbor Julian Temperley, who pours a libation of his splendid ten-year-old Somerset cider brandy around a tree to bless the crop. Julian grows many of the old varieties, and their names read like those of figures in a fairy tale: wife of bath, slack-m'girdle, stoke red, Kingston black. For lunch there are crisp eating apples served with wedges of Jamie Montgomery's cheddar. This is true *cuisine du terroir*: the absolute best, freshest ingredients with as little as possible done to them. The harvest is in, and we are eating and drinking it.

Blackberry and Apple Cake
SERVES 8–10

Loaded with ripe fruit, this moist cake is a cross between two classic English desserts, sponge cake and summer pudding.

¾ cup softened unsalted butter, plus more for greasing pan
1½ lbs. fresh blackberries (about 6 cups)
1 tbsp. dark brown sugar
3 granny smith apples, cored, peeled, and quartered
⅓ cup apple brandy, such as calvados
2¼ cups cake flour
2¼ tsp. baking powder
1 tsp. ground cinnamon
½ tsp. fine salt
¾ cup milk
1½ tsp. vanilla extract
Zest of 1 lemon
1 cup plus 2 tbsp. superfine sugar
4 eggs
Crème fraîche, for garnish (optional)

1. Heat oven to 350°. Grease a 9" springform pan with butter. Line bottom of pan with a parchment paper circle; grease paper. Wrap outside of pan with foil to prevent drips; set aside. In a small bowl, toss 2 cups blackberries with brown sugar; set aside to let macerate.

2. Meanwhile, cut each apple quarter into 1/8" slices; toss with apple brandy in a bowl; set aside. Sift together cake flour, baking powder, cinnamon, and salt into a bowl; set aside. In another bowl, stir together milk, vanilla, and lemon zest; set aside. Using a standing mixer with a paddle attachment, cream butter and sugar on medium speed until fluffy, about 2 minutes. Add the eggs, one at a time, beating for 15 seconds after each addition. Reduce mixer speed to low. Alternately add flour and milk mixtures in thirds, beginning and ending with flour, until just incorporated. Scrape down sides of bowl with rubber spatula and gently fold in the apple-calvados mixture.

3. Transfer batter to the prepared pan; spread evenly. Scatter remaining blackberries over top of batter. Bake until golden and a toothpick inserted into center of cake comes out clean, about 1 hour and 30 minutes. Let cake cool in pan on a rack for 30 minutes; unmold, then cool completely. Mash macerated blackberries through a sieve into a bowl; discard seeds. Serve cake slices drizzled with the blackberry juice and dollops of crème fraîche (if using).

The Meat of the Matter

BEEF: IT'S WHAT'S FOR DINNER

By Betty Fussell

From *Raising Steaks*

A tenacious journalist and insightful food historian with a
simply gorgeous prose style, Betty Fussell follows up her
previous classics, *The Story of Corn* and *My Kitchen Wars*, with
this incisive horn-to-hoof study of one of America's most
iconic meals: the steak dinner.

It's not just about the beef, but about the ritual. It's not just
a stroll to the Upper East Side of Manhattan, but way
across the East River into the unknown wilderness of Williamsburg, Brooklyn, and you have to ride something to get there. You
wish it were a horse. A horse and carriage would suit its begin-
nings in 1887 within sniffing distance of the river, six years before
the Williamsburg Bridge was built, when the area was still a
bustling waterfront of breweries and warehouses, shipyards and
sugar refineries. It was crowded with Irish, Austrian, and German
immigrants, among them Carl Luger, who hedged his bets on the
food angle by calling it Carl Luger's Café, Billiards and Bowling
Alley. It was just as well, since the neighborhood declined once the
bridge was built, the rich burghers crossing over to Manhattan and
leaving behind working-class slums and tenements. In 1950 Sol
Forman, who ate steak at least once and often twice a day at the
café, because it was across the street from his factory for stamping
metal giftware, bought the place at auction so that he could continue his diet until his death at ninety-eight in 2001.

Whatever he may have done to the myth that steak is bad for
you, Sol certainly furthered the mythos of the American steak-

house, which was founded in market centers where cattle were turned into meat. Thomas De Voe, writing in 1862, numbered 1,200 butchers "both of the olden and modern times" in the many meat markets of the city and described the driving of cattle to market as a professional: "About 60 carts, accompanied with music, and flags and streamers, conveyed through the streets the 32 head of cattle fattened by Philip Fink of the Washington Market." However secular its format, the modern steakhouse bears vestiges of this ceremony of celebration. It gives meaning to the same animal sacrifice that our most ancient ancestors commemorated by offering the best parts to the gods. In Ulysses' day, the "best" was the fattiest piece of the slain ox, offered up hot and smoking on the altar. Nowadays a chef will slice off and discard the extra fat from the slab of meat he throws on the hot and smoking grill, because now it's trimmed meat that is deemed "best." But it's still an offering, and the scented smoke of its grilling is still meant to tempt whatever gods there be to a feast that echoes, however faintly, all that is heroic, primordial, carnal, and carnivorous in man's eternal urge for blood. "We're all basically animals," Sol is quoted as saying. "We want to eat meat." And in this country, we want to eat beef. Not just any beef, we want to eat steak, because steak for all of us immigrants means America. From the middle of the nineteenth century onward, steak was not only the commonest meal in America, it also represented every man's right to have the best. And while the Great American Steakhouse may have grown out of the inns and taverns and bars of early-nineteenth-century market cities, it was a late-nineteenth-century phenomenon celebrating what was already lost to the new industrialism, a vision of a gutsier time when every man had a right to claim the best, in a wilderness where men were men and meat was red as blood.

In New York City an annual beefsteak orgy had been staged for decades by butchers in a tavern at Shannon's Corner on Catherine Street to reward their favorite sea-captain customers. But by the 1880s and '90s men's eating and drinking clubs allowed newly enriched merchants and Wall Street tycoons to play red-neck primitives at the beefsteak feasts with which this book began, staged in halls made to look like old-time taverns. Just as cowboys anticipated letting go at the end of the cattle drive in an orgy of booze and gals in railroad-town bars, so urban herders of the money market looked forward to letting go at the end of the Wall Street week. The steakhouse is about letting go, about eating and drinking too much, about the joys of carnival excess. The romance of the steakhouse, like the romance of the cowboy, is rooted in a deep American nostalgia for male rituals, the more primitive the better.

When you enter Peter Luger's (Carl's heir Peter, who died in 1941, renamed the restaurant after himself), you walk into a bar—a long wooden bar under bare wooden beams next to a room with bare wooden tables and bench booths and brass chandeliers. You don't ask for a glass of house red or a wine list. You ask for a martini straight up. Or beer—pint or pitcher. The ceilings are tin, the floors strewn with sawdust. You don't ask for a menu, and you don't expect the waiter to introduce himself by name and tell you his life story. The waiters have been here for decades and scorn such guff. The entire ritual was set a century before you walked in the door, and thank god Sol Forman didn't change a thing. Men in shirtsleeves, women in housedresses, huge families packed with fat kids yelling loudly as they tuck in. You relax. You feel good, privileged, king of the fort. Everything is big: the chewy onion rolls, the thick-sliced tomatoes and onions in the salad slathered with Luger's special steak sauce, the 1¾-inch porterhouse sliced and sizzling on a platter so hot it can cook, the sides of German fried potatoes and creamed spinach, the bowl of whipped cream next to the apple strudel or chocolate mousse or pecan pie. You are in for a Big Evening and you pay in cash. Joseph Mitchell in the 1939 *New Yorker* piece "All You Can Hold For Five Bucks" recounted a typical Peter Luger's conversation: "At a table near the kitchen door I heard a woman say to another, 'Here, don't be bashful. Have a steak.' 'I just et six,' her friend replied. The first woman said, 'Wasn't you hungry? Why, you eat like a bird.' Then they threw their heads back and laughed." One 2007 blogger just didn't get it. "The place is a barn," she wrote, complaining about the poor wine list, the lack of menu, the arrogant waiters. "I prefer a finer atmosphere." The American steakhouse was born for no other reason than to give "finer atmosphere" the finger.

The Luger's menu is bare-boned because you're there single-mindedly for steak, not for lamb or salmon, which got added as concessions to the weaker sex. Cowboys don't have a choice; it's one gun or two. Here it's Steak for One, Two, Three, or Four, with "Steak for Two" the best cut because it's a bone-in porterhouse with a large filet, so you just double that for Four. The only real choice is rare or, for the hopelessly overurbanized, medium rare. If you want well-done, eat at home. Significantly, creamed spinach is the only green stuff, made tolerable by cream and butter. The potatoes are made tolerable by chopped bacon and onion. But nothing distracts from the platter of meat brought straight from the old Garland broilers set to 500 degrees that guarantee this is something you couldn't easily manage on your home stove or grill. The steakhouse is not meant to simulate home cooking or backyard barbecue. It's a communal feast celebrating superabundance and topsy-turvy, as in Roman Saturnalia or the medieval Land of Cockaigne, where nuns go bottoms up, servants beat their masters, the world flips upside down, and skies rain cheeses and pies and everything your animal gut desires.

What sets the steakhouse apart beyond all else is the quality of the beef, which you cannot buy in a supermarket but may in one of the few remaining butcher shops in cities as large as New York. Top steakhouses, along with upscale white-tablecloth restaurants, skim off the cream of beef stamped USDA Prime, which totals less than 2 percent of the beef market to begin with. Industrial beef cranks out Choice and Select. Within the Prime category, there are varying degrees of quality. Not only is it hard to get Prime beef of the highest quality, it's also hard to get beef that has been properly dry-aged. You need a temperature-controlled aging room for that, not to mention skill and knowledge. When you read stories about Peter Luger's, most of the story is about selecting the beef.

I meet Jody Spiera Storch, granddaughter of Sol, at Walmir Meat, Inc., at 839 Washington Street, in what remains of the old Gansevoort Meat Market. Jody is a vivacious, pretty blue-eyed brunette, mother of two young children, not at all the person you'd expect to see poking at half carcasses hung on a rail above the cement loading deck of a meat wholesaler's. But the lady meat buyers of Luger's are a family tradition. It was Sol's wife, Marsha, who took on the meat buying when Sol bought the restaurant, and it was Marsha who went to a retired government meat grader for instruction. "My grandmother used to bring me here from about age ten on non-school days," Jody said. "She was a really special lady, very regal, she'd come down here in a fur coat, pearls, and a fur hat." Jody dons a white butcher's coat and knit gloves while we talk with Ray DeStefano, a longtime Walmir's worker, who chimes in, "She'd come in her Cadillac, twenty-five years old and had 3,000 miles on it."

Grandma Marsha established the matriarchal tradition followed by her daughter Marilyn Forman Spiera, Jody's mother, and now by Jody herself. Jody's father is a surgeon and all her siblings are doctors; they call Jody the Meat Doctor, despite the fact that she thought she wouldn't be able to stand the blood and gore, and in fact after her first visit went vegetarian for a month. She'd gone to Barnard and was set to go to law school, but got distracted by the family business, which turns out to suit her. "I don't like being in an office," she says. "I like being out here with the guys." There are a lot of guys to be out with, since Luger's buys around 10 tons of beef per week, using half a dozen suppliers, three in the Gansevoort Market and the rest at Hunts Point. The restaurant uses at least 600 short loins a week, she says, each serving eight to twelve diners. The short loin is the section just below the steer's bottom rib, about a foot and a half long, which is cut into two or three porterhouses, T-bones, and New York strip or shell sirloins.

"This used to be an old Armour building," Ray says, "Armour meats, Armour foods, used to bring the meat downstairs and we'd cut it up and ship it out. Used to be all meat places here, but money talks and bullshit walks, and now a guy spends $6 million for the building on the corner for a dress shop."

"This is much more fun than Hunts Point, this neighborhood," Jody says.

"The kind of guys that are down here are all fun," Ray says. "They joke around, somebody you'd want to take home. But everything is boxed now, there's not enough top quality to go around, that's why they box it to get rid of it." Jody gets the first selection, Ray adds. "She pays top dollar."

Jody pokes one of the hanging sides. "My grandmother used to call this 'Christmas cattle,' *real* Prime."

Finding real Prime, even when all the carcasses are stamped USDA Prime, turns out to be an exacting task. Jody goes beneath one of the carcasses to touch the exposed thirteenth rib with her finger. "See how silky this is? Good fat, good color." Beware of dark cutters, she warns. Sometimes she'll cut a thin slice off the surface to see if the color beneath will brighten when it's exposed to air, but if it doesn't, she rejects it. Some she rejects because the texture is "ropy" instead of silky or because there's so much outside fat on it that it's "wastey," for the fat will have to be discarded. She inspects the backbone; if the meat's been sliced away, it won't age properly, the flesh will deteriorate faster. The meat she selects she stamps twice with her grandmother's long-handled brass die, which marks "F4F" within a purple ovoid, the stamp of Forman's metal factory.

"The calves used to be very rich, very grainy, but now they rush them, they force-feed them, the grain is stringy, looks like valleys and crevasses, instead of pinpoint marbling," Ray says. "It's all speed feeding now. They've changed the rules on what it takes to be Prime, and it doesn't take that much today."

"In the yield grading we always liked 3s," Jody says. "We never even looked at 2s, but now we're forced to because there aren't enough." She exams a rib on a carcass. "This is a 2, looks very pretty, but I prefer more outside-fat cover because we age them with the kidney and kidney fat on it. The fat protects the meat during the aging period."

"See how the kidneys are bright red on this one?" Ray asks me. "When the kidneys are black, the quality could be there, but the meat isn't going to taste as good. The blood type is different." Jody has moved down the carcass line. "Oh, this is beautiful, silky, marbley— not ropy—heavy like velvet, tiny points of marbling, nice rosy color."

Ray points to another one. "This one's nice, but it's got a small eye."

"Looks a little Choicey to me," Jody tells him. "Not great. This one felt very gummy, rubbery, got a lot of bruises. See where it's yellow? The animal got kicked or something."

"They butt each other," Ray says. "They know they're going to die, so they butt to get out."

"You don't want to get involved with that," says Jody. Of the next one, she exclaims, "This is graded Prime, but my grandmother would roll over if she saw that. This is Prime *crime.*"

We step inside Walmir's warehouse to look at the metal trees of short loins, hooked on a central spike like a coat hanger, hanging upside down. Each loin weighs around 45 pounds, Jody says, depending on the size of the kidney, which might weight 12 to 15 pounds. At Luger's they render the kidney for fat, use some of it for cooking and for suet; the rest gets picked up. Luger's famed aging room, Jody says, is just "a long skinny room with fans blowing on it, nothing weird about temperature, humidity, no set rules. A lot depends on the meat. If it has a lot of thick, heavy marbling, it takes more time than meat with fine flecking. So when the meat comes in, we divide it into lot numbers, then keep logs on everything. Some lot might need an extra week. It's a family business, not a committee. If I see meat very ropy, I'll say, 'This needs a little more time.' A lot of people don't understand what meat should be. They think it should be soft, bland, but it should have a little texture to it."

Besides the quality of the meat, what sets the steakhouse apart from home cooking is the quantity of heat. Typically, steakhouse kitchens go for quick-searing in upright commercial broilers that use infrared or radiant heat. Infrared uses ceramic bricks and is hotter than radiant, but the bricks are more fragile than the cast-iron burners that radiant broilers use. BTUs for either broiler are in the range of 70,000 to 104,000 per deck, which generates a quick sear that can be followed by a finishing oven. Jody and Ray compare the best way to simulate the heat of restaurant grills on home broilers, which are rarely more than 25,000 BTUs tops. Jody suggests preheating the boiler for as long as half an hour, then putting the meat close to the flame, although that creates a real risk of fire. Ray's technique is to take some of the kidney fat, melt it down, brush it on the outside, and put the meat right up to the fire in a broiler pan. "I like it singed, nice and pink in the middle, all those juices locked in."

Ray's been making a living at Walmir's for forty years. His grandfather had a little butcher shop on Houston called DeStefano's, where he was a plumber and his grandmother was the butcher. "I used to have the smallest fingers in the family, so I stuffed the sausage," Ray says. Real butchering he learned in the Army in France, where he'd been sent after he got wounded in Korea.

His sergeant said, "Anybody know how to cut meat?"

"'Yeah, I know.' I didn't, but before you knew it, I took over the place, just for officers and their wives, and stayed there four years, in Orléans, near Paris."

He misses the old days of butchering in the Washington Meat Market. "There were so many jobs around in the sixties," he says. "If you didn't like your boss, you'd go next door and work for the other guy. But now there's only three places left here. Cryovac spoiled everything. I went to visit IBP after they said, 'Come and see how our meat is processed.' They put us up, fed us, gave us a lot of brochures, predicted that by 2010 they're going to have machinery to bone out cattle. Butchering's a dying art. I heard those things and I was getting sick. I love this business. I don't want to go, like, *down*, you know what I mean?"

THE LAST OF THE GREAT $10 STEAKS

By Jason Sheehan

From *WestWord*

Few restaurant reviewers are as consistently entertaining as
Sheehan, the dining critic for Denver's *WestWord* weekly
newspaper. His sprawling reviews—like this one of a local
steak joint—zoom right past menu notes and get to the heart
of why we dine out.

It's 1983, I'm ten years old—and it's steak night at the
Sheehan household.

Steak nights didn't happen very often at my house. But every
now and again, Mom would go to the freezer and pull out a frost-
rimmed, plastic-wrapped Styrofoam tray of thin, choice-grade steaks
bought on sale at the neighborhood Wegmans and then saved
against need. She would scrape some of the ice off with a thumb-
nail, check to make sure that the beef inside was still vaguely meat-
colored (never pink, of course, or bloody, beautiful red, but rather
gradations of purply-gray) and then leave the package to thaw on
the kitchen counter. Mom was a great believer in technology, in
the near-magical powers of the upright freezer in the kitchen. That
miraculous white box—jammed full of mysterious packages, ancient Tupperware and wrapped balls of what might've been cookie
dough, might've been meatballs—could keep food safe and edible
for years. Decades. It was like a time machine for comestibles.
Reach in blindly, pull out a package, and suddenly you were back
in the middle of the Carter administration or thawing leftover beef
stew first eaten on the night the Steelers beat the Cowboys in Su-
per Bowl XIII, January 21, 1979.

The steaks would sit on a plate on the counter, slowly losing their pre-Cambrian frost. My brother and I would come home from school; Dad would come home from work. He'd see the steaks, change out of his work clothes and go out into the backyard where his grill sat. His elderly, gas-fired charcoal grill. His elderly, gas-fired charcoal grill that, depending on how the household finances were shaking out, how the weather had been, might not have been used for weeks or months. He would bend down, start fussing with gas lines and igniters, tapping at the tank with the metal end of a pen or a pair of pliers. Because Dad was a mechanic and a repairman, we got almost everything—every appliance, every piece of home electronics—second- or third-hand. We got the things he hadn't been able to repair during the regular course of his job so had brought home to tinker with in his spare time. Sometimes he got them to work grudgingly, sometimes he didn't. Like a dedicated preacher, though, he considered these castaway domestic devices as part of his flock and never gave up on the possible salvage of their mechanical souls. The grill was one of his more recalcitrant projects. It never worked well, sometimes didn't work at all, and so there was always the chance that, on steak night, Dad would go outside, start poking around the guts of that intractable grill and accidentally blow himself up.

My brother and I were always waiting for it, knowing full well that such an explosion wouldn't kill the man—nothing could do that, not to a guy we'd once seen cut one of his fingers nearly off while working in the garage, then tape it back together with black electrical tape and go right back to work—but just drive him back into the house, smoke-black and probably bleeding and laughing, looking for the tape, maybe a staple gun, with which to reassemble any of his own missing parts. But the explosion never came, and Dad would eventually gimmick the grill into action, take the steaks and stand outside in the lowering dark cooking, smoking, gently hitting a can of Genny Cream Ale, doing what a man does on a good night when he has done good work and is proud to be able to offer steaks to his little suburban tribe.

The smell of cheap steaks burning on a grill, of char smoke on the spring air mixing with the smell of hyacinth and burley-and-bright. That will always remind me of my dad, of my mom watching him through the little window in the kitchen looking out over the back yard, of good days when I knew in some deep and mostly inaccessible part of my childhood self that things were, for the moment, okay. Steak nights were like quiet celebrations of small victories— solid knowledge that there was enough money to pay the bills, that the grownups had done whatever it was that grownups do to make things all right for a few hours or a few days.

If I were Proust, that smell would be my madeleine—the trigger for a crashing flood of recall, of me in the warm comfort of boyhood. And walking past the back door of the Columbine Steak House, I get a whiff of it. Just a hint—a trick of the breeze sucking a breath of blood and smoke and fire out through the open door where a busboy stands smoking a cigarette in the afternoon sun— but it is enough to stop me in my tracks and nearly drive me to my knees from the weight of memory. The scratched black paint of Dad's grill. The pop and hiss of him opening his can of Genny Cream. The taste of bloody, low-rent beef on my tongue.

The Columbine claims to have been "nationally known for fine steaks since 1961"—since my dad was the age that I'm remembering being, standing in its back parking lot almost fifty years later. It is a survivor, the kind of place they don't make anymore, that no one has made in decades: a steak diner, a pure-strain joint, with a faded and smooth-worn dining room in front and a dim lounge in the back with a bar, a juke, a few booths and bottles of old-man liquor in the racks like a museum of classic alcoholism: Canadian Club and Ballantine's and John Powers Irish. It is menu service in the lounge, short-order up front, with an abbreviated stretch of bright aluminum counter the color of a new Airstream and a cafeteria setup. You look at the menu hung above the two cooks working the grill and just tell them what you want: T-bone, tenderloin, New York or porterhouse, plate of shrimp (shades of *Repo Man* ...) or burgers or fries. Pay at the register five feet away—cash only, no checks, no plastic. Then wait.

When I walk in the front door, the dining room is running near-capacity, and two cooks are working the grill like it's said something nasty about their mother. They have close on twenty steaks already mapped onto the grate, putting some to the flame, others holding warm and par-cooked.

"Getcha?" asks the cook.

"T-bone," says me.

"How you want it?"

"Mid-rare."

"'kay."

And done. Fourteen bucks and change to the register for my steak dinner and a fountain Coke, three dollars into the tip jar. At this point, the smell is washing over me like rain—smoke rising up, the sizzle and flare of fresh meat being pulled bare-handed out of the cooler and slapped down onto any empty acreage on the grill. I get my drink, grab the second-to-last table, and before I've even settled into my seat, one of the cooks is calling me back: "T-bone, medium!"

For my money, I get a straight iceberg salad (dressing ladled out of inserts set between the cafeteria rail and the short-order pass, no sneeze-guards here) with a little shredded carrot and red cabbage; a thick slice of Texas toast off the grill and soaking with butter; a baked potato in a foil jacket, already split and mounted with more butter—a ball of it, as big as a small scoop of ice cream—and my steak: big enough to overhang the lip of my plate, marked with an inexpert quadrillage but lovely to me regardless. My T-bone is tender except for the twists of fat and gristle near the bone. It tastes of flame and char and blood and meat and history. The potato has soaked down butter like a sponge, and I eat it with bites of Texas toast just because too much butter is never quite enough. Later, I will return for an even cheaper steak, a ten-dollar New York that I'll cut with a rickety, wood-handled dollar-store knife, tear into pieces and eat with my fingers, the meat pressed into torn hunks of Texas toast. And then I'll come back again, collapsing into one of the deep booths in the lounge for cold, happy-hour beers and a porterhouse: top of the menu at fifteen bucks.

No one comes to the Columbine for the service, the artful plating or the charming company. And no one steps into this raggedy, patched dining room expecting a fat, USDA Prime steak-of-the-year slab of beef. You either come to the Columbine because you love the good, cheap stuff—because you remember when most restaurants were like this one, before everyone started putting wasabi or truffles or lemongrass in everything—or because you understand that the difference between paying fifty dollars for a steak and paying fifteen dollars for a steak is mostly about paying for the crowd, the tablecloths, the fine plates and the sommelier's salary. But I like the Columbine for both reasons. I love iceberg salads with blue-cheese dressing out of a plastic jug more than I love almost any other kind of salad. I love baked potatoes that are used mostly as a cover for people too embarrassed to eat butter with a spoon. And I have always loved cheap steaks because, to me, cheap steaks are the only kind that actually taste like *steak*. Yes, I enjoy a Prime porterhouse or a fat rib-eye, perfectly rare and on the bone. But because of the way I grew up, those heroic cuts of incredibly expensive cow flesh taste more like luxury and fat-ass braggadoccio than they do steak. I am always faintly embarrassed when I walk into a serious steakhouse, knowing good and god-damn well that I would not *ever* be in that restaurant were it not for this job.

But at the Columbine? Christ, I just feel like I'm home.

HIGHWAY TO HOG HEAVEN

By John Linn

From *Broward Palm Beach New Times*

The new restaurant critic for the *Broward Palm Beach New Times*, Linn slid handily into food writing from his South Florida nightlife beat for both the *Palm Beach* and *Miami New Times* weeklies. His weapons? An egalitarian palate and well-honed comic punch lines.

Scene: Four friends plunge through the outskirts of Savannah, Georgia. They're on the hunt for what is reputed to be the best barbecue joint in the area, Two Bubbas BBQ, and their journey is taking them far off the beaten path, past the din of commuter traffic, past vacant auto lots, and into a thick umbrella of moss-draped sentinel oak trees. They have no idea where they are going, and they are very hungry.

To a hungry stomach, any drive can seem like forever.

We were driving *maybe* 30 minutes, but you couldn't tell that to any three compatriots, whom I had dragged, stomachs rumbling, past no fewer than four barbecue joints on the way. With each glowing "BBQ" sign fading into the background, I could feel the pressure building in the car, like so much smoke in a barrel. They were pissed.

I can't really blame them. At the time, my buddies didn't understand the difference between merely OK barbecue, the hastily prepared stuff that's scattered across the landscape whether you're in Savannah or Fort Lauderdale, or truly transcendental barbecue, the kind whose smoky promise commands you to do selfish things to your very tolerant friends.

In about 30 more minutes, however, they would come to for-give me . . . and then some. Serving as emissaries for my official apology: spare ribs laden with the rich ichor of hickory, wedges of chopped pork shoulder gang-tackling an overmatched bun, an infant-sized baked potato cradled in smoked chicken meat, and the magical blue-green twilight of rural Georgia at dusk. I was in good hands.

Back home, I set out to discover what smoky secrets South Florida's less-traveled pathways have in store. Only, I ran into a bit of a snag. Despite being home to a handful of respected, long-established barbecue eateries, the tricounty area has come to be characterized as a place from which no real barbecue can grow.

Talk to any out-of-state transplant (all experts, mind you) and he or she will tell you that SoFla's 'cue can't hold a cleaned rib bone to the stuff from Texas, the Carolinas, or the entire South, for that matter. It's a frustrating mindset, though not one that's re-served solely for barbecue. Pennsylvanians know that no sun-tanned cheese steak can touch the offerings from their native land. British expats would rather boff the Queen than eat Indian on our shores. And no list of this sort would be complete without New Yorkers—the most pugnacious one-uppers of them all—who won't let our pizza or Chinese food cross their lips without chal-lenging the legitimacy.

If you listen to these haters, you'd be better off spending your nights tucked into a Stouffer's lasagna on your couch than braving the multitude of subpar dining options available. But I've got a better theory: Florida *does* have great barbecue. It's just that those transplants spend too much time at home reminiscing about how much better they had it at home to discover the truly plentiful spread of food finds out there. Could it be they just don't know where to look?

Recently, underground Florida barbecue has been popping up all over the map. Last week, I visited Big Belly Jerk BBQ, a humble food truck parked in the Sunoco lot of Sunrise Boulevard and Powerline Road, and walked away with a spicy-sweet feast of jerk chicken, pork, and ribs that I couldn't finish in three days. Then I joined another group of pals on the hunt for a man who cooks 'cue out of his Hollywood home on Saturdays, selling off ribs by the rackload. You've got to know someone who knows someone, and most of his racks are spoken for by noon, but if you can snag one, it's well worth the trip. But my best find came two Fridays ago, when I stumbled across Deep Down South BBQ.

I say *stumbled* across it, but the reality is, you can't miss it. DDS is a 40-foot, barn-house-red trailer that ties up at the east corner of the Exxon lot on Sunrise Boulevard and 31st Avenue. If somehow you overlook the trailer, you can spot it by finding the swarm of cars parked alongside or the line of folks queuing up ten deep at its takeout window (the only option available). They're there en masse—though DDS has been open barely two months now and only Thursday through Sunday—because the barbecue concocted by owner Albert Houston is the honest-to-goodness real deal.

"Real barbecue?" you scoff. "Not in this town!" Well, my friend, Houston's baby back ribs ($12.99 half rack, $18.99 full) tell another tale: The juicy spears of rib meat are basted for nearly four hours in thick hickory and applewood smoke until a vibrant rose ring forms beneath the spice-rubbed crust. Teaming with rendered fat and tissue, the meat falls from the bone with even the slightest suggestion, yet retains its fleshy and toothsome texture. You can't eat one rib without letting out an "*mmmm*," pausing only to lick your fingers and the corners of your mouth.

Houston's 'cue is served with a side of his smoky barbecue sauce—a mixture that shares traits with those from Kansas City: It sports a tomato base and a sweet, honey-and-fruit flavor that pairs well with the richness of the meat. It's a fine sauce, but I find I don't need it, especially on DDS' moist spare ribs ($8.99). These puppies get the same treatment as the baby backs, only they come chopped down into two-inch-long sections and coated with a bit too much sauce. Maybe it's a great thing for folks who always need extra, but not for those who prefer their meat tasting of meat. If you're in the latter group, get it on the side and you'll be in absolute pig heaven.

Ask Houston about his craft and you can tell he's studied barbecue inside and out. The ribs are so good because he knows the tricks: He takes the time to remove the membrane, that slightly chewy coating along the underside of the bone that keeps smoke from penetrating the meat. He never brines them, because then they just end up tasting like ham. He wouldn't dream of parboiling them, a common restaurant shortcut used to cut the cooking time. Instead, Houston is exacting in his preparation, a trait he no doubt picked up while cooking chow in the Marine Corps or working on restaurant development for Marriott Hotels. It's why his number-one goal, he says, is consistency. "If I can't be consistent to the *T*," he says proudly, "then I'd rather not do it at all."

Houston first launched DDS in Fort Myers in 2005. Cooking "competition-style" 'cue from his big red trailer, he developed a devoted following serving ribs, chicken, pulled pork, seafood, and daily-made fixings. When he was forced to leave his well-known spot because of nearby construction, Houston looked to sites in Atlanta and at the Swap Shop in Fort Lauderdale. Though he couldn't secure a space inside the Shop, he decided the area was just too ripe to pass up, so he moved into the Exxon lot adjacent to the market. His goal is to open his first brick-and-mortar store in Broward and eventually expand his concept elsewhere.

Meanwhile, we'll have to settle for ordering DDS' pulled pork sandwich ($4.99) from the raised takeout counter on his truck. I'm convinced this is the best food deal in South Florida right now: You get two inch-thick slices of buttery, garlicky Texas toast to go with a mound of dripping pulled pork so big it looks as if a forklift plopped it in the foil-lined to-go container. I could talk for days about how the shredded meat is eminently tender—though never clumping into a tuna-salad-like mash like some pulled meat does—and so wet with its own "gravy" that it needs no sauce at all. For a dollar more, you can perfect it by adding some of Houston's own mayonnaisey coleslaw on top.

You need more reasons to get up and visit DDS right now? How about the mac 'n' cheese ($1.50 with any meal, $2.50 otherwise), a velvety, heart-stopping wad o' pasta, cheddar, and jack cheeses baked until golden? Or the deep-fried seafood box ($13.99)—hardback blue crabs caked in crunchy corn meal and rolled around in garlic oil, ultra-fresh fillets of moist grouper and tilapia, and pink shrimp cut to look like some exotic flower? Braver folk may opt for the souse ($4.99), that Southern classic of odd pig parts brined and stewed. For dessert, I suggest the creamiest, richest slice of sweet potato pie you'll find, only $2.75.

About the only complaint I can muster is that there's no telephone—so instead of being able to call your feast in, you'll have to hoof it down there and wait in line for your food, sometimes for quite long. It's not inconsequential, but it's hardly a deal breaker with grub this good. Still, feel free to write me and tell me I don't know anything about great barbecue, that DDS is nothing compared to the joints you've been to in Dallas or Atlanta or Asheville. Well, go ahead and haul yourself to said destination. I'll hold down the fort here, along with a lot of other *very* happy Floridians.

Scene: Four friends drive out of the wilds of unincorporated Broward, hands sticky and bellies full. As a pink-hued blanket envelops the horizon, they have an epiphany: Great barbecue is neither fast nor easy. But it's always worth it.

By Meat Alone

By Calvin Trillin

From *The New Yorker*

Despite years atop the elite roster of writers at
The New Yorker and *The Nation*, Calvin Trillin—journalist,
essayist, humorist, novelist—is still a Kansas City native,
and thus a born-and-bred connoisseur of barbecue. Who
better to investigate the meteoric rise of a new contender
for America's barbecue crown?

I approached *Texas Monthly's* cover story on "The Top 50 BBQ Joints in Texas" this summer the way a regular reader of *People* might approach that magazine's annual "Sexiest Man Alive" feature—with the expectation of seeing some familiar names. There was no reason to think that the list's top tier—the five restaurants judged to be the best in the state—would look much different than it had the last time a survey was published, in 2003. In recent years, Hollywood may have seen some advances in physical training and cosmetic surgery, but barbecue restaurants still tend to retain their luster much longer than male heartthrobs do. In fact, I've heard it argued that, absent some slippage in management, a barbecue restaurant can only get better over time: many Texas barbecue fanatics have a strong belief in the beneficial properties of accumulated grease.

In discussions of Texas barbecue, the equivalent of Matt Damon and George Clooney and Brad Pitt would be establishments like Kreuz Market and Smitty's Market, in Lockhart; City Market, in Luling; and Louie Mueller Barbecue, in Taylor—places that reflect the barbecue tradition that developed during the nineteenth century out of German and Czech meat markets in the Hill Country of central Texas. (In fact, the title of *Texas Monthly*'s first article on barbecue—it was published in 1973, shortly after the magazine's founding—was "The World's Best Barbecue Is in Taylor, Texas. Or Is It Lockhart?") Those restaurants, all of which had been in the top tier in 2003, were indeed there again in this summer's survey. For the first time, though, a No. 1 had been named, and it was not one of the old familiars. "The best barbecue in Texas," the article said, "is currently being served at Snow's BBQ, in Lexington."

I had never heard of Snow's. That surprised me. Although I grew up in Kansas City, which has a completely different style of barbecue, I have always kept more or less au courant of Texas barbecue, like a sports fan who is almost monomaniacally obsessed with basketball but glances over at the NHL standings now and then just to see how things are going. Reading that the best barbecue in Texas was at Snow's, in Lexington, I felt like a *People* subscriber who had picked up the "Sexiest Man Alive" issue and discovered that the sexiest man alive was Sheldon Ludnick, an insurance adjuster from Terre Haute, Indiana, with Clooney as the runner-up.

An accompanying story on how a Numero Uno had emerged, from 341 spots visited by the staff, revealed that before work began on the 2008 survey nobody at *Texas Monthly* had heard of Snow's, either. Lexington, a trading town of twelve hundred people in Lee County, is only about fifty miles from Austin, where *Texas Monthly* is published, and Texans think nothing of driving that far for lunch—particularly if the lunch consists of brisket that has been subjected to slow heat since the early hours of the morning. *Texas Monthly* has had a strong posse of barbecue enthusiasts since its early days. Griffin Smith, who wrote the 1973 barbecue article and is now the executive editor of the *Arkansas Democrat-Gazette* in Little Rock, was known for keeping a map of the state on his wall with push-pins marking barbecue joints he had been to, the way General Patton might have kept a map marked with spots where night patrols had probed the German line. I could imagine the staffers not knowing about a superior barbecue restaurant in East Texas; the Southern style of barbecue served there, often on a bun, has never held much interest for Austin connoisseurs. But their being unaware of a top-tier establishment less than an hour's drive away astonished me.

I know some of the *Texas Monthly* crowd. In fact, I once joined Greg Curtis, the former editor, and Steve Harrigan, a novelist who's had a long association with the magazine, on a pilgrimage to Lockhart, which some barbecue fans visit the way the devout of another sort walk the Camino de Santiago. I know Evan Smith, who was the editor of the magazine when this latest barbecue survey was published and has since been promoted to a position that might be described as boss of bosses. I couldn't imagine Smith jiggering the results for nefarious purposes—say, telling his staff to declare a totally unknown barbecue place the best in Texas simply as a way of doing what some magazine editors call "juicing up the story." I took him at his word when, a few months after the list was published, he told me how Snow's had been found. His staff had gone through the letters written after the 2003 survey complaining about the neglect of a superior specialist in pork ribs or the inclusion of a place whose smoked sausage wasn't fit for pets—what Smith, who's from Queens, refers to as "Dear Schmuck letters."

He did acknowledge that his decision to name a No. 1—rather than just a top tier, as in the previous barbecue surveys—came about partly because everyone was so enthusiastic about Snow's product but partly because its story was so compelling. Smith himself was not in a position to confirm the quality of the product. Being from Queens is not the only handicap he has had to surmount in his rise through the ranks of Texas journalism: he has been a vegetarian for nearly twenty-five years. (The fact that he is able to resist the temptation presented by the aroma of Texas pit barbecue, he has said, is a strong indication that he will never "return to the dark side.") As a longtime editor, though, he knew a Cinderella story when he saw one. It wasn't just that Snow's had been unknown to a Texas barbecue fancy that is notably mobile. Snow's proprietor, Kerry Bexley, was a former rodeo clown who worked as a blending-facility operator at a coal mine. Snow's pit master, Tootsie Tomanetz, was a woman in her early seventies who worked as the custodian of the middle school in Giddings, Texas—the Lee County seat, eighteen miles to the south. After five years of operating Snow's, both of them still had their day jobs. Also, Snow's was open only on Saturday mornings, from eight until the meat ran out.

MY CONVERSATION with Evan Smith took place in a Chevrolet Suburban traveling from Austin toward Lexington. I'd been picked up at my hotel at 7:20 A.M. The *Texas Monthly* rankings had attracted large crowds to Snow's, and, even four months later, we weren't taking any chances. Greg Curtis and Steve Harrigan were with Smith in the back seats. Harrigan was one of the people who, having been tipped off between the time the feature was completed and the time the magazine came out, hurried over to Snow's like inside traders in possession of material information not available to the general public. He seemed completely unrepentant. "I took my brother and brother-in-law and son-in-law and nephew," he said, smiling slyly. Next to me in the front seat, Paul Burka was doing the driving. Greg Curtis once reminded me that "all barbecue experts are self-proclaimed," but *Texas Monthly* had enough faith in Burka's expertise to send him to Snow's late in the selection process as what Smith calls "the closer." It was up to Burka to confirm or dismiss the judgment of the staffer whose assigned territory for the survey included Lexington, and of Patricia Sharpe, the editor in charge of the project, and of a second staffer sent in as a triple-check. Some people at the magazine had predicted that Burka wouldn't like Snow's barbecue simply because it bore Pat Sharpe's imprimatur. "Paul thinks Pat's judgment of restaurants is fancy and white tablecloth and Pat thinks Paul is a philistine," I heard from the back seat. "And they're both right."

When I spoke to Pat Sharpe a couple of days later, she bristled at the accusation that she is a person of elevated taste. "I'll eat barbecue in the rattiest joint there is," she said in her own defense. Burka, on the other hand, seemed unconcerned about being called a philistine. He is a large man with a white mustache and a midsection that reflects a forty-year interest in Texas barbecue. Having grown up in Galveston, which is not a barbecue center, he innocently started eating what he now describes as "barbecue that was one step removed from roast beef" while he was a student at Rice, in Houston; he had his true conversion experience on a trip to

Lockhart with Griffin Smith in 1967, when they were both in law school at the University of Texas. Burka, who worked for five years in the Texas state legislature, writes about politics for *Texas Monthly*. Speaking to him as the Suburban rolled toward Lexington, I was reminded of the Austin brought to life in *The Gay Place*, Billy Lee Brammer's marvelous 1961 novel about an LBJ-like governor called Arthur (Goddam) Fenstermaker. That Austin was essentially a two-company town—the university and the state government—and I always pictured those connected with both companies sharing irreverent observations of the passing scene while consuming a lot of beer in the back of Scholz's beer garden. It is an Austin that is sometimes difficult to discern in a much larger city of slick office buildings and computer-company headquarters and the mother church of Whole Foods, which actually offers barbecue in the meat department of its Austin stories. ("Organic barbecue," Burka muttered, when somebody brought that up.)

The first time Burka went to Lexington to check out Snow's, he arrived just before noon. "It looked like it had never been open," he said. "It was deserted." When he finally got there at a time when meat was still available, he was convinced. In fact, he was rhapsodic, particularly concerning the brisket ("as soft and sweet as cookie dough") and the pork butt. Smith believed that Burka's description of the latter—"the butt was tender and yielding"—was in need of some editing, but, without having to consume any critters personally, he was persuaded by Burka's report. Snow's was to be named the best barbecue in Texas, and Evan Smith never had any doubt about what would happen as soon as that designation was on the newsstands. "I basically said, 'Congratulations and I'm sorry,'" he told me, "because I knew what would happen."

"That brings up the subject of remorse," I said.

"You mean remorse on their part?" Smith asked.

"No, remorse on your part—remorse for having turned the place into an ugly scene."

"We don't publish *Best-Kept Secrets Monthly*," Smith said, as he got out of Burka's Suburban. He sniffed confidently, presumably to reassure himself that, despite the aroma, he would have no trouble limiting himself to coleslaw and potato salad. Then he marched across the street toward Snow's BBQ.

REGULAR CONSUMERS of Hill Country-style Texas barbecue know what to expect when they walk into an establishment that is said to offer the real article. I had never been to Louie Mueller's, in Taylor, before this trip, but when Greg Curtis and I went there the day before the Snow's outing for what we referred to as some warm-up barbecue, the place looked familiar. At a Texas barbecue joint, you normally pick up a tray at the counter and order meat from one person and sides from another. The person doling out the meat removes it from the smoker and carves it himself. It is sold by the pound—often brisket and pork ribs and sausage and beef ribs and chicken and, in some places, clod (beef shoulder). The carver serves it on some variety of butcher paper. If, despite having worked with smoke in his eyes for many years, he is of a generous nature, as the carvers at Mueller's are known to be, he might slice off a piece of a brisket's darkened outside—what would be called in Kansas City a burnt end—and, before you've ordered anything, place it on your tray as a small gesture. (Given the quality of Mueller's brisket, it is a gesture that can make a traveler feel immensely pleased about being back in Texas.) A couple of slices of packaged white bread are also included. Usually, the only way to have a brisket sandwich in central Texas is to make your own.

A Texas barbecue joint is likely to have neon beer signs on the walls, and those walls are likely to have been darkened by years of smoke. At Mueller's, a cavernous place in a former school gym, there is a large bulletin board festooned with business cards, and most of the cards by now look like specks of brownish parchment. In a restaurant serving Hill Country barbecue, there may be bottles of sauce on the tables, but the meat does not come out of the pits slathered in sauce. I remember a sign at Kreuz Market announcing that the management provided neither sauce nor salads nor forks. In central Texas, you don't hear a lot of people talking about the piquancy of a restaurant's sauce or the tastiness of its beans; discussions are what a scholar of the culture might call meat-driven.

Geographically, Lexington is not in the Hill Country—it's in ranch land, northeast of Austin—but ethnically it is. Burka told me that a politician from Lee County once said to him, "It's the Germans against the Czechs, and the Americans are the swing vote." Snow's BBQ turned out to have the sort of layout found in a place like Kreuz Market, except in miniature. It's a small dark-red building that has room for a counter and six tables—with a few more tables outside, near the cast-iron smokers that in Texas are referred to as pits, even if they're not in the ground. A sign listed what meats were available, all for $8.45 a pound: sausage, brisket, pork, pork ribs, and chicken. The sides offered were "Mrs. Patschke's homemade coleslaw and potato salad," plus free beans. There were only a couple of people ahead of us in line. Burka stepped up to the counter to order.

"Are there five of you?" the young woman slicing the meat asked, as Burka tried to figure out how many pounds we needed.

"Well," Burka said, glancing at Evan Smith. "Four, really. One is . . . he has a big meal coming up."

"You're ashamed of your friend," I whispered to Burka. "You've abandoned him."

"I just couldn't say the V-word," Burka said. He looked sheepish—not, I would guess, a normal look for him.

I had warned the *Texas Monthly* crowd that if they were looking for confirmation of their ranking by an objective outlander, someone from Kansas City was not likely to provide it. A jazz fan taken to a rock concert might admire the musical technique, but he probably wouldn't make an ecstatic rush to the stage. As we sat down at one of the outside tables, under a galvanized-tin covering, I told them that they could expect the sort of response that a proud young father I know has received during the past year or so whenever he e-mails me pictures of his firstborn: "A perfectly adequate child." Still, what Burka had ordered was good enough to make me forget that we were eating a huge meal of barbecue at a time on Saturday morning when most people were starting to wonder what they might rustle up for breakfast once they bestirred themselves. I particularly liked the brisket, although I couldn't attest that it was as soft and sweet as cookie dough. In Kansas City, it is not customary to eat cookie dough.

ALTHOUGH SNOW'S HOURS may seem odd to a city dweller, they seem normal in Lexington. Saturday is traditionally when farmers and ranchers from the surrounding area come into town, and at twelve-thirty every Saturday there is a cattle auction in yards that are just down the street from Snow's. From 1976 to 1996, in fact, Tootsie Tomanetz, who is known far and wide in Lee County as Miss Tootsie, served barbecue every Saturday at a meat market that she and her husband ran in Lexington. Miss Tootsie's husband is half Czech and half German. She was born Norma Frances Otto, German on both sides, and her father liked to say that when she married she went from having a last name that could be spelled backward or forward to having one that couldn't be spelled at all. Before the Tomanetzes opened their store, Miss Tootsie had put in ten years tending the pits at City Meat Market, in Giddings. In other words, Kerry Bexley, who's forty-one, could have a certainty about Miss Tootsie's gift that was based on having eaten her barbecue virtually all his life.

After lunch, if that's what you call a large meal of meat that you finish just before 9 A.M., I had a chat about Snow's origins with its management team. We talked near the pits, so Miss Tootsie could pull off sausage links now and then. "I felt like with her name and barbecue and my personality with people we could make it work," Bexley told me. He's a short, outgoing man whose résumé includes—in addition to rodeo clown—prison guard, auctioneer, real-estate agent, and shopkeeper. He already had the location—a place where he'd run a farm and ranch store in 1992. The name came from a nickname he'd had since before he was born. According to the family story, his brother, then four years old, was asked whether he was hoping for the new baby to be a boy or a girl, and he replied, not unreasonably, that he would prefer a snowman. Kerry (Snowman) Bexley and Miss Tootsie opened Snow's in March of 2003—Bexley had built the pits—and it did well from the start. "For the most part, we cooked two to three hundred pounds of meat," Bexley told me. "We sold out by noon."

In the weeks after the *Texas Monthly* feature was published, Snow's went from serving three hundred pounds of meat every Saturday to serving more than a thousand pounds. At eight in the morning—six or seven hours after Miss Tootsie had arrived to begin tending the pits—there was already a line of customers, some of whom had left home before dawn. Bexley said that one Saturday morning, when there were ninety people waiting outside, a local resident asked permission to gather signatures along the line for a petition, only to return a few minutes later with the information that there wasn't one person there from Lee County. Some locals expressed irritation at being shut out of their own barbecue joint. At times, Bexley and Miss Tootsie felt overwhelmed. There were moments, they say, when they wished that the tasters from *Texas Monthly* had never shown up. Then Bexley added three brisket pits, Miss Tootsie got some help, Snow's for a time quit taking pre-orders by phone except for locals, and the amount of meat prepared every Saturday leveled off to about eight hundred pounds.

Most of the time, Bexley and Miss Tootsie are grateful for the additional business. Not long after the survey appeared, Snow's BBQ started selling T-shirts that had on them not only "Voted #1 BBQ in Texas" but a motto that Bexley's wife had suggested— "Smokin' the good stuff." Looking around for a way to extend the newly famous Snow's brand without sacrificing the quality of the product, Bexley has hit on mail order, and is hoping to have that under way soon. Snow's already has a Web site. Bexley and Miss Tootsie are also pleased by the personal recognition. They've worked hard. Most people in Lee County work hard without anybody's noticing. Whether or not Kerry Bexley and Tootsie Tomanetz ever feel able to give up their day jobs, they have received the sort of pure validation that doesn't come to many people, no matter what their field of endeavor.

"Miss Tootsie gets some recognition now for what she's actually done all her life," Bexley said. "She's now"—he turned to Miss Tootsie—"seventy-four? Excuse me for asking."

"No, I'm just seventy-three," Miss Tootsie said, smiling. "You add a year every time."

"What did you do when you heard that you were No. 1?" I asked.

"When we found out we were No. 1," Bexley said, "we just set there in each other's arms and we bawled."

The Disappearing Art of the Country Ham

By Kathleen Purvis

From the *Charlotte Observer*

Originally a two-part feature, *Observer* food editor Purvis'
inquiry into the state of Carolina ham is the sort of definitive
statement on Southern foodways that she serves up to her
readers on a regular basis.

Salty. Leathery. The skin dried so hard, it can take a band saw to cut through it. Before cooking, you have to heft it into a sink and scrub off the mold. This is not most people's definition of food. But in the Carolinas, it's a good description of one of our most important contributions to the American food story: Slow-cured country ham.

It once kept people in this part of the world alive through tough winters. It added flavor and protein to meager plates of grits and greens. It was so prized, colonists made scarce cash by shipping it to Europe for the gentry.

Today, slow-cured country ham is not much more than a lingering taste of Carolinas history. In supermarkets, you usually find mass-produced versions that use climate controls to hurry the process. What's hard to find is the original kind, treated with nothing but salt and maybe sugar, and hung in a room with open windows, exposed to months of spring breezes and humid summer nights. The craft is a victim of strict regulation and modern tastes that prefer sweet to salty and convenience in all things.

But maybe the world is ready to come back to country ham. Slowly made foods are finding fans in chefs who love strong, unique flavors. At gourmet markets, people pay a premium for imported prosciutto. When Spain's most famous ham, Iberico de Bellota Paleta, finally was allowed into the U.S. last year, aficionados lined up to spend up to $125 a pound for paper-thin slices. What do people pay for Carolina country ham, for all that history, all that flavor and all those months it takes to make it? Less than $3 a pound.

Nostalgic Business

Charlotte used to have its own ham tradition. You can still find elderly cooks who remember when a ham curer in the mountains, W.G. Long, would drive hams down from Ashe County in the northwestern North Carolina mountains and sell them off the back of a truck. About 15 years ago, soon after I started writing about food, I drove a loyal customer of Long's up to Glendale Springs, to buy a ham from Long's son, Clayton.

Last year, I heard Clayton Long was finally getting out of the ham business and handing off his customers to a younger man, Byron Jordan, who runs a barbecue restaurant in West Jefferson and slow-cures hams on the side as A.B. Vannoy Hams. So I called Jordan and asked how he makes a ham. Only four ingredients go into them, he said, repeating his favorite slogan: "Brown sugar, salt, mountain air and time."

Ashe County used to have four ham makers, including the Longs and Vannoy. Today, Vannoy is the only one left, and it may be the last open-air curing operation left in North Carolina. Jordan and his wife, Nancy, bought the ham house from A.B. Vannoy's daughter in 1994. They wanted a small business they could run along with their restaurant.

But for Jordan, 55, there also was a little nostalgia. He remembers his father, a veterinarian in Lexington, coming back with hams after visiting clients in the country. "Because of my history, being around it as a kid," he says. "Thinking it was a neat and unique business. I'm hoping it doesn't become a slide rule."

I made Jordan a proposition: How about letting me follow a ham through the process? He was willing. So I took it a step farther: How about letting me start with the pig?

He was slower to agree to that. His business is watched closely by inspectors and regulated strictly. Any change is a risk. But Jordan also knows there is another world out there, full of gourmets who would pay more than $2.59 a pound for ham. He doesn't know how to reach that world, but he wants to know more about it. So he agreed. I'd find an old fashioned pig and Byron Jordan would make the ham. We'd both learn something.

But he ended the call with a caution: "You know, we lose about 30 percent of our hams every year."

"That's OK," I said. "I'm willing to take the chance."

Start with a Good Pig

On an unusually warm December morning a year ago, I drove 35 miles northwest of Charlotte, to Grateful Growers Farm in Denver, North Carolina.

Along with the growing audience for slowly made artisan food, there's also an interest in the ingredients that go into that food. All around Charlotte, people are raising animals in small batches, using older breeds prized for their flavor and letting them live more naturally than they would on a factory farm. Natalie Veres and Cassie Parsons of Grateful Growers have made it a specialty, focusing on humanely raised livestock, particularly an old English pig called a Tamworth, a red-haired breed with a genial personality.

Veres, 42, is the farm's pig handler. A stocky blonde who favors dusty work boots and well-worn jeans, she likes to say she does the muscle work of farming "50 pounds at a time," hauling almost a half-ton of feed, a mix of corn, soy and grains, around to the pens every day. She's quiet and gentle, a slow talker who comes to life around her pigs. "Hi, babies," she calls, her normally low voice ticking up an octave, as we walk to a pen full of 5-month-old shoats.

She perches on a metal trash can, her favorite spot to watch while the pigs play and tussle like big puppies. They oink with a deep, guttural rumbling from down inside their noses. The action around their feed bowls never stops. Pushing, nudging, sidling in. Every day is Thanksgiving for pigs, Veres says: Eat and sleep, eat and sleep.

When I step into the pen wearing black suede work shoes, one pig presses a flat, muddy snout against my foot to see if it is food. It isn't, so he nudges to get under my foot, just in case I'm standing on food. He leaves a gray snout print and I start to brush it off, then stop. How many jobs involve getting this close to your food?

Veres points out our pig, his brassy red hair shining in the sun. What's his name? He doesn't have one. Veres never names the pigs. She names the sows, who stay on the farm. But raising pigs is how she lives and pays the mortgage. She has learned not to treat them like pets. "I truly appreciate these animals and I don't take any pleasure out of the end of their lives. But giving them a good life, that's something I can do."

Part of that is ensuring them a peaceful end. Pigs that are stressed when they're slaughtered have tougher meat. If they're scared, their meat gets high in adrenaline and lower in glycol, the sugar in their muscles. And Veres doesn't want them to suffer. So getting them to the slaughterhouse takes several days. First, she parks a trailer near the pen, so the pigs get used to the sight of it. Then she starts feeding them on the trailer, so they get used to being in it. Finally, she feeds them in the trailer and closes the gate, letting them sleep there. When the trailer starts to move the next morning, they don't get as stirred up. At the slaughterhouse, the pigs are allowed to rest at least three hours and usually overnight.

Making that effort is part of what Veres calls being conscientious. "Being mindful of each system's role," she calls it. "Respect, sustainability. Food that feels as good as it tastes."

Preparing Ham the Old Way

In late January, our pig—who had grown to well over 300 pounds—made the 76-mile trip to Thomas Brothers' Meat Processing, in North Wilkesboro. A couple of days later, we drove to the cinderblock building in the back of a neighborhood of small houses, a loose-skinned hound loping beside the car. Inside, it was like a small country store, stocked with red-waxed hoop cheese and a country feast of pork products—slabs of snowy fatback, smoked and peppered side meat, liver mush and liver pudding. Behind a glass door, I could see workers breaking down a side of beef.

Owner Ted Thomas' grandfather started the business in the 1930s and his father still works there with him. Thomas, 50, is

6-foot-2 with a bundle of braids tied at the back of his head. His business was up, because drought and higher corn prices had driven many farmers to thin their herds.

He knows Byron Jordan well, he says. There aren't many people left who cure hams the old way. "It's the consumers and the weather," he says. Consumers are picky about ham—"it's either too salty or not salty enough. And the weather—hot one week, cold the next." Most farmers don't bother with curing hams from their pigs anymore. "They all grind them into sausage or slice them into chops."

Our ham—the back leg of our pig, with the hoof removed and the hock, or cut-off bone, left on—is 37 pounds, a lot bigger than the 25 pounds we were expecting. Thomas unwraps it so we can see: Pink meat under a 3-inch-thick layer of fat, with pale skin covering one side. Thomas hefts it into the trunk and we drive 40 miles farther north on U.S. 421, past breath taking views of deep mountain valleys and around breath-holding curves patchy with ice. On a side street off West Jefferson's main road, across from a Dr Pepper plant, we find A.B. Vannoy's Ham House, a small, two-story brick building so close to the road, there is barely enough room for a car to pull up beside it.

It's winter outside, but it's almost as cold inside the concrete-lined front room. A wall thermometer reads 40 degrees. Temperature is everything in handling meat. This is why most hams are made in mountain areas: You need at least 30 days below freezing or the meat will rot.

"A lot of the way you control bacteria growth is temperature." That's Byron Jordan, who has come out of the curing room to meet us. He's tall and thin with graying hair and a soft voice. He looks a little harried—this is one of his busiest days of the year. His small crew is being paid by the hour, he has to get 1,600 hams—about 42,000 pounds of meat—coated in curing mix, and he has to get back to his restaurant, Smoky Mountain Barbecue, for the lunch rush. He's apologetic: In the ham business, you're very busy for about five days a year and there's nothing to do for the other 360.

In the meat locker, wooden pallets line three sides of the room and stretch down the middle, each covered with a plastic sheet and stacked three deep with hams trucked in from the Midwest. The crew has a metal bin on wheels filled with a mixture of brown sugar and salt. Ham by ham, the workers pick up each hunk and ram it, hock down, into the mix. The movement is a curving swoosh, like spiking a football—a 25-pound football made of fat, bone and meat. Slamming the meat down is important. You have to force salt and sugar into the cut surface of the hock, where the curing mixture will work into the circulatory system and spread throughout the meat. They scoop a little extra mix around each ham, then they heft it back into the pile, where it will sit for 35 to 39 days, while the salt works its way into the meat.

Federal regulations require that a country ham has to spend at least 30 days coated in the cure mix. Then it has to hang through the hottest months—June, July and August—while the heat activates the salt. The idea behind curing meat is simple: Salt draws out moisture. Without moisture, bacteria can't survive. The trick is to remove enough moisture to keep the meat from spoiling while leaving enough to make the meat palatable. These days, since people want sweeter ham, they lower the salt and increase the sugar as much as possible, while still making the ham safe to eat. The most the law will allow is 6 parts salt to 1 part sugar.

The crew works its way around the pallets and it's finally time for our ham. It stands out: Twelve pounds heavier than the rest, it's also cut wider. Jordan does a quick calculation: It will have to spend 57 days in the cure. And because it's different, from an old-breed pig, there's a higher chance it will spoil. To be safe, a ham has to lose at least 18 percent of its water content, although most usually lose 25 to 27 percent.

I cross my fingers as Jordan picks it up, plunges it into the mixture, and places it alone on a pallet, separate from the others. It's 11:55 a.m. on Jan. 23.

The workers leave the room, pulling off their white smocks and lining up to get paid. In the meat locker, it's cold and quiet. There is a soft caramel smell of dissolving sugar and a constant drizzling sound as juices head to the floor drains. Moisture is coming out. Salt is going in. Jordan clicks off the fluorescent lights and slides the metal door closed. Our ham will wait in the dark.

Pig to Plate

In the A.B.Vannoy Ham House, on a steep side street off U.S. 221 in Ashe County, the ham room is upstairs. Hundreds of hams hang from wooden beams, each wrapped in brown paper and a loosely woven, white stocking. To get there, you climb narrow wooden stairs as steep as a ship's ladder. Halfway up, you start to smell an aroma of meat, salt and wood that has been accumulating for more than 80 years.

When you reach the top, you have to move carefully. A ham starts out as 25 pounds of bone, fat and meat. It's a hard thing to bump with your head. From spring until fall, when the room is filled with the latest batch of curing hams, moving around is like trying to cross an attic strung with oversized baseball bats.

The only light comes from a dangling light bulb and deep windows on two sides. Through the windows, you can see the hill that stretches behind the ham house, covered with Christmas trees and thick meadow grasses.

Vannoy hams are all about those windows. These country hams are climate-cured, which means: Open windows. Windows that let in spring breezes and the humid heat of summer. There aren't many places left that do it this way, letting the hams hang for at least eight months and especially through June, July and August, when heat activates the salt that has been driven into the ham through the cut end of the bone, driving out moisture to stop bacteria from growing.

March

In March, I headed back to the mountains, on a drizzly day when cows huddled in pastures tucked into the crooks of the hills. There aren't a lot of tourists here. These are the mountains of working people, where brick houses sit next to tumbling-down homeplaces with caved-in roofs.

North Carolina leads the nation in making country hams, according to Dana Hanson, an associate professor of food science at NC State University. Out of about 60 ham processors nationwide, 20 to 25 are here. But most are climate-controlled houses that use heated rooms to hurry the process or to ensure consistency. The length of curing time, when hams develop deeper, more unique flavors, can vary from 75 days to 18 months or longer. Open-air ham houses like Vannoy are rare. Hanson believes it may be the only one left in the state. He only knows of a couple of others, one in Kentucky and one in Missouri. There used to be four ham houses in Ashe County, about 120 miles northwest of Charlotte. But the other three are gone now, closed by owners who no longer want to wrestle with state regulations and wait months for a product that few people want to buy.

Each year, the Jordans buy more than 1,600 hams, most from pigs raised in the Midwest. They coat the hams in a mixture of salt and sugar for 36 days. They rinse them, wrap them in brown paper, slide them into loosely woven stockings, move them upstairs and hang them. There the hams wait, for at least seven months and as long as two years. "Folks don't understand," says Jordan. "They'll say, 'Well, shucks—I can get one at Ingles.'" But they don't know what goes into it, he says, or how long he has his money tied up in these hams. And sales are gradually declining, particularly for whole hams. "The people who know what to do with a whole ham are dying off."

He can't ship his hams to New York. His ham house is state inspected, so he can't sell across state lines. To get federally inspected, he's afraid he would have to change his operation, cover the old concrete walls and take out the wooden beams. That, he fears, might change his ham. . . .

Once the hams are hanging, Nancy Jordan runs the business. She spends a lot of her time in the old ham house, where it's cold in winter and cool even in summer. She fills the ham orders, weighing, inspecting and wrapping the hams and shipping them to the customers. When customers call, with praise or complaints, they talk to Nancy. She often looks worried, fretting about inspectors, about sales, about customers. What she really worries about is whether their business will survive.

She's from Plymouth, in eastern North Carolina, and she grew up on country ham. But when Byron wanted to buy the business, she wasn't sure. "I was raised on ham that was very, very salty. When we were approached about buying this business, I thought, 'I don't want that salty mess!' But then I tasted it. The sugar keeps it from being so salty. That's when I thought, 'I do like this ham. And I believe I can sell it.'"

She still likes it, but she only eats it at Thanksgiving and Christmas. "I don't want to get tired of it," she says. "Believe me—I've had barbecue (from their restaurant) for 18 years. When you're trying to sell a product, you don't want to get tired of it."

I came in March to see my ham make its trip upstairs to the ham room. The other hams have already been moved, but mine was bigger, so it had to wait longer. The old-breed pig it came from grew faster than I expected, yielding a 37-pound ham. It started out pink, then turned dark red and brown from the cure. Now the meat under the thick layer of fat looks kind of gray— normal for a curing ham. When Byron rinsed off the curing mix, the fat looked startling white against the darkening meat.

Next, he wrapped the ham in brown paper, as they were taught when they bought the business. People in the mountains believe that brown paper stops larder beetles. Indigenous to the mountains, larder beetles bore into hams to lay their eggs. In the old days, people didn't mind the eggs. They called them skippers, and they just cut them out and ate the rest of the ham. Meat was precious, and you didn't waste it. Today, of course, it's different: "My customers would faint if they found a bug in their ham," says Nancy. The only sure way to stop the larder beetle is to fumigate the ham house, which happens in May. It sounds strange, but it's required by law. Jordan has to close and tape up the windows and set off a canister of methyl bromide. It's odorless and colorless, and it kills bugs, but it doesn't affect meat. It's one of the only pesticides approved for use around food. But the manufacture of it is now regulated. When the Jordans bought the business, it cost $150 for enough to treat the whole ham house. Now, it costs almost $1,000 and they have to do it twice.

August

In August, I returned for a visit. It was late summer, and the trees were festooned with gray clouds of tent caterpillars.

In the ham house, it was much quieter. "It's like a barn," said Nancy Jordan. "No heat, no air conditioning. We have to roll with the seasons." Upstairs, a tall fan was roaring steadily, to keep the air moving and help the hams cure evenly. The trick to curing all these hams is consistency. You need heat to activate the salt, driving out moisture, but you don't want the meat to dry too quickly. If it's rainy, the hams can mold. Of course, mold on a ham is part of the process. When you unwrap a country ham, it will be covered with it. Nancy dreads the calls from customers, upset because there's mold on the ham. She includes a label telling them to scrub the mold off, but she's had calls from people who told her they threw the ham away. "Every Christmas, somebody calls with that. Oh, I just cry."

October

On a chilly day in early October, nine months after it went to the mountains, it was time for the ham to come home to Charlotte. This time, I took along a guest, chef Joe Bonaparte of the Art Institute. Bonaparte has made several trips to Italy, where he has become enthralled with old-style meat curing, so he wanted to see a Southern curing house.

In the ham house, the chilling room downstairs had been turned into a meat-cutting room. Since so few people want a whole ham, Byron and Nancy Jordan have decided to branch out, cutting some of their ham into center-cut slices and vacuum-packing it for holiday gift packages.

Byron shows Bonaparte the oldest artifact of the business, handed down from the original owner: a stubby ice pick with a wooden handle. Before inspections and water analysis, this was how you checked hams. He still uses it, sliding the pick into the ham, pulling it out and sniffing it for the sour smell of spoilage. In Italy, Bonaparte tells him, they use a horse bone, because it's porous and the smell clings to it. "A horse bone?" Nancy Jordan gapes at him. "You are kidding me."

In the cutting room, they look at the hams that have been cut in half, pointing out the anatomy, the way the meat has darkened closest to where the salt goes in, the way crystallizing proteins have left little white spots. A worker suddenly calls Jordan over. He's found a bad ham. Jordan leans in close, giving a whiff with his long nose, and nods solemnly. "You treat two hams the identical same way. You salt them the same, you hang them side by side, and one will cure out and one won't."

Upstairs in the ham room, Bonaparte has to be careful—he's tall, and the aged hams hanging from the beams are now as solid as bowling balls. The brown paper has tightened around them, almost as if they've been vacuum-packed. He strolls around, looking at everything, and tells Jordan about ham houses in Parma, Italy, where hams cure in the breezes from the Mediterranean. "What do they do for pest control?" Jordan asks him.

"I don't know," Bonaparte says, laughing. "I'm going over in two weeks. I'll try to find out."

What Jordan really wants to know: "What can we do to keep it going? To keep it profitable?"

He lifts our ham up off the nail where it has hung since March and carries it downstairs. Slitting open the netting, he peels back the brown paper, revealing patches of gray-green mold. He slides the ice pick into the center and pulls it out, and we all lean in to smell. No sourness, just metal and the sweetness of meat.

Jordan moves the ham to a scale, then gets out a calculator. I hold my breath: It started at 37 pounds and now it's 29 pounds. It lost almost 22 percent of its weight—just a little over the 18 percent minimum. "Thank you, God," Nancy murmurs.

Bonaparte suddenly has an idea: They have the meat saw set up, why not cut into it? Jordan is willing, so he carries our ham to the saw, fires it up and then shaves off a few slices. Bonaparte picks up a sliver and eats it as the workers in the room—even Nancy Jordan—stare at him. He's eating raw ham? Why not, Bonaparte reminds them. It's cured.

I take a piece, too. It's sweet and more delicate than I expect. The fat is creamy and clean-tasting.

November

The ham that started in a field in Denver, NC, ended up on my back porch near Cotswold. The weekend before Thanksgiving, I invited a houseful of guests, including farmers Natalie Veres and Cassie Parsons, who raised the pig, chef Joe Bonaparte and one of his culinary students, Marla Thurman.

I had paid Veres $144 for the original ham, and $27.83 to the Jordans for the time it spent in their ham house. I had driven just over 1,000 miles to follow it through its yearlong journey.

I cooked the ham the traditional way, soaking it in water overnight and simmering it in a big pot all day. Then I cut away the skin, scored the fat and baked it until it was sizzling.

I made buttermilk biscuits, a grits souffle and collards. Then we all sat around the table, eating and admiring the ham. Under the table, I was wearing my black suede work shoes, with the gray imprint of a pig's snout still visible on one toe. So you could say the pig was there, too.

It wasn't prosciutto. It wasn't Iberico. It was North Carolina country ham, a little salty, a little chewy, and a taste all our own.

Want to order one?

A.B. Vannoy Hams can't ship hams out of state. But you can order one within North Carolina. Cost: Whole hams are $2.59 a pound; most are 13 to 18 pounds. They also have 12-ounce vacuum-packed packages of center and biscuit slices for $4.99 to $7.99. Gift boxes with several packages of slices and trimmings for seasoning are $26.

Orders: Call Smoky Mountain BBQ toll-free at 888-793–5371, or e-mail orders to smokymtnbbq@skybest.com. Hams also are sold at the restaurant, on U.S. 221 in West Jefferson, or at Thomas Bros. Meats, 347 Thomas St. in North Wilkesboro.

For more resources, try this NC Department of Agriculture site: *www.ncagr.gov/markets/gginc/index.htm.*

Morality Bites

By Monica Eng

From the *Chicago Tribune Magazine*

Tribune food reporter Monica Eng—a well-traveled Chicago
native whose "World Eats" column is essential reading for
Chicago ethnic specialties—tests her own mettle as a self-
described "ethical meat eater" in this Sunday magazine piece.

What I feared most was the screaming.
Desperate cries from a freaked-out pig might ruin bacon for me forever.

I'd spent the previous two days hanging out with happy hogs at
the idyllic Newman Farm on the Arkansas-Missouri border. I
watched them trot around the fields, wag their curly tails and flop
in pools of mud. I even held one in my hands when it was only a
few hours old.

But here I'd come, five hours across Missouri to Trimble, just
outside Kansas City, Mo., to witness the other end of a pig's life cycle. Comfortingly, the place was called Paradise Meat Locker.

So why was I here? I asked myself the same question as I nerv-
ously pulled on shoe guards, tucked my hair in a shower cap and
snapped up my lab coat right outside the kill floor door. I didn't
want to see a pig get killed. Heck, I don't think anyone does.

But I felt like I couldn't continue eating meat if I didn't. So this
summer I embarked on an unpleasant pilgrimage to bear witness
to the death of every kind of animal I ate. And in some cases, to kill
the animal myself.

Before you start with the angry letters, please hear me out. We're probably more similar than you think. Like most of you reading this story, I love animals. I love to pet them. And I love to hold them.

But I also love to eat them.

So the thought of their execution—something my appetites demand—both frightened and revolted me.

But if I couldn't take the reality of what was on my plate, how could I justify eating it? And how could I feed it to my kids?

I'd been asking myself this for years, but urban life made it easy to avoid the issue. Meat here comes in manicured cuts covered with shiny plastic. It doesn't have a face (as long as you avoid those ghastly ethnic markets) and certainly doesn't make noise. It's easy to imagine that these cuts come from the rib machine or the chicken tender factory or even the brisket dispenser down the street.

But after reading Michael Pollan's *The Omnivore's Dilemma* (2006) in which he personally kills and forages his dinner, I found it harder to tune out the question. My own foodie concerns about the provenance of my meat drove my curiosity further. But the biggest factor was my conviction that it's wrong to ask someone to do something for you that you morally could not do yourself.

This plan felt very personal, but in doing it, I was actually joining a blooming movement of ethical meat eaters. Cool, conscientious folks who used to slump guiltily next to their righteous vegan friends, knowing they were baddies for eating factory-farmed animals, but not seeing much choice.

Today, however, many proudly proclaim their meat love—especially for pork—with the near-virtuousness of vegetarians. That's because ethical meat options have expanded faster than you can say "ex-vegetarian." Between 2002 and 2007 U.S. organic meat sales grew tenfold (from $33 million to $364 million), according to Chicago-based Mintel research group.

This doesn't even count the sales growth in meats that are free-range, grass-fed and natural—less restrictive standards than organic, in which livestock is required by the U.S. Dept. of Agriculture to have been fed organic feed and be free of hormones and antibiotics.

The new options have even partially lured vegetarians to the carnivore camp. While no one keeps figures on such things, anecdotal converts include Mollie Katzen, author of *Moosewood Cookbook*, and Amy Standen and Sasha Wizansky, founders of *Meatpaper* magazine, a young quarterly examining the recent "fleisch geist," the trendy term for the new "meat consciousness."

Although watching an actual slaughter lies at the far end of the ethical meat-eating spectrum, a growing number of foodies and chefs are embracing the challenge as a political, environmental and moral exercise.

Anecdotally, Pollan's book pushed many into the killing-and-flesh-eating camp. But mostly, it got them thinking about what it means.

"There were several people I heard from who were inspired to try killing their own meat, and several others who became lapsed vegetarians," Pollan told me. "The book seemed to create a certain number of new vegetarians and a certain number of new carnivores, which gratifies me—that people would have used the same information to come to such diametrically opposed conclusions."

In the name of conscious cooking, some chefs are proudly raising and slaughtering the animals themselves. Chris Cosentino, of Incanto in San Francisco, who has personally slaughtered dozens of animals and writes about it at offalgood.com, leads the movement in the U.S. while Jamie Oliver (who slaughtered a chicken in front of a TV audience this year) is at the forefront in England. Both have earned praise, but also a fair share of death threats.

"Be careful," Cosentino warned when I told him of my mission. "Some people have threatened to murder me because I kill the animals I'll serve. People love to eat their sausage and T-bones and hot dogs, but they don't want to know how they got to the plate. They refuse to come face to face with their food and where it comes from."

For those who do, the journey usually starts with buying organic milk and eggs. It often progresses to buying natural, organic, grass-fed, antibiotic- and hormone-free meats.

That's how I started. But soon I'd moved on to buying meat at local farmers markets. Then I'd graduated to secret "tuppermeat" brunches in Wicker Park where a farmer set out coolers of meat and eggs in a living room. We'd load up our bags, drink Intelligentsia coffee, write the farmer a hefty personal check and go home with heavy bags of organic meats and virtue.

One pal swooned with pride: "These eggs are so fresh they still have chicken poo on them." For an urban foodie like me, this was as close to the source as I could get.

Or so I thought until I read Pollan's book. His indictment of factory farming, his first-person exploration of his food sources and his unflinching examination of what it means to eat meat inspired me—and many others—to take that next step.

So I called some local farms and asked if I could attend a slaughter. I was greeted by chuckles and head shakes at the idea that these farmers actually do the slaughtering anymore. A typical response came from Diann Moore, of the Moore Family Farm in Watseka, Ill.

"Since *The Omnivore's Dilemma* came out people are much more interested in their food sources and the animal raising," says Moore, who sells her sustainable produce and meat at the Urbana Farmers Market, among other outlets. "But we send most of our livestock out to a processing facility. Just about the only people who ask for live animals are Muslims, Hindus and Hispanics. And they need to get the right licensing in order before they do it."

This was not a promising start.

I thought I might never see a slaughter. But then providence stepped in.

A chance call to New York-based Heritage Foods revealed that this sustainable specialty meat broker was offering the first ever pig-farm tour that finished with a trip to the abattoir. I signed up right away.

Then a few days before driving through Minnesota this summer, I learned about a slaughterhouse that offered viewing facilities for select visitors. I called and the owner said I could come and watch.

All the pieces came together to produce a six-week period in which I ruefully watched the death of a pig, cow, chicken, fish and crabs—yes, crabs. The most traumatic was the biggest surprise to me.

As we toured the holding pens at Paradise Meat Locker, it was as if the black Duroc pigs were playing tricks on our guide. Each time he described Paradise's calming environment, the oinkers around the corner would start squealing again.

To be fair, the seven bristly porkers had already moved beyond the holding pens and were in an alley leading to the abattoir. I was touring the plant with a group of chefs on this blisteringly hot day and a few of us went to investigate. It appeared to be a fight over who had dibs on the water bucket. The fact that their fellow hogs were disappearing through a small black door ahead of them seemed less of an issue.

Back in the cool of the building, we were offered a buffet of cured meats before donning our safety clothes and heading onto the kill floor. I skipped eating the meat and chatted with the anxious chefs. None was looking forward to this. But each saw it as a rite, a show of respect and an education.

The first thing that hits you on the kill floor is the temperature. The body heat of open hogs, the torches used to burn off their bristles, the steamy "dehairing" machine (like a horizontal washing machine full of boiling Nair) and the hot Missouri air that slips in with each new pig, crank it up to around 100 degrees.

Our first station is the innards table, where freshly harvested organs are dropped for the U.S. Department of Agriculture inspector to examine. In back of that table are the knife-wielding eviscerator and the hair-and-hoof removing guys. Also, the man who deals with the live hog. He lifts the door, zaps the hog with an electrical wand on the back of the neck, hoists him by his leg over a barrel and then "sticks him," cutting deeply through neck arteries that unleash an avalanche of blood.

Above the din of machines and power hoses, meat scientist and PhD candidate David Newman explains the procedure. Newman, the son of Newman Farm owners Mark and Rita, has been our instructor on this pig tour, teaching us about everything from feed options and pH balances to marbling and slaughter theory. "The pig will lose most of its blood in the first 15 seconds," he says. The hog's heart is still beating. It shudders and kicks a leg as the desanguination continues.

My knees are trembling, but overall I feel relief. Since Bristly is shocked into unconsciousness before he flops into view, we encounter minimal struggling—and mercifully, no screaming.

Still, as soon as we leave the kill floor and step into the open air, the chefs are silent. They reach for beer and cigarettes to help digest what they just saw.

On a torrid Minnesota day in suburban Minneapolis, Mike Lorentz meets us at the employee entrance of Lorentz Meats. With brown hair and a sturdy build, Lorentz is a thoughtful talker, often allowing a few moments of silence before he answers a curious journalist's question. He's completely transparent about his meat operation, but knows this can make him extra vulnerable to those who oppose meat eating in general. Although I've explained my mission, he still seems leery about my motives.

Pollan had given me Lorentz's name a few days before. I had already planned this road trip with a friend to pick up his 13-year-old from summer camp. Providentially, our trip takes us near Lorentz Meats precisely during steer-slaughtering hours.

As we approach town, we warn the boy about the visit. "Cool," he says with teenage bravado. "Can I kill a cow?"

"No," we say. He opts to stay in the car.

As we enter the two-story rectangular industrial park unit—built in 2002 to the specifications of Temple Grandin, the czarina of humane abattoir design—it feels like a refrigerator and smells like a butcher shop.

Lorentz leads us up to the viewing room where, he's told me, only one person of the thousands who have been through has fainted. The windows (one overlooks the kill floor and the other the butchering area) are located in the employee lunchroom. This may sound stomach churning for some but it seems to speak to the quotidian nature of animal death here.

The possibility of allowing my children to witness a slaughter drew outrage and derision from my urban colleagues but here those sentiments seem absurd. "My own kids [who are all under 7] look out there and say, 'Daddy, is that going to be our hamburger tonight?'" Lorentz says.

The workers are on a 15-minute break. So one organic cow hangs by his legs and another lies half-skinned and belly-up in "the cradle"—a stand that allows workers to cut and carve different parts of the animal after he bleeds out. I discuss the different stations of the kill floor with Lorentz using my newly acquired terms, like "immobilization," "desanguination" and "evisceration." He says, "We don't use those fancy words here. We say stun, bleed and gut." OK.

Soon the workers return to finish off the steer in the cradle. Carefully gutted and almost totally skinned, he gets hoisted back up and a roller contraption grabs his hide and pulls it cleanly away from his body.

Time for the next steer.

As he enters the "knock box" (a one-cow-sized pen connected to the holding area by a sliding door) all we see from the lunchroom window is his curious white head barely poking over the wall. The worker recharges the stun bolt (à la *No Country for Old Men*) and calmly assumes a position near its head to get a clean stun.

"One of the ways this differs from a large factory slaughterhouse," Lorentz tells us, "is that, if the bolt doesn't stun him right, we have the time to go back, correct it and make sure he is really out."

The stun works and Whitey has fallen on his side to the floor. But he still kicks.

Like the pigs at Paradise, Whitey is hoisted into the air with his heart still beating. His carotid artery and jugular are severed by hand and he dies of blood loss over a barrel. The steer is then processed by strong, skilled men who wield knives like artists, efficiently removing head, skin and organs before the carcass moves into the cooler. The men handle one steer at a time.

The only noises come from hoses and the machinery that moves and cleans the beasts.

The scene is a little easier to bear the second time around, especially since we are watching it from our lunchroom opera box. Still, I feel a certain buzz in my limbs and that familiar knot has returned to my stomach. When we stop at Culver's for lunch, I order a salad.

WHEN I ARRIVE at the live poultry shop on Chicago's Lawrence Avenue, I spot a bad omen immediately. Painted on the window are the words "POLLO Y PATO" (chicken and duck) and "ENG" (me?). It's probably some sort of mistake, but it doesn't make me feel great.

Inside the waiting room, the stench is intense. I figure it has something to do with the cage of pooping quail staring us in the face.

My friend and I join a half dozen others waiting and breathing through their mouths. Most seem to be picking up several fresh birds they've ordered in advance. They leave with bulging black sacks delivered by a mustachioed man. He seems to run the whole operation.

When it is finally our turn, I ask if I can choose my chicken. He leads me through the processing room (which includes a cash register, a scale, a cutting table, a scalding vat and several tin buckets) into the chicken room. It holds several cages of noisy brown and white birds. We point to a fluffy chicken that is drinking water. The mustachioed man reaches in, grabs Fluffy and takes her to the scale.

She flaps her wings and clucks during the weigh-in, all the while eyeing me with contempt. The mustachioed man carries her to the back of the room, pulls back her head and slides a sharp knife across her white neck. He whispers "bismillah, allahu akbar," a Muslim blessing that must accompany each halal slaughter.

Looking up, he places her head down in a tin bucket to let her bleed out—another halal requirement. "This will only take a few minutes," he says. I ask if we can watch her last moments. He nods.

My eyes turn to Fluffy as she shudders, stretches her claws out of the bucket and waves wildly. She falls still, but resumes the seizure-like dance. Stillness again. I hold my breath.

My friend squeezes my hand and whispers, "It's over. She's gone."

But, as if on cue, Fluffy summons her strength for one last theatrical hand jive.

Who can blame her for trying to make me feel as bad as possible. I'd do the same.

Finally, with Fluffy at rest, the mustachioed man places her in the scalding bath to loosen her feathers. Next stop is a spinner (kind of a small washing machine) that pulls off her feathers. Inevitably bits of chicken fall on these floors and the man hoses them down frequently. My rubber flip-flops feel like a bad shoe choice.

While Fluffy spins, the mustachioed man asks us to return to the waiting room. Ack, that smell again. But soon she's ready to leave. I pay my $11.50 (chickens cost $1.59 a pound), thank the mustachioed man and put Fluffy in the car. She is warm and heavy.

At home I put her in the refrigerator and close the door. I avoid the fridge all day.

By late afternoon, I call my mom to come over for moral support. But she is late and I must cook dinner. So I enlist my children. Under orders from his mom, my 9-year-old son, Joe, removes Fluffy from her double black plastic bags. He drops a clear, chicken-filled bag on the counter before me and Fluffy's head stares me down again.

Her legs, thighs and wings, though, look comfortingly like anonymous chicken parts I've known. My kids each take out a leg and roll it in seasoning. I gather the strength to remove a few more pieces and slide them in the oven. My mom arrives and we make a coq au vin with the rest, leaving the head, neck and feet in the bag.

The baked chicken smells pretty good. The coq au vin smells great. I force a few bites down but Fluffy seems oddly dry and tough. I feel like she's trying to vex me again—but later realize it's just rigor mortis that I was supposed to wait out before cooking her. The leftover coq au vin is tastier and tenderer when I try it again the next day. But I'm only eating it out of respect.

We get to the Chinatown fish store late. The guy at the tanks has already put his cutting board and knives in the sink. He speaks to me in Chinese and then tries English. Two words: "no cutting." I'm hoping this means he won't trim nice fillets today. So I respond in piercing, language barrier-busting volume, "No problem!"

He nods. We scan the tilapia tank. Joe wants the one tilting on its side so we can "put him out of his misery." I choose a healthier-looking fish. Swiftly the man scoops him out the tank and drops the flopping creature in a plastic bag for me.

"No, no, no," I say, pushing the bag back into his hands. "I can't." Even as the words escape my mouth, I know that killing

Floppy myself is exactly what I should be doing for this exercise. But my fear is strong. Giving me a dirty look, the fish man shakes his head and pulls his board and knives out of the sink.

He holds down Floppy's head and performs a cursory scaling. My son mock-barfs and dashes for the door with his sister close behind. I threaten future toy purchases if they dare leave. At the same time I try to keep one eye on the fish man, so as not to miss the actual execution. I feel like a failure on all fronts. Crazy screaming mom. Lax journalist. And cowardly carnivore.

Out of the corner of my eye, I see him remove more scales. His knife slices half-way through the gullet and then down Floppy's belly exposing innards that are gone in one quick move.

The man slides the red-spattered fish back into the plastic bag and hands it to me. I sheepishly take the still-wriggling purchase to the counter. The clerk weighs it, charges me $8.57 and places it into another plastic bag. I put Floppy in the trunk hoping he won't make much noise as we drive the six blocks to my friend's house.

There we wash him and dress him with soy, MSG, fresh ginger and garlic. We slide his body onto a steamer over a burbling wok and top it with a glass lid. When I return 10 minutes later, I find a fin perpendicular to Floppy's body pushing at the glass. He steams up beautifully. The flesh is white, sweet and delicate. But I take little pleasure in the eating.

When my children and I walk up to the three boxes of live blue crabs at the Vietnamese market, we're not sure which ones to grab with our tongs. An experienced shopper takes pity and advises us to choose only live crabs with orange markings on their shells. We try, but the whole thing is so disturbing that we end up just filling two bags as fast as we can without getting pinched. If one crab latches on to another couple of pals, they go into the bag too. This seems to account for the pungent smell of dead crab that wafts from the sack.

I call my friend and ask him to start boiling a huge pot of water to which we add Old Bay seasoning, corn, potatoes and finally the feisty crabs. The kids gather in the kitchen and we thank each crustacean for its sacrifice as it heads into the pot. Through the steamy glass lid I watch one wave and struggle as it succumbs to the heat. I've cheerfully eaten a lot of blue crabs in my life. I even wrote a story on how to do it properly. But this crab meal is not cheerful at all. This time I'm wholly responsible for the dirty work and can feel a guilty knot in the pit of my stomach.

I have a close friend at the *Tribune* who once worked as a chef. One night he had to kill dozens of soft-shell crabs as he cooked them to order. With each crab he said he could feel the death and bad karma creeping up his arm. Maybe that's what I felt as I dutifully nibbled each cooked crab out of respect. Was this what it was like to kill your dinner? Why didn't these taste good? And why did I feel like Lady Macbeth as I spent the night trying to wash this damn crab smell off my hands?

In the end, the crabs would be the only thing I actually killed. And they were the thing I felt worst about.

My summer of slaughters left me with mixed feelings. But not the feelings I'd imagined.

I thought I might emerge from it with a greater sense of entitlement and accomplishment. Like if you can face the realities of meat, you're allowed to eat it. But I felt no sense of entitlement. I felt more hesitance, a deeper reverence and a new conscientiousness.

Yes, I will probably continue to eat meat—I am a food writer. But in these weeks after the experiment, I already find I'm eating a lot less. I select it very carefully, eat it only occasionally and consume it in the kind of precious quantities that my grandparents did. Most of all, I approach the meat with a renewed sense of gratitude that extends to the farmer, the slaughterhouse workers, butcher, broker, chef, artisan meat curer and, most of all, to the animal that lived and died—I will try to ensure, well—to bring it to me.

I involved my children in parts of this process—despite disapproval from friends—because I want them to make food choices based on knowledge. The lasting effects are still unclear. My son, Joe, is still upset about the crabs. Before we killed them he insisted that I look the crustaceans in the eyes and confess what I was up to. He is currently contemplating vegetarianism. The 5-year-old, Miranda, keeps asking if we can play with the next

"Fluffy" for a few days before "we kill her." I assure her this is a terrible idea.

I don't know how this will affect their greater meat consciousness in the long run. But I drew hope the other day when I heard my daughter whisper to a paper-thin slice of prosciutto: "Thank you, pig. I love you, pig. Now I'm going to eat you."

THE BEAUTY OF THE BEAST

By Bethany Jean Clement

From *The Stranger*

Clement's sassy, loquacious features, reviews, columns, and
blog posts for this hip Seattle alternative weekly (where she
also multitasks as managing editor) are well worth the price of
the paper. Granted, it's a free paper. But still.

My grandmother raised Angus cattle east of the mountains, outside Sunnyside. We often went over on weekends. We mended fence, and we took the cattle from pretty
pastures out to prettier sagebrush and back in the ancient International Harvester truck, which I learned how to drive at a very
young age. When we branded—heating the branding iron to red-
hot over a fire in the corral, guiding the cattle through a labyrinth
of fences with more yells than whipping, squeezing them tight one
at a time in the metal-barred chute—my job was to clip off the fur
on their sides in a square so my dad or brother could apply the
iron. It smelled pretty bad, and the cow would bellow mightily, its
eyes rolling back in its head. Then, released, it would forget instantly, walking away calm and docile.

Aside from that, they only had one bad day, those cows. They'd
go away—killed and butchered elsewhere, by those whose job that
was—and come back in pieces, wrapped in white paper. We were
not well-off when I was a child, but we always had a large quantity
of beef in the freezer. After I left home, I hardly ate beef at all for
several years. I was sick of it—even steak—and when I did have it
elsewhere, it tasted terrible.

When she was mending fence or bucking hay or hauling cattle or branding, my grandma wore an old bandana on her head with a cowboy hat on top of that, rubber boots, utilitarian clothes. As she got old, when it was cold, she wrapped and pinned rags around her arthritic wrists. She raised cattle pretty much by herself into her late 70s (and lived alone on the ranch until she died at 96). The only cow that ever had a name was the last one, a blind steer that I took to calling Ray Charles. He stayed in the pasture by the house and liked to be near the fence; maybe he was bored or lonely. His eyes were like a cat's caught at night in bright light, discs of beautiful mirror. Eventually, we ate him. He was extra tasty, maybe because he didn't walk around a lot, maybe because he was the end of the line for family beef.

My grandmother had a very low tolerance for any kind of foolishness. I'm pretty sure if I could tell her about a bunch of city people paying $50 a head to stand around in the mud and watch a pig die, she'd say, "Oh, for God's sake." And the rhetoric that Culinary Communion—the Seattle cooking school that put together such an event at a farm in Port Orchard in January and is doing so again this Sunday—has bandied about gives me much the same reaction. They've called it a "sacrificio," invoked "ancient tradition," made much ado about community, named the pig (Hector the first time), given a subsequent dinner a title worthy of a grad-school thesis ("Snout to Tail/Celebrating the Demise of Hector; Long Live Hector"). It's profoundly indulgent, both over- and underintellectualized, arguably voyeuristic, and plain old disturbing, and not in a knee-jerk PETA way: When we've arrived at slaughter-as-edutainment for the well-off, while the regular food supply is contaminated regularly and, still, all those people are starving, is the end of days far away?

That said, Culinary Communion's pig kill in January was marvelous. The farm was antipicturesque, with piles of both figurative and literal crap everywhere, the mark (my grandmother would agree) of a real working farm of the you-never-know-when-you-might-need-it variety. People brought their children, who jumped up and down in mud puddles, which was picturesque. It was cold but sunny, and the mulled wine provided straightaway in the early morning was sour and bracing. The pig, meanwhile, had a last meal of fine slop: rice, old hamburger buns, and melting ice cream. The killing part of the gathering was solemn and respectful. Culinary Communion head chef/main man Gabriel Claycamp—not a regular gunshooter, looking pale and grave—thanked everyone for coming "to celebrate the life and demise of Hector," crouched down to look the pig in the eye, and then got a very clean, close-range shot to the pig's head with a .22. No one cried but me, and I thought of my grandmother and quickly cut it out. Claycamp got kicked in the ear hard during the pig's (brief, silent) death throes. (Revenge!)

Then the pig was bled, the blood saved for blood sausage. The hair was singed off the carcass. Gutting and sawing ensued. The kids were front and center for all of this, completely captivated and not at all grossed out. At one point, the saw-wielding man—a professional who travels with a killing/butchering truck brought in to do the heavy lifting—asked Claycamp, "You want me to saw through the head?" Before Claycamp could answer, a kid yelled, "YEEEEAAAAH!"

Then Claycamp did the breakdown—dismantling the pig while explaining every piece, giving a whole new perspective on bacon, ham, guanciale, etc. Anyone who wanted to could help with the butchering and charcuterie, and many people joined in, with varying degrees of knife skills ("I mangled the ham!" said one man with furrowed brow). The kids loved this, too. Everyone kept saying that the texture of the meat was extraordinary, which it was: all jellylike, more akin to raw tuna than the rigor-mortis meat one usually handles. And it was still warm.

Annoying rhetoric it may be, but it's true: A temporary community was formed. Only the couple who arrived postslaughter never really joined it; they stood clinging to each other and drinking wine at a safe distance from the carcass. They were at my table at the dinner the next night, looking much more comfortable, talking about being lawyers, and using the name "Hector" a lot. Watching a pig die was vastly more interesting than dining with these people in Culinary Communion's lovely dining room.

This Sunday, as back in January, a band will play and lunch will be served, including some bits of the newly dead pig, which will be delicious. (The rest of it, whatever its name may be, will become prosciutto and other meat products, available for purchase by participants only.) If you get the chance—if you're not squeamish—you should go.

Home Cooking

Kitchen Smackdown

From the *New York Times*

As befits one of America's best-regarded weekly food sections, the *New York Times* fields quite a roster of food-writing heavy hitters. Last spring two of its most accomplished food reporters, Kim Severson and Julia Moskin, challenged each other to a cook-off—and enlisted restaurant critic Frank Bruni to judge the results.

Take That! Sort of French, Sort of Italian

By Kim Severson

I was not going down over a tortilla. And I was certainly not going to fail in front of Julia Moskin.

She sits two desks away from me. We are comrades, battling side by side on the front lines of food journalism. We plot stories and share lunch.

And now, in a cruel twist of fate, we were pitted against each other.

The assignment was straightforward: Create a dinner party for six for $50. There were only a few rules in our culinary Thunder-dome. Pantry basics like spices, butter and olive oil didn't count toward the total price. Guests would bring any wine or liquor.

Oh, and there was one more thing. Frank Bruni, the restaurant critic of the *New York Times*, would be coming to both dinners and writing a critique of each.

The day you get handed an assignment like that is the day you wish you had called in sick. But, as the kids say, game on.

Bring it, Moskin!

I started thinking about pork shoulder, a versatile cut that can be braised into all sorts of main attractions. But I didn't want to create the kind of Ital-Cal meal that is my default style. Besides, Frank has spent a lot of time in Italy. He is Italian-American, for heaven's sake. Anything less than a stellar pasta would mean certain defeat. And if I knew Julia, she was going French. Well, here in Brooklyn, baby, we were heading south. I figured if I looked toward Mexico, I could make clever use of inexpensive ingredients like jicama, beans and peppers. If I combined them with big flavors and artisan techniques, I could easily hit the $50 mark. Julia would fold like a cheap tent.

The heart and soul of my strategy would be a big pot of carnitas perfumed with oregano, orange zest and the delicate Mexican cinnamon called canela. As a bonus, the carnitas came with a built-in coach. The recipe belongs to Tara Duggan, who writes a column called "The Working Cook" for the *San Francisco Chronicle* and has a cookbook out with the same name. She's an old friend who taught me a lot about cooking when I worked at the *Chronicle*.

I knew that I had to elevate the carnitas from a pot of long-simmered pork into something special enough for a dinner party. "I'm going to make my own tortillas and serve them hot off the griddle," I told my coach.

She gasped. Brilliant! O.K., she didn't actually gasp. But she did remind me that trying out an untested dish on guests is never a good idea. So I spent the entire weekend before my party rolling out practice tortillas. This was war, and sacrifices had to be made.

The carnitas meat posed a challenge. I buy pork at my food co-op or at a farmers' market. Because of the way these pigs are raised, it's very expensive.

Unless I split a chop six ways, that kind of pork was not going to fit my budget. So I headed to the local Pathmark, where the picnic roast—the lower part of the shoulder—cost $1.49 a pound. Even better, the four-pound one I bought was covered in skin. This led to my next genius move.

I had already planned to set out a series of Mexican bar snacks for appetizers. I figured variety would make up for the lack of luxury ingredients.

I had stumbled across a recipe for spicy candied peanuts in a new book called *Simply Mexican* by Lourdes Castro. I added lime juice, zest and chili powder to jicama, and set out pepitas I bought already roasted. And for the centerpiece of my little snack tray? Homemade chicharrones from the skin of that grocery store pork.

(Cut the skin into inch-wide strips. Season, set in a pan and cover with an inch of water. Bake at 400 degrees until fat is rendered and water evaporates. Stir now and then.)

My tray of Mexican snacks cost less than $5, which left a little money for a second appetizer. I cut some store-bought tortillas into wedges and fried them up. (Take that, $4 bag of tortilla chips!) Then I searched for the cheapest, sturdiest, freshest fish I could find to make ceviche. Luckily, Atlantic tilefish was only $7.99 a pound.

For a little extra flourish, I threw thin slices of red onions into white vinegar spiked with Mexican oregano overnight. The pickled onions and my two inexpensive blender salsas would be perfect on the carnitas.

But tacos alone would not be enough. My original plan was to stew some dollar-a-pound pinto beans cowboy style, with canned tomatoes, onions, peppers and chorizo. But I realized I could afford $4 for a pound of big, gorgeous Rancho Gordo Christmas lima beans.

For something refreshing, I turned to that budget star, the cabbage. I dressed up two kinds with a confetti of watermelon radish and raw poblano peppers, then tossed the slaw with Coach Duggan's cilantro-lime vinaigrette.

By this point, I had abundance on my side. But I needed to stick the landing if I was going to beat Moskin. After flailing around with a cake that called for a cup of expensive pecans, I hit on it: a dark, spicy gingerbread with soft whipped cream and dulce de leche.

The only thing I needed to buy for the cake was molasses and eggs. For the dulce de leche, I used an old trick. I submerged an unopened can of sweetened condensed milk in water and boiled it for three hours. I let it cool, opened the can and boom, dulce de leche for $3. (You don't literally want it to go boom, so make sure you keep the can completely covered with water while it cooks.)

The night of the party, I was flinging masa like a tortilla machine and freaking out when Coach Duggan called.

"Don't forget to relax and let the food take you where it wants to go," she said. "This is about enjoying the process and the food and your guests."

Note to self: Never pick a coach from California again.

But she was right. The tortillas were hot and delicious, and her carnitas didn't let me down. I had come in $2.45 under my $50 budget, and everyone seemed to be having a great time. Especially Frank, who was spooning up the dulce de leche like a schoolboy with a bowl of pudding.

I was sure victory was mine.

Then I heard that Julia was planning a move so brilliant and confident that it immediately knocked me off my game.

Next week, at her party, she was going to serve pasta.

Tacos de Carnitas
Adapted from Tara Duggan, the San Francisco Chronicle
Time: 2 ½ hours

3 pounds pork shoulder, either butt or picnic
7 strips orange zest
5 garlic cloves, minced
1 large onion, chopped, plus finely chopped onion for garnish
1 ¼ teaspoons crushed red pepper flakes
1 cinnamon stick, preferably Mexican canela
2 bay leaves
1 ½ teaspoons crushed dried oregano leaves, preferably
　　Mexican
1 ½ teaspoons kosher salt, more to taste
¼ teaspoon ground cloves
24 small corn tortillas, warmed, for serving
Chopped cilantro for garnish
Salsa for garnish.

1. Trim any thick fat from surface of pork. Cut meat into 1-inch cubes, discarding any that are pure fat. Put pork in a large pot. Add enough water to cover by 2 inches, orange

zest, garlic, chopped onion, red pepper flakes, cinnamon, bay leaves, oregano, 1½ teaspoons salt and the cloves.

2. Bring to a boil, then reduce to a simmer. Skim off any scum that forms on surface. Simmer uncovered for 1½ hours, until pork is very soft; add water if necessary to keep meat submerged. Season with salt, then continue to cook until water has evaporated, about 30 minutes. Cook a little longer to fry meat slightly; cook even longer if you prefer crisper meat. Stir often and add a bit of water if meat sticks or seems about to burn.

3. Remove bay leaves and cinnamon stick. Spoon a few tablespoons of carnitas onto each tortilla. Top each taco with cilantro, finely chopped onion and salsa. Serve.

Yield: 6 to 8 servings.

———⁂———

Take This! Starting with Five Appetizers

By Julia Moskin

Her fifth appetizer was like a knife in my heart.

When Kim Severson and I were set the challenge of making dueling dinners for six for $50—about the least one can spend on dinner for two in a Manhattan restaurant—I was, frankly, unconcerned. As many readers know, a decent cook with a deep bench of pantry ingredients can easily make a great meal with $50— or $5.

Then I sat down at her table, and the icy reality of competition sank in. She was playing to win: her meal was big, delicious and interesting.

By the time she served a ceviche of tilefish, marinated in lime juice and triumph and spooned onto a handmade tortilla chip, I knew I would have to sweat as never before.

Also, by then I was mad. She had accused me of lying down and refusing to fight. Kim comes from a family of hardworking dairy farmers and Olympic skiers. In mine, a game of Scrabble and an errand is considered a full day, and I have shunned competition since going down in the first round of the 1977 New York City spelling bee.

Cooking skills would not determine the victor. We are both enthusiastic home cooks, not trained chefs. My only chance lay in rock-solid menu planning.

This called for a visit to the Museum of Bad Ideas: mistakes in recipe choices or execution that I hope never to make again. A dessert recipe from Jean-Georges Vongerichten that calls for 13 Granny Smith apples, peeled and thinly sliced. (I still have hand cramps.) Steak au poivre for eight in a freshly painted white kitchen. (I still have smoke stains.) Embracing simplicity by serving a platter of naked steamed vegetables and a bowl of mayonnaise for dinner. (You can always order Chinese food afterward.)

I spent a couple of hours surrounded by grease-stained cookbooks and clippings, recalling the peaks of my lentil soup years, the best lamb stews of the 1990s, the finest lemon cake in living memory.

But would lentil soup impress? Could it win?

"What's the one best thing I have ever made?" I demanded of friends and family, soliciting only the flattering details of my past.

The answers that came back proved my suspicion that French and Italian classics, combined with some twists on American tradition, would be popular. (It works for Thomas Keller.) That approach would also enable me to buy some key ingredients at Costco, where basic luxuries like nuts, cheese and dried fruit are good and cheap.

The flavors of tomato soup and grilled cheese sandwiches were paired: a cold soup made with canned tomatoes that suggests (but beats out) gazpacho, with a huge hit of cilantro; and gougères, buttery egg-cheese puffs that make the house smell great. There is simply nothing better with a glass of wine—sparkling, white or red—and they can be made with any cheese lingering in the drawer, or something as inexpensive as plain American cheddar at

$3.99 a pound. As a fan of cheddar, especially in melted form, I was happy to insert it into a French recipe for gougères that I've made many times with expensive Gruyère, Roquefort and Parmigiano-Reggiano; it performed admirably.

At the last minute, I ditched some too-spicy chocolate cookies and spent the savings on half a pound of toasted walnuts, tossing them in white pepper, coarse salt and olive oil—pantry ingredients all, but offering crunch and novelty next to the other appetizers.

Now, the menu needed something crisp and refreshing after the salty, cheesy pleasures of the appetizers. I was committed to using supermarket produce, but a trial run of celery salad did not go well. ("Not everyone," said my husband, choosing his words carefully, "likes celery as much as you do.") Tender, pale, ever-so-slightly-bitter hearts of escarole were better; perfect with a basic purée of anchovies, garlic, lemon and olive oil. (The escarole yielded a bonus, a mountain of dark outer leaves that were braised to fill a kind of lasagna the next day.)

Roast chicken is widely beloved, but has been played to death—the Norah Jones of entrees. I knew it could not win on its own. Then I remembered a curiously satisfying experience I'd had of ripping up a roast chicken with my bare hands—carving is so finicky and leaves so much behind—and mixing the results with pasta, pine nuts, currants and rosemary. Using all of a chicken and its golden fat to sauce a pound and a half of pasta—what could be more economical than that?

The only improvement I made on the original recipe, which comes from the Jewish community of Venice via the cookbook writer Claudia Roden, was to use thighs instead of a whole chicken: more meat, more fat, less money.

As someone who eats many gougères or an entire breadbasket during the ravenous stage before dinner, I am not exactly hungry by the time dessert rolls around. In a cookbook by the Los Angeles chef Suzanne Goin, I found a speck of a recipe that sounded like a very upscale Creamsicle float (fresh tangerine juice, homemade vanilla ice cream).

Honey tangerines happened to be in season last week, so I was able to take advantage of a super-low bulk price. Knowing I could not afford a vanilla bean, I found an ice cream recipe that called for

Dairy's Queen

By Michelle Wildgen

From *O! The Oprah Magazine*

In Michelle Wildgen's hands, the borderline between food
writing and personal essay is fluid, bridged by sensory details,
culinary expertise, and a flair for dramatic detail. The senior
editor of *Tin House* literary magazine, she has published two
novels, *You're Not You* and *But Not For Long*.

When I was 26 I got married, moved to Yonkers, New
York, and tasted devastatingly fresh mozzarella for the
first time. The cheese remains the most vivid memory of the three.

It came from the tiny Little Italy neighborhood in the Bronx,
which is far superior to Mulberry Street's gaggle of hawkers and
shamefaced tourists. My husband, Steve, and I would make the 20-
minute drive there every month for olive oil, pasta, cured meats,
and mozzarella. The store we always went to, Casa Della Mozzarella on East 187th Street, is essentially a long, packed hallway,
and at the back men stand over vats of water, stirring and ladling
balls of cheese. The choices are large or larger, salted or unsalted. I
tried unsalted once, thinking vague thoughts about purity and
simplicity, before remembering that if anything improves pure and
simple foods, it's salt. No one bothered to tell us to eat the cheese
immediately, or not to refrigerate it, both of which we learned
through trial and error. At the height of my devotion I would save
that store for last and dash back to the car, cradling my cheese like
an infant.

I soon realized that there is a ruthlessness to fresh mozzarella, much as there is with tomatoes: The best of science and ingenuity cannot fake that optimal moment when the food is at its peak. From the second mozzarella is formed, it is never again as good as it was the moment before. It's not that mozzarella gets bad after a few hours in the fridge, but it becomes . . . less. The delicacy of the flavors begins to blend into an overall mildness, the texture firms, and the cheese ceases to release those silky ivory droplets that give the impression of a food so dense with glory it cannot help sharing a little. I'm pretty sure this is not hyperbole. The stress I felt just trying to orchestrate my cheese-eating makes me glad I never tried to be an EMT.

The day I learned how much timing matters to a mozzarella, Steve and I had purchased our cheese and then hurtled back up the Bronx River Parkway. Still wearing our coats and surrounded by unpacked grocery bags, we each tore off a velvety shred. The cheese glowed on the cutting board, demurely shedding whey.

At the first taste, we both said, "Oh, my God" and locked eyes. The cheese was barely springy but yielding, with a gentle, fresh, milky tanginess. Silently, dazedly, we nibbled another piece. It was difficult to believe that something so pillowy in texture, so graciously light, was in fact a dense concentration of butterfat. When I turned away for a split second, Steve lost all reason and took a bite straight from the cheese, as if it were an apple.

Ever since I learned to cook, I'd pursued gastronomy's holy grails—the elusive raw milk Camembert, the enormous black truffle. The actual encounters were often disappointing—perhaps the result of a subpar specimen, perhaps of my subpar palate. Either way, like an agnostic slipping toward atheism, I had begun to wonder if nothing was as glorious as everyone said, a melancholy view I renounced that day. It was like finding out unicorns had been hanging out in the Bronx all along.

AFTER SEVEN YEARS in New York, we moved to Madison, Wisconsin, where I had gone to college. Of course I knew there were certain areas in which Wisconsin could not compete—but I hadn't expected one of them to be cheese. I could buy "fresh" mozzarella, but it tended to be a week old, a touch sour, and sometimes mushy. It's the dairy version of those Mulberry Street tourist-trap restaurants, and the cheese and I both felt a bit degraded in the end.

Then tomato season arrived, and the lack of that celestial mozzarella took on phantom-limb proportions. I felt a great weight lifting once I accepted the eventuality that I had to make my own. The very idea made me feel both homespun and chic, a self-sustaining hippie with a yen for cocktail rings and leather boots. A little research turned up Ricki's Cheesemaking Kit, for both ricotta- and mozzarella-making. Inside a box replete with hearts and stars and cows were citric acid, cheese salt (no additives), cheese-cloth, tablets of rennet (an enzyme that separates curds from whey), a dairy thermometer, and directions. I headed to the farmers' market for local milk, which tends to be pasteurized at a lower heat; ultrapasteurized milk may be spot-on for transcontinental journeys but is of little use for cheese.

The process seemed simple on the page: Add citric acid to the milk, heat milk to 90 degrees in a stainless steel pot, add rennet, stir for about a minute, then back off. After several moments, big, soft curds were supposed to separate from lemony-colored clear whey. I would fish the curds out with a slotted spoon and heat them in the microwave, knead the hot curds and pour off the whey, repeat, then cool my cheese in ice water. Ricki emphasized the cheerful ease of the whole process.

My first attempt was marred by uncertainty and a small pot. Pouring the milk mixture into a larger pot devastated the nascent curds, which are apparently temperamental and wary of bonding, like hollandaise or sixth graders. My beautiful golden milk remained mostly milk, but was now shot through with tentative pearls that dissolved on contact with my slotted spoon. I drained the mixture, hoping for ricotta, and ended up with what I can only describe as firming glop.

Did I mention I had invited people to a dinner featuring homemade cheese? Secreted in my refrigerator was subpar water-cheese from the supermarket, as if I'd known all along I couldn't hack it. I was tempted to ditch the entire mozzarella-making idea, but I washed all my pans and thermometer and cleaned the kitchen counters and took a breath.

This time I got tough: I doubled the rennet and let the mixture sit for twice as long before draining. Now soft, breakable curds did form, so I made a desultory stab at the microwave method. It was late in the day and I was getting sweaty and depressed.

After heating and kneading, the curds became marginally firmer and more cohesive. But then, somewhere between the second and third heating, something happened: I suddenly was holding not a bunch of dissolving curds throwing off milk but an amorphous ball of something that was having a distinctly cheese-like moment. I began to see just what one should see in fresh mozzarella: the paper-thin layers of stretchy proteins that allow you to smoosh the hot cheese around like bread dough.

At this point things became extremely exhilarating. I began to knead and heat compulsively, even breathlessly, maybe for a bit too long, and soon I was cradling an ivory orb the size of a small grapefruit.

An hour or two later, I cut the mozzarella into chunks to serve with fresh tomatoes and pasta. It was compact and mild, with the firmness of a provolone, a tangy, dairy-sweet kind of flavor, and not quite enough salt. It was cheese, but not quite the cheese—the rapture—I'd envisioned. My guests, tactfully silent about its unorthodox solidity, marveled at the fact of its existence.

Not long after, I stopped at a midweek farmers' market and for the first time noticed a table bearing ziplock bags of the satiny white grail itself. The cheese had been made two days earlier, and I guessed it would have about the same texture by now as what I'd made at home. I considered explaining to the cheesemaker that I used to procure a truly life-changing cheese in the Bronx, or that I had made some mozzarella one time myself, which he would likely greet with the same expression I have when people tell me they've always thought they'd get around to writing a book someday. In the end, I bought half a pound. It couldn't compete with the freshly made cheese in the Bronx, but it was nice. It was better than mine, if you must know.

Now that I've experienced mozzarella's unpredictable temperament and the huge quantity of milk needed to turn out a semisuccessful half pound of cheese, I admit I'm a bit daunted. But there's still no obtaining that perfect mozzarella moment unless I perfect my own. I suspect that the mozzarellas of my future will proceed like clockwork, once I figure out precisely what the cheese wants and when and in what quantity and according to what moods and weather patterns—except that my cheese isn't telling me a thing. That sort of mystique can enthrall a person, particularly when the reward is so transporting. Just the idea of it makes me want to play a little soft music, put up my hair, and saunter into the kitchen to try again.

Mozzarella and Arugula Salad with Croutons and Black Olives

2 tbsp. plus ¼ cup extra-virgin olive oil
4 thick slices crusty bread, cut into ½-inch cubes
    (or 8 thin slices)
1 tsp. finely minced shallot
¼ tsp. salt, plus more to taste
¼ tsp. freshly ground black pepper, plus more to taste
1 tbsp. sherry wine vinegar
1 large bunch (about 8 cups) arugula, ends trimmed, washed,
    dried, and chopped into 2-inch pieces
⅓ cup black olives (preferably oil cured), pitted and halved
½ pound fresh mozzarella at room temperature, sliced

1. To make croutons: Heat 2 tbsp. olive oil in a medium skillet until simmering. Add bread and fry, tossing until crisp and golden on all sides. Set aside to cool slightly.

2. To make dressing: In a small bowl, combine minced shallot, salt, pepper, and vinegar. Whisk in ¼ cup olive oil.

3. Toss arugula with dressing in a large bowl. If desired, add more salt and pepper to taste. Divide greens among 4 plates. Scatter olives and croutons over each plate, then lay mozzarella slices on top.

Makes 4 servings.

Eggs Enough and Time

By Margaret McArthur

From eGullet.org

As thoughtful a writer as she is a cook, Margaret McArthur—
longtime editorial director of eGullet's *Daily Gullet* online
literary journal—was a major factor in solidifying eGullet's
publishing credentials. Even a simple boiled egg becomes
something special under her scrutiny.

She can't even boil an egg!" Before she stopped being able
to boil water, that was the last word on kitchen clueless-
ness. Between you and me, that cook with the bad rep got a bad
rap. It's easier to poach an egg, fry an egg, whip up an omelet, or
serve forth a soufflé than it is to soft-boil an egg. It's easier to shuck
oysters, pass the CPA on your first sitting, or train cats to pair socks
than it is to produce a perfect soft-boiled egg.

A perfect soft-boiled egg has a completely cooked white and an
oozing warm yolk. A few seconds too few, and you'll tap open a
nauseating translucent-white/cool-yolk combo that goes straight
into the dog's dish. A few seconds too many, and the yolk's soft but
stiff—a medium-cooked egg. (I've never understood the medium-
cooked egg; it seems like a soft-boiled or hard-boiled gone wrong.
But with lots of butter and regrets, it's edible.)

Last winter I craved a soft-boiled egg. I wanted to wash my
dusty collection of bird-bodied eggcups, some unused since I
scored them at a long-ago tag sale or my first visit to a Sur la Table
in Santa Monica. I wanted pain de mie, toasted, buttered and cut
into soldiers. I got greedy: why not two soft-boiled eggs, scooped
warm from their shells onto a nest of toast points? I'd lost my job,

the Black Dog of depression was my faithful mutt, and the grey days of February were broken only by oral surgery and the bloody orgies of Tess Gerritsen thrillers. Even the best-adjusted lady—and I'm medium-adjusted at best—would get wiggy. In my darkest hours I considered going into the egg cozy business. What better way to keep my fingers occupied (and my smoke count under forty a day) than to create egg couture? What better way to while away a few months of meds, monster.com and unemployment checks? I realized I was reverting to craftswoman consolations, and that I'd better slap on some eye makeup, pull out an egg carton and check out any new thinking about how to soft-boil an egg.

My father was the family egg cook, and I remembered his recipe for a Four-Minute Egg: lower an egg into a pot of water at a gentle boil, set the timer for four minutes. Remove when the timer dinged. Daddy made a reliable soft-boiled egg.

Research beguiles me, so I whiled away a few hours with cookbooks. According to the experts, from the Rombauers to Harold McGee, Daddy had it all wrong. What I'll call the "Slow Start" is accepted wisdom in egg cookery. Put a 70-degree egg into a saucepan, cover with an extra inch of cold water, bring to a boil, then simmer for two to three minutes.

North Americans don't leave eggs on display in cunning wire baskets, nor do I know how to find an egg's armpit and take its temperature. Sure, I could have warmed one in hot tap water for a couple of minutes, but that seemed like fussiness; we're talking about a boiled egg here, not zabaglione. My plan was to cook the egg for the longer suggested time and if necessary, try, try again. I'd paid $1.79 a dozen at Walgreen's for my test subjects and I could afford to be fearless; I wasn't experimenting with sturgeon eggs.

I filled a small deep saucepan with water and slipped in the egg. The problem with the Slow Start Method is that it requires devoted pot-watching, because the timing starts when the water reaches a boil. The cook has to see when the rolling bubbles form. I'm sure there's a remote thermometer out there that would beep as the water reached 212, but that seemed like mucho materiel for a fifteen-cent test subject.

I lurked, the water boiled. I turned it down so that it maintained a tranquil bubble, and set the timer to three minutes. I busied myself buttering toast then stood, tea strainer in hand, to pull out the egg when my squat red kitchen timer chimed.

A boiled egg is hot, wet and slippery. With the help of a potholder I wrangled it into an egg cup and stood there counting back the years—the last time I'd boiled an egg, Oasis and Blur were thumping from my daughter's bedroom. I performed a gentle tap tap tap with my paring knife and reached for the toast fingers.

Raw egg white. Slimy, snotty, raw egg white and a thin liquid yolk that was barely warm. I tossed the egg, tossed the toast—almost tossed my cookies—then refilled the saucepan with water and deposited Test Subject 2. I didn't spend a lot of time waiting for the water to boil because the phone rang. By the time I'd convinced a landscaping company that I was planning to let my property revert to prairie, the water was preparing to churn out big-boy bubbles. I adjusted the heat, set the timer for three minutes, and made more toast. When the timer pinged I started counting. When I reached twenty (one thousand) I pulled the egg, beheaded it and danced a victory Watusi: the white was cooked firm, its texture neither rubbery nor shiny and glutinous. The yolk was runny, lightly thickened and clung to the toast like White-Out on a black satin jacket. I topped up the butter and salt and pepper in the perfect Brancusi serving vessel and thought: "I stressed less the last time I made Beef Wellington!"

Washing up, I pondered. Slow start, rolling boil, and three minutes and twenty seconds to soft-boiled bliss—too much pot watching and counting for fifteen cents worth of perfect protein. I don't have a timer that ticks off to the second. Waiting around for the pot to boil was dandy; I could wipe off a couple of cabinet doors or start a batch of yoghurt. But the counting method was primitive. I cast about to find a better metric for that three-minute twenty-second paradigm.

I reeled with my brilliance—I was a freaking genius. I have the perfect set-up in my kitchen, a CD player with a remote. All I'd need was to find a 3:20 track, cue it up and hit Play. No need to buy a more sensitive timer, no dorky counting. All the February misery and meds were as nothing. I was on my way back, baby!

I tore into the glittery stacks of CDs, only to face another challenge. My beloved Motown/Stax selections rarely hit two minutes, let alone three. After spending four hours I'll never reclaim, I found two possibilities for my digital egg timer: The Who, "My Generation" (3:18) and The Bagpipes and Drums of Scotland, "When the Battle is Over"(3:21).

My husband couldn't see the coffee table for the CDs when he got home. Neither would he buy into my brilliance—he gave me the same wary glance that I'd last seen when I told him that our path to a whiz of an old age was going to be strewn with designer tea cozies. He thought I was nuts.

He was right. I'd entered culinary Cuckoo Land.

I just wanted a soft-boiled egg I could eat without the bagpipe overture. The Slow Start Method wasn't making it, so I decided to forget the Rombauers and McGee and try my father's Fast Start Method. I wouldn't have to mooch around the kitchen, catching the water as it hit 212. I could stick a pan on the stove, walk to the mailbox, answer the phone or run out for cat food and cigarettes, tasks short enough to assure me a pot of boiling water.

Father didn't know best, or he'd used smaller eggs. A four-minute egg done Fast Start was the exemplar of what I can't gag down. I was negotiating sutures and bleeding gums, unable to chew a steak or gum Rice Krispies, I was empty and angry. I was hungry. Why couldn't I boil an egg?

I make my own marshmallows. I can knock off puff pastry without the maidenly dew of sweat. I can bone animals and fish big and small. My Paris-Brest, my babas au rhum, my bacon and eggs get good press. Not only can I make a perfect pâté, I can source caul fat in the 'burbs. But I couldn't boil an egg.

I was as committed to my goal as Newton was to The Calculus. As to mathematics and time, I discovered that my microwave—a machine I've owned for ten years—had a timer that counted to the second. (That's what happens when you store your microwave at knee level.) As severe as Marie Curie in her lab coat, I in my apron set out to make lab notes.

- February 15: 4:20. Threw it out. White nowhere close to done. Oatmeal for lunch.

- February 17: 4:35. Tossed it. 15 extra seconds didn't make much of a difference. Yoghurt and a banana.

- February 18: 4:50. Almost! White still too soft, but I ate it! (Pick up some pepper later.)
- February 20: 5:00. White cooked. Yolk thick and runny! Perfect!

I'd conquered the soft-boiled space/time continuum. I'd come up with a nice round number—five is an elegant array of minutes. I could pull an egg straight from the chilly Styrofoam carton. I could eat an egg for lunch until the sutures melted. I could look forward to ancient decrepitude sans teeth, sans everything, knowing that I'd still be able to gum a soft-boiled egg.

Nathaniel Hawthorne wrote a story called "The Birthmark," in which the husband becomes so disturbed by a tiny stain on his gorgeous wife's cheek that the birthmark blinds him to her beauty. When I had topped my excellent egg, the albumen was still a micro-millimeter unset where it met the yolk. My obsession egged me forward: I knew in my bones I hadn't achieved perfection—I was roosting on mere excellence. That slippery remnant of white became a preoccupation, the niggling doubt that I'd failed to capture the egg-cup grail.

How to firm up the ends without risking a medium-boiled egg? I wasn't going to mess with my five minutes learned the hard way, no Siree Bob! I considered finding the wire holder that comes with the Easter egg dye kit, and parboiling each end for fifteen seconds before lowering the entire egg into the pot, but that would feel like cheating because it would require extra counting. (Nor did I want my husband to suggest that I should adjust my meds.) But that twist of wire was my Newton's apple—it sent me free associating about Easter baskets. I prick one end of the eggs I hard boil for Easter, to protect them from cracking. What if I pricked both ends, exposing the white to some extra heat? There was no hard science to back up my hunch, just intuition and desperate, piteous hope. I wanted to crack this ovoid mystery and move on with my life.

I punched two neat holes with the very needle I'd used to appliqué satin braid to my baroque egg cozy. I lowered the egg into boiling water. I set the timer for five minutes. I found a forlorn

English muffin at the back of the fridge, and started it to toasting. I fretted. When the magic minutes were up, I stood my egg in its cheery cup, and crossed myself. I topped my prize, and checked the white. God must listen to the prayers of atheists: it was perfect. Not excellent, perfect.

As Simon said: "Time, time, time, see what's become of me, while I looked around for my possibilities. I was so hard to please." Time flies. Time is of the essence. Had I but world enough and time. There's a time for every purpose under heaven.

The time for my purpose was five minutes flat.

Deep in the Heart of Texas, We Bread Steak

By Joe Yonan

From the *Washington Post*

Food editor of the *Washington Post*—where he earned a 2009
James Beard award for best newspaper food section—Yonan
came to D.C. via Boston (cooking school, then a stint as food
and travel editor at the *Globe*), but his roots lie in West Texas—
prime chicken-fried steak country.

I've always told people that chicken-fried steak, one of the
iconic dishes of Texas, was the first thing I learned how to
make, at age 8 or 9, even though that's not entirely true. Mashed
potatoes and whipped cream came slightly earlier; I had a thing for
my mother's stand mixer. But those were mere accompaniments: a
side dish, a garnish.

Anyone who has ever eaten CFS knows that it's nothing if not
a whole meal: a crisp, tender-but-chewy mess of meat drowning
in rich, peppery cream gravy. When those mashed potatoes I had
mastered took their place on the plate, too, then you'd be more
than set. Save the diet food for another day, or another state. My
teacher was my stepfather, Vernon Lee Jones, from the little West
Texas town of Miles, about 20 minutes from the relative metropolis of San Angelo, where we lived. Tall and lean, Vern's a man of
few words (think of Clint Eastwood's character in *The Bridges of
Madison County*), and in my memory we conducted this lesson
largely in silence. But what is there to say, really, that can't be
shown? Pound a piece of round steak with a spiked mallet, dredge

it in seasoned flour, get some oil real hot in a cast-iron skillet, pan-fry the steak on both sides until golden brown. Pour out most of the oil, add flour and pepper and milk or cream, whisk, scrape, let thicken, serve.

Not until I got to Austin for college did I realize there were other ways to make CFS. In the 1980s, the dish was having a moment in such restaurants as the famous comfort-food palace Threadgill's and the retro-hip Good Eats Cafe. At those places, the breading was flakier and more distinct than Vern's, probably because the cooks were dipping the steaks in egg before flouring them. Not bad, just different.

At Good Eats, in fact, one of the most popular dishes was chicken-fried chicken, made with boneless breasts rather than steak. Think about that name: It wasn't just fried chicken, it was chicken that was fried like chicken-fried steak, which was in turn fried . . . like chicken. Perhaps only a Texan could appreciate the distinction.

I haven't lived in Texas for 20 years now, so my experiences with chicken-fried steak have been few and far between and largely of my own making. That is, until the Smithsonian decided to feature Texas (along with Bhutan and NASA) at this year's Folklife Festival, which starts today. Among the recipes in the arsenal of things they're planning to demonstrate on the Mall is good old CFS.

This recipe came with an official-sounding story of origin, one that ran somewhat counter to what I had come to believe: that chicken-fried steak must be related to schnitzel, brought by all the Germans who immigrated to the Texas Hill Country. The story tells of Jimmy Don Perkins, a short-order cook at a cafe in Lamesa (even farther west than San Angelo), who on one fateful day in 1911 wrongly assumed that a waitress's ticket for two orders ("chicken, fried steak") was for only one. He had never heard of it, but figured the only way to make it was to cook the steak like fried chicken. So that's what he did.

The venerable Texas food authority Robb Walsh, in what may be the definitive treatise on CFS in a 2007 article for the *Houston Press*, broke down the dish into three distinct versions, theorizing that each may have a separate heritage. The East Texas one, dipped in egg and then flour, is probably connected to Southern fried chicken. The central Texas version, sometimes using bread crumbs in the mixture, probably comes from those German immigrants. And the eggless West Texas version I learned to make is probably more closely related to what the cowboys called pan-fried steak.

But there are exceptions to everything. The citified versions I tasted in Austin didn't use bread crumbs. Neither does the Smithsonian recipe, provided by Tom Nall of Burnet, also in central Texas. What's more, Nall uses Bisquick for a final coat.

That raised my purist's hackles, but when I tested his recipe, I loved it. The breading was extra flaky, no doubt from the baking soda in the Bisquick, and the gravy was perfectly spiced thanks to a few dashes of Tabasco and a pinch of sugar. It took me back to Texas: if not quite all the way to my childhood home in San Angelo, at least to Threadgill's in Austin.

I made it last week for a friend. He was enthusiastic about the steak and the breading but less so about the characteristically thick gravy. "It's so heavy and peppery," he said, "and it fights with the beef. Can you rework the recipe to make it thinner, maybe a little lighter?"

He's Canadian, so I should have cut him some slack. Instead, I told him yes, I most certainly can make the gravy thinner or lighter, but I won't. Not without the approval of Vernon Lee Jones of Miles, Texas, and I already know what he would say. Or what he wouldn't.

THE BEST CHOCOLATE CHIP COOKIE I'VE EVER HAD

By Raphael Kadushin

From epicurious.com

Food writer? Travel writer? Why choose, when you can carve out a career like Raphael Kadushin's, jetting away from his hometown of Madison, Wisconsin, to chronicle food scenes in cities around the world for *Bon Appetit* and other magazines.

I was recently evicted from a Wisconsin buffet line, which, I suppose, is like being asked to leave the bullring if you're a matador. I didn't realize it at first, though, because the woman evicting me was very polite about it. "You might want to leave some food for some others," she said, which, now that I consider it, is a remark that crackles and then virtually explodes with roiling sarcasm and quiet rage. But I was too busy chewing at the time to notice that the entire sentence was grammatical garnish except for the one operative word (that would be "leave") and so I just smiled and kept eating, one oblivious pie-hole, until two beefy men sort of walked me away from the admittedly diminished smorgasbord of deviled eggs and cream pies, talking quietly, in the soothing tones people use to calm down angry drunks.

The woman of course was absolutely right to bounce me, though that didn't stop me from sending an actual drunk, willing to do anything for my bottle of Bud, back to the buffet for one more deviled egg. The reason I got so carried away relates to one of the points of this blog: the traveler's tireless search for the one memorable mouthful. Usually that will mean something I've tasted on the road somewhere, at a restaurant or deli or bakery, and something everyone can sample if they're in the global neighborhood.

But I think it's good to start a travel blog where your trip always starts, at home, especially when home represents the start of all our culinary trips: the farms that are the source for all that busy local sourcing driving contemporary cuisine. And one of the meals I like best is the classic Midwest farm buffet and a particular kind: not the ethnic Scandinavian smorgasbords or the serious organic buffets but the snaking potlucks triumphantly rooted in the fifties, the ones that mix pudding whips and marshmallow creams and wonton noodles and the contents of any soup can into a proudly artificial, brightly glowing, exuberant cook-off.

This may have something to do with the fact that my mom was the original purist cook who spent most of her culinary life quietly contemplating what you can do with a kosher chicken (a lot, as it turns out) and I felt cheated of the whole world of fun food.

So I was excited when Jim McGhee, the brother of my inimitable partner T.P. McGhee, and his wife Mala threw a midsummer buffet this past weekend on their farm in south central Wisconsin. The McGhees are the kind of politically progressive farmers who represent a great Wisconsin tradition, family farmers who helped pioneer the push for sustainable and organic agriculture, and who fought the inevitably losing battle against the tin-souled corporate farms. But if they're progressives, then their buffet is an oddly thrilling throwback. I suppose it's odd to opt for the miniature marshmallow puffs and ramen noodles when there is a whole ripe universe of corn, wheat and dairy cows ringing the farmhouse (at least there was until the corporations took over) but in a way it makes sense; if you can sit down to a mug of fresh milk every morning something big and overstated is probably an exotic relief, the definition of a party.

And Mala, along with her daughter Liz Jones and their neighbors, outdid themselves. There were pasta salads and sloppy joes and the kind of Asian salad you'd never see east of Michigan, the one that's an addictively sweet and sour toss of cole slaw, ramen noodles, almonds, green onion, sugar, and rice vinegar. But the thing I can still taste, five days later (partly because they gave me a plate to go) is Mala and Liz's rendition of the classic chocolate chip cookie, the emblem of Americana that a lot of Americans screw up. Too often what people call chocolate chip cookies are these oddly leathery things, as blistered as a bad Boca tan, or the doughy ones that turn mealy, or the overly sweet ones, or the so dry they're desiccated ones. But the McGhee chocolate chip cookie has a pure vanilla flavor that tastes, somehow, slightly caramelized and a texture that elevates it: a feathery, pillowy texture that isn't too porous, that still has a chew to it, and that stays ethereal even the day after it comes out of the oven.

Offering up a chocolate chip recipe on a food site is a dangerous thing, it basically means you're itching for a fight, so I'm going to lard this recipe with all kinds of caveats. First I won't be in the habit of featuring recipes because my forte is judging recipes, not collecting them. And to be honest I'm not sure why these cookies turn out the way they do because on the face of it the recipe looks fairly banal and standard. Maybe it has something to do with the purebred Wisconsin milk, and maybe Mala and Liz have to be in the kitchen actually doing the baking, staring out at their wheat fields. So don't blame me, Mala or Liz if you try this recipe and you don't taste ambrosia, and feel free to offer your own superior recipes (or places that sell memorable cookies). For me, though, this is the best.

The recipe according to Mala (another caveat: she was rattling this off on the phone and seemed distracted): 1 cup of butter-flavored Crisco shortening (I'm just reporting); ¾ cup of brown sugar; ¾ cup of sugar; 2 eggs; 2 teaspoons of vanilla (note the extra vanilla which is one of the things that I think elevate these cookies); 2 or 3 teaspoons (Mala got a little vague here) of water; 2 teaspoons of milk (another signature). Beat all that until it's creamy. Then add 1 teaspoon of baking soda, 1 teaspoon of salt, 2 cups of flour, add Nestle semisweet chocolate chips, and bake at 350 degrees for 8–10 minutes, though, and this is crucial, both Mala and Liz say err on the side of undercooking, just slightly. And I think timing might be the key. Like the best cooks, Mala and Liz know intuitively when something is perfectly done.

They Remember Home

By Annia Ciezadlo

From *Saveur*

Political journalist Ciezadlo has her own avenue for exploring
the intricacies of Middle East politics, which she covers from
her base in Lebanon: Examine how everyday realities like
cooking, shopping, and eating carry on throughout civil war
and armed strife.

The most stressful and dangerous period of my life was
the seven and a half months that I spent in Iraq reporting on the war there in 2003 and 2004, and ever since then I've
been burning to go back. Because it's still not safe in Iraq for a
freelance journalist like me, I satisfy this irrational yearning by
seeking out Iraqi food wherever I can: tender okra slow-cooked in
thick tomato sauce; beef and lamb layered with tomatoes, eggplant,
and green peppers; lush stews of tomatoes and apricots poured
over yellow rice, to name a few. These cravings led me to al-Najaf
al-Ashraf, the only Iraqi restaurant in Beirut, Lebanon, which I
now call home. That is where I met Ali Shamkhi.

The first time I saw Ali, he was sitting at a table nuzzling a bowl
of golden yellow tashreeb dijaaj, an aromatic dish of broth-soaked
bread and slow-cooked chicken that has been traced all the way
back to ancient Mesopotamia. Khubuz al-tannour, the thick,
wheaty Iraqi flat bread baked in a *tannour*, the Sumerian stove still
used to this day in Iraq, is broken into pieces and drowned in a
rich stew of chicken that has been simmered with onions and ba-

har asfar (a spice blend made of a variety of ingredients, including cardamom, cumin, and turmeric). In the end, the meat is so tender you can pull it off the bone with the bread before stuffing it all in your mouth, which is what Ali was doing when I met him. Iraq has had many great civilizations, he told me between bites: the Sumerians, the Akkadians, the Babylonians, and others, all layered one on top of the other like so many ingredients in a traditional Iraqi stew.

You don't have to tell me about Iraqi civilization, I told him. I've been there. I liked it, especially the food.

I should have known better than to say that: being an Iraqi, he immediately invited me to his home for dinner.

The next day, I was in the cramped kitchen of Ali's apartment in the Hayy el-Selloum neighborhood of Beirut, watching him wash chicken with the help of his two roommates, Jassim and Ahmed Jaafar. He was going to make tashreeb, the dish I'd seen him eating when we met. As he held each piece of chicken under running water, Ali whispered "Bismillah [In the name of God]"—a small prayer of thanks for this flesh, so recently alive, that we were about to eat.

In a blacked aluminum skillet missing its handle, Ali seared each thigh the way his mother taught him, skin side first, pressing down on the meat with a slotted spoon—"just enough to release the fragrance," he said. Then he paused, closed his eyes, and inhaled a deep, hungry lungful of home. "The scent of tashreeb," he said, waving his spoon in the air, "will drive you mad."

ALI IS A REFUGEE. Of the 2.2 million Iraqis who have fled to neighboring countries since the war in Iraq began, about 50,000—many of them single men like Ali and his roommates—have ended up here in Lebanon. Back home, in times of peace, their mothers (or, once they were married, their wives) would serve them plates heaped with tender beef or lamb and fragrant rice every day after work. Here in exile, however, men like Ali are long on appetite but short on women, so they cook for themselves.

"It's not usual for men to cook in Iraq," Ali said, "but we're in a strange country, and we have to familiarize ourselves with things we're not used to." In Beirut, these home-cooked meals do more than just nourish Ali and his friends. Iraqi cuisine keeps them whole, keeps their scattered world intact. The shared ritual of eating has turned these hungry, homesick men into a household.

Ali, Jassim, and Ahmed have been cooking together for four years. Ali, who was a truck driver in his hometown of Karbala, makes a living driving trucks and bulldozers at construction sites these days; Jassim and Ahmed work as house painters. Whoever gets back from work first each day goes to the local market, buys vegetables and meat, and starts dinner. The others pitch in when they get home, dividing the labor: one slices, one cooks, one cleans. Then other men, drawn by the smells of familiar dishes, arrive: a distant cousin of Ali's from Karbala, maybe, or the neighborhood's Iraqi barber, or fellow teammates from the local soccer team that is made up of Iraqi refugees. Iraqis, they assure me, rarely eat alone.

Among these exiles, Ali, tall and tanned and all of 28 years old, is the mother hen. During that first visit, he bustled around the kitchen, affectionately barking orders and making extravagant pronouncements: "I could cook a kharouf"—a whole lamb—"in one hour!" he said with a wave of his cigarette as he presided over the simmering tashreeb. Later, when the subject of Iraqi hospitality came up, he said, half seriously, "If we have a guest, we give them our own children. This is our way."

Jassim, 25, is the joker. Graceful as a cat, flirtatious, he clowned around in the kitchen, brandishing plates of food and pretending to be on a cooking show by imitating the clunky classical Arabic of Lebanese celebrity chefs. At 32, Ahmed is the oldest, the responsible one. He didn't kid around as much as Jassim or boast as much as Ali, but on the rare occasions when Ahmed said something, everyone else listened.

Through it all, Ali urged the others to pick up the pace. "Come on, Jassim!" he said, as Jassim sliced more eggplants, onions, and tomatoes. "Yallah, yaa roohi [Come on, my soul]!"

At 8:30, the electricity cut out for the fourth time that evening, Jassim lighted a candle and set it carefully next to the sink. They continued their cooking by candlelight, the kitchen bathed in a buttery glow.

"Jassim, get me the water," commanded Ali, as he emptied a spoonful of spices over the chicken in the skillet. Jassim poured water into the pan. "Look at this tashreeb," he said, pleased. "Yaa aini [O my eyes]!"

OVER THE NEXT THREE MONTHS—June, July, and August—I visited the guys every few weeks. We would eat dinner on the floor, on a drop cloth made of plastic garbage bags. The men ate with the fingers of their right hands, expertly scooping up hunks of meat and rice and piloting the food into their mouths without dropping a morsel. They always gave me a spoon.

In Iraq, a typical meal for a guest might be kharouf, lamb roasted and layered atop an enormous oval platter of rice. Or dolma, a complex architecture of eggplant, tomatoes, green peppers, and grape leaves, stuffed with meat and rice and simmered together in a pot on top of lamb chops. Or pacha, a sheep's head stewed and served, like everything else in Iraq, with rice. But on these nights we ate the kind of food their mothers would have served them at home: bahmieh, a lamb and okra braise; kabset beitenjan, a stew of eggplant, tomatoes, and beef; and, of course, tashreeb.

Whenever stewed meat dishes were served, Ali would fish out the choicest hunks—great white gobs of fat dripping with sauce—and hand them to me, urging, "Eat, eat, it has flavor!" And it did; after cooking in a rich, spicy sauce for several hours, the fat was savory and delicious.

One evening toward the end of the summer, Ali told me why he had left Iraq. Not long after the American-led intervention in 2003, he said, Shiite militias took over Karbala. When he refused to sign up with them, gunmen came to his house and shot him at close range, just below his shoulder, in a not so subtle recruitment pitch: Join us, or next time we'll have better aim.

Instead of joining, he fled, leaving behind everything he knew—his job, his family, his home. He arrived in Beirut with little more than a suitcase and the hope of someday settling in Texas, where a friend from Karbala has lived since the first Gulf War, in 1991. He doesn't know when he'll return to Iraq or when he will see his mother again. She is still in Karbala, and when Ali calls her, which is as often as he can afford, the first thing he asks is "What's for dinner?"

"She might tell me, 'I am preparing rice and eggplants,'" Ali said, busying himself by turning over the chicken thighs, "so that's what we'll make here." At the thought of his mother, Ali grew quiet.

After dinner, over industrial-strength Iraqi tea, the guys peppered me with questions about Texas. Is Dallas a country, or is it a village? Would Ali be safe if he moved there? Do Americans respect people of other religions?

I asked Ali what he would eat if he made it to America. Would he try McDonald's? Puzzled, Ali appealed to Ahmed for help. "Mek Donalds?" he repeated, his tongue stumbling over the unfamiliar consonants. "What is that?"

WITH SEPTEMBER came the news: Ali had been accepted into a U.S. resettlement program for Iraqi refugees. He would be going to Texas in less than a month. The guys invited me to dinner to celebrate the news.

I arrived to find Ahmed slouched against the door frame in the living room, listening to a wistful-sounding Iraqi song on his cell phone. The customary pot of tashreeb was bubbling on the stove like a volcano. Ali took the lid off the stew and stood back theatrically, beckoning me over to appreciate its majesty. "Listen," he said, gesturing to Ahmed's phone. "The song says, 'I can't leave my parents.'" Ali began to sing along:

> I got used to unfamiliar places,
> But I still yearn to go back to you, Mother.
> I'm used to wandering around unfamiliar places.
> I'm staying up all night.
> I can't sleep . . .

He turned the pot down to a simmer and lit a cigarette. "I already miss the guys," he said, stirring the tashreeb. "We've been living together for a long time, and they're good company." The men stared at the floor for a while. Ahmed and Jassim had applied for the resettlement program, too, but they didn't know whether they'd be accepted or when they'd see Ali again.

The next day, I had the three of them over for a Tex-Mex meal of chicken mole and quesadillas. I wanted them to taste the kind of food Ali would likely encounter in Texas. After dinner, Ali called his mother on his cell phone. After a few seconds, his face was aglow; she'd picked up. "Have you had dinner?" he asked eagerly. "What did you eat?"

As his mother spoke, Ali closed his eyes and smiled, picturing the meal his mother was describing, interrupting his reverie occasionally to prod her for more details. "And what else? What else?"

When he was finally off the phone, I asked, "So, what did she eat?"

"Chicken, with dates and apples," he said. And we laughed, because we too were eating chicken.

Later, after the guys had gone, I thought about the phone calls I'd made to my own mother from Baghdad when I lived there and was feeling scared and far from home. I pictured Ali calling home to Iraq from Texas just as he had from Beirut, asking, "What's for dinner?" and cooking tashreeb in a yet another unfamiliar kitchen before sitting down to eat with another group of homesick refugees.

Ali, oh, Ali, I thought to myself. You've left your world behind once already; now you're about to do it again. Then I remembered something Ahmed had told me a few months earlier, over tashreeb. "When I eat this food," he said, "I feel like I'm home."

Tashreeb Dijaaj
(Spiced Chicken and Chickpea Stew)

Serves 4

This dish, sometimes called thareed, is similar to chicken curry. Instead of the spiced chicken and chickpea stew's being served over rice, though, it is ladled over torn-up pieces of flat bread. As the dish sits, the bread soaks up the fragrant liquid.

¼ cup canola oil
6 cloves garlic

3 small onions, quartered

4 medium waxy-style potatoes, peeled and quartered

2 bay leaves

2 tbsp. spice mixture or curry powder

1 tbsp. ground turmeric

1 tbsp. kosher salt, plus more to taste

4 skinless chicken legs (about 1 lb.)

4 skinless chicken thighs (about 1 lb.)

1 19-oz. can chickpeas, drained

4 pieces khubuz al-tannour (Iraqi flat bread), naan, or pita

1 lemon, quartered

1 tbsp. dried sumac (optional)

Heat oil in a 6-qt. pot over medium-high heat. Add garlic, onions, potatoes, bay leaves, spice mixture, turmeric, and salt. Cook, stirring and scraping bottom of pot occasionally, until onions and potatoes are golden, about 10 minutes. Add chicken and 3½ cups water; stir to combine. Bring to a boil over high heat, reduce heat to medium, and simmer, uncovered, until chicken is tender and cooked through, 20–25 minutes. Add chickpeas; cook for 5 minutes more. Taste the stew and season with more salt, to taste. Line 4 bowls with torn pieces of the flat bread. Ladle stew over bread. Squeeze a wedge of lemon over each bowl and sprinkle with sumac.

What Is Real Cooking?

By Monica Bhide

From *Modern Spice*

Updating and translating traditional Indian cooking for the
contemporary kitchen, Monica Bhide offers a fount of
pragmatic shortcuts and substitutions. At heart, one senses,
is her very real respect for the home cook—like the friend she
describes in this essay.

What is "real cooking"? Who is a "real" cook? I write
about food for a living; I should know the answer to
these seemingly simple questions, yet I am not entirely sure.

Each time I visit New York I look forward to trying the food in
the city's legendary restaurants, but mostly to eating at the home of
my friend Vrinda. She is a highly successful investment banker, a
bundle of confidence and a complete misfit with traditions. And she
is not a cook; not a real one anyway, she repeatedly tells me. You
know the ones, she tells me, who can whip up a gourmet dinner for
twenty in the blink of an eye; the ones who can prepare rice ninety-
seven different ways and then have sixty-five recipes for leftovers.

A few years ago my husband and I visited her at her home near
New York City. We arrived in the late morning and were greeted
with the warmth of a blossoming friendship. Her apartment over-
looked a gorgeous golf course and as her husband began speaking
in glowing terms about the view, she retreated to the kitchen to
cook lunch. I offered to help. She shrugged her shoulders, "It will
be nothing special. Just sit and chat with me as I cook."

I watched her, casually at first and then intently. Meticulous and fast, she was cooking her food in traditional plain stainless-steel utensils that she had brought with her from India. No nonstick pans, no Cuisinart, no high-end chef's knives in this tiny kitchen. She had, however, managed to nail into the counter a mean-looking coconut scraper with a razor-sharp edge.

Her gestures were precise. She has done this before many times, I thought.

Creamy yellow lentils simmered on the right back burner, growling at the spices floating on top of them. Deftly she calmed them by pouring in some oil. The left back burner had a large skillet containing a little oil. She quickly began to sauté thinly sliced onions in it. Then she added a generous helping of cumin seeds and the rice that had been soaking on the side. She sautéed it briefly and then added water that she measured at the sink, one raise of an eyebrow at a time. Impatiently she tapped her fingers on the range. "Come on, *boil*," she commanded. It boiled fast as if to obey. A pinch of salt appeared from nowhere as did a squeeze of lemon juice. She covered it with a lid, reduced the heat, and then turned her attention to the potatoes.

We talked as she diced with mechanical precision. I wonder if she had ever noticed that my potatoes rarely are all the same size. Another pan went on the range. In went a few tablespoons of oil and then mustard seeds. As if in defiance of the heat the seeds began to sputter and rebel. She sprinkled something that I could not see and then added a few whole dried red chiles. The room began to smell divine. Panic set in as she began to look around frantically for something. The garlic! The garlic was needed before the spices began to burn. She found it still crushed under the rolling pin, quickly scooped it up, and added it to the pan. The potatoes went in next; following in quick succession were the ground spices. She talked up a storm as she cooked, not stopping to measure or taste or analyze. The potatoes were beginning to brown. She turned the heat down, covered the pot and turned to me. "Now," she said, "the salad."

She came to the tiny kitchen table with a large bowl of cucumbers, tomatoes, onions, and cilantro. As she discussed the nuances of the stock market, the life of a commuter in New York, her old neighbors, and the pain of being away from family, she peeled, chopped, diced, and assembled the salad, which went into a large glass bowl. A mortar and pestle—produced from under the table no less—was used to pound salted roasted peanuts, which then went into the salad. A squeeze of lime juice, a pinch of salt, and it was ready. She covered it and set it in the refrigerator to chill. I must have been staring. Self-consciously she apologized. "I am not a cookbook author like you," she said, "I just make these simple dishes. I hope you will like them."

The men returned and we began discussing the price of real estate in New York, a topic that never seems to go out of style. The tempting smell of tempering garlic and red chiles on the lentils brought us to the table, ravenous.

In the dining room, Vrinda had laid out traditional large steel plates and shining steel bowls for all of us. Indian-made steel glasses, filled with ice water, glistened with condensed droplets on the outside.

Tempered lentils, cumin rice, mustard potatoes, homemade yogurt, peanut salad, and of course two types of pickles were lunch that day. We were about to start when she appeared from the kitchen, apron covered in dusted flour, carrying hot *chapattis* (Indian griddle breads) doused with homemade *ghee* (clarified butter) on a platter.

We ate with quiet reverence. Her table with the simple dishes and well-worn tableware and her repeated insistences that we take seconds, reminded me of my grandmother's dinners.

Vrinda would disappear every few bites to roast more breads and then reappear, sweaty and yet ever hospitable. Her ingredients seemed to have fallen head over heels in love with one another. The (now) empty serving dishes vouched for it.

The meal was over and we moved to the living room. The shades were drawn to keep out the blistering August sun. The luxurious cool breeze of the air conditioner dared the heat of the summer sun. The room smelled of homemade bliss. We sat still embracing the peacefulness of the moment.

I turned to her and said, "I thought you said you can't cook?"

"I can't cook," she said nonchalantly. "This is a simple homemade meal. This is not really cooking. You should see the way my friends cook such lavish meals with gourmet curries and breads, exotic vegetables. Now that is real cooking."

But you can cook, I thought as I looked around at the contented faces. This, my dear friend, *is* real cooking.

V's P's

These are the potatoes Vrinda served at lunch.
Serves 4

2 tablespoons vegetable oil
1 teaspoon black mustard seeds
4 whole dried red chiles
3 garlic cloves, crushed
1 pound baby potatoes, peeled and quartered
¼ teaspoon ground turmeric
8–10 fresh curry leaves
2 tablespoons minced cilantro
Table salt

1. In a large lidded skillet, heat the oil over medium heat. When the oil begins to shimmer, add the mustard seeds. When the seeds begin to crackle, add the red chiles.

2. Add the garlic and potatoes and sauté for 3 to 4 minutes.

3. Add the turmeric and mix well. Add the curry leaves and cilantro. Mix well and cook for another minute.

4. Add salt to taste and about 2 tablespoons of water. Cover and cook over low heat until the potatoes are tender, 12 to 15 minutes. Serve hot.

Someone's In the Kitchen

Mac 'n' Jeez

By John DeLucie

From *The Hunger*

Like a modern-day Manhattan fairy tale—with a sardonic,
sex-and-rock-'n'-roll edge—DeLucie traces the improbable
course of his career from bored corporate headhunter to
executive chef/co-owner of the city's sizzling-hot Waverly Inn
in Greenwich Village.

I'm sitting on the stoop of the brownstone next door to
The Waverly, enjoying a late-day espresso before I go in.
This is my ritual prior to the predinner meeting with the waitstaff,
when I go through the evening's specials. The place, without fan-
fare or publicity, has gone through the roof. We still have no
phone, so there's no way to make a reservation other than access to
the e-mail address only the restaurant's closest allies are privy to.
The menus still say "Preview" in bold red lettering. Despite the
fact we have been open for three months, technically, we are not. I
think we had all grown comfortable with this arrangement. If
you're not open, you can't screw up. Or at least be judged as
harshly as the food media predators would enjoy. Our invisible status, along with the fact that we were jammed to the gills every
night, made for a rollicking good time for all.

I have to admit I was relishing this. I had somehow become a
part of something very special that was elusive to most everyone
else. In my days as a corporate chef, cool was often purchased with
cash on the barrelhead. If you could wield it, you had it. At The
Waverly, it was a whole different scene. People would ask me for

reservations for their friends and they'd justify it by saying, "Oh, he's got money, he'll be your best customer." But it was not about money. It was more about what The Waverly insiders had accomplished. The "big swinging dicks" from Wall Street whom Tom Wolfe had immortalized in *The Bonfire of the Vanities* were not really welcome here. Generally, they were seen as crass, and when we did get a table of them, they would order an expensive bottle of wine and high-five each other every ten minutes. We tended to look more highly on the creative types, like the designer Tom Ford, who was not only immensely successful in business, but magnificently stylish and elegant in his manner. Al Di Meola, the guitarist I idolized in high school, came to the restaurant. This is a guy who played with Return to Forever, Chick Corea's 1970s jazz fusion supergroup. Al is known for his blistering speed and virtuoso technique and has played with the world's most prolific musicians. Of course no one recognized him except me. I shook his hand and asked about a million questions, breaking my own rules about schmoozing with guests. He told me about how he dropped out of Berklee College of Music at nineteen years old and played his first gig as a professional musician at Carnegie Hall. For me this was like meeting Phil Rizzuto. Al likes his steak medium rare. But don't tell the press.

Shortly after we opened, we expanded and took over the apartment above the restaurant. We used it to make room for more vintage wines and, conveniently, to serve as our makeshift office and changing room. I was already in my uniform, chef's jacket and jeans, enjoying the end of a sunny afternoon—my battery-charging time before the shit hits the fan—when a shady-looking guy comes down the completely empty street, stopping at the bottom of the stoop. "You-ah the-chef-ah-here," he asked in an accent that sounded just like my grandfather's, and I immediately recognized it as southern Italian. He gestured toward the restaurant. Our celebrity reputation had become so overblown, I nearly hesitated. Between the food press and reviewers and bloggers and a media starved for access, I was very spare and blatantly apprehensive about who I dished so much as a morsel of information to.

"Maybe," I said hesitantly. "Can I help you?" I asked, thinking he might be a waiter looking for a gig. He came up a step on the stoop and unzipped a frayed, dirty backpack. Was I about to get shot because our hostess had turned some B-list actor away at the door? It was New York, after all. He reached into the bag and a strong earthy smell hit me. I knew instantly what was coming next.

"Tartuffi bianco," he announced, slowly, methodically removing a wrinkled brown lunch bag, the kind my mother used to pack my sandwiches in on my way to grade school. He opened it for me as if he'd just walked out of *The French Connection*. Only it was not heroin he was offering, but white truffles from Alba, fresh off the plane from Italy.

"You like-ah?" he said, handing me the bag full of heavy, dark knotty knobs. I didn't need to sniff it. The funky earthy scent was clear—this was the real deal—the stuff every cheap chemically manufactured truffle oil maker tried to imitate. These nutty little roots were going for around $2,500 a pound. Cash only. The guy's backpack looked heavy. I bet he was carrying close to $40,000 worth of tuber contraband. I asked him where he got them. He smiled a mischievous smile and said nothing. I wondered if he'd held up a produce truck on the Belt Parkway on its way in from Kennedy.

"Pass," I said.

"You ah-sure, maestro? I can-ah do maybe-ah little bet-tah for you." He pulled out a small scale from his lumpy backpack, ready to do business.

Odd as this street-corner transaction may seem, it was not totally off the map. I had guys coming to the restaurant all the time trying to hawk their goods. Yesterday, I had a food broker bring in a legitimate cowboy who had hauled ass all the way from a ranch in Montana. The guy wore Wranglers, a four-inch belt buckle, shit-stained boots, and a beat-up Stetson. He had flown to New York with a cooler that had seen better times. It was full of dry ice and thick juicy steaks from his own cattle, from his own ranch. He was trying to cut some big volume business in the Big Apple. And for good reason. If you have a decent product and a top-drawer restaurant makes you their specialty purveyor, it can be worth a fortune in sales and publicity. Just ask the pork guys from Nieman Ranch. We had a local vintner from Long Island who wanted us to carry his wines so badly, he chartered a helicopter to take us out to his vineyard. The chopper picked us up on a windy Saturday morning at the Eastside Heliport and dashed off to the East End in forty-five short minutes, barely enough time for the Xanax to kick in, flying at about a thousand feet with a bird's-eye view of Long Island's gorgeous topography. We landed smack in the middle of the vineyard and walked from the helicopter to the tasting room, where a delicious lunch of Italian *salumi* and antipasti was waiting with tastings of about thirty wines. After coffee and espresso we got back on the chopper and an hour later we were back at work.

"No thanks," I told Truffle Guy. This was a little too shady even for me. But as I walked into The Waverly to start my evening, I had truffles on the brain. Our menu had taken off mainly because of its simplicity and timing—New Yorkers were hankering for a nostalgic take on American dishes from a more innocent time. Nothing too fancy or "chefy" as the partners liked to say. Truffles are fancy, opulent, and downright luxurious by anyone's standards. They were statement food and I didn't see a place for that statement on our menu. But what if I could do something more down-home with truffles? Our biscuits were written about in glossy magazines, and people were clamoring for them. I even made a tray for Helena Christensen, the supermodel, who was having a dinner party at her West Village town house and simply had to have some. She was so desperate that she promised to cook me dinner in return. I delivered the goods but I am still waiting for the dinner invite. Could I devise something that was, like our biscuits, comfort food, jacked up with a bit of the truffle mystique?

The next day I dug out several boxes of Barilla pasta. I decided to go with the cavatappi noodle because I liked the shape and it also happened to be the only pasta we had in dry storage. While the water boiled, I whipped up a light béchamel sauce with milk, flour, and butter, using just enough of the roux to thicken it but not too much, lest it become gummy. I didn't want a heavy, gut-busting plate. I was looking for something small but impactful. When the pasta was cooked al dente I dumped the load into a mixing bowl, adding a healthy dose of an artisan cheddar, parmagiano Reggiano, and a few other ingredients I liked to keep up my sleeve. I transferred the whole concoction into a hotel pan and baked it at 400 degrees in the convection oven until the dish was bubbling and the top had browned just crunchy and right. I called Emil in and scooped a little out onto a plate for each of us. I grabbed a small knob of truffle that I had purchased on the way to work, along with a stainless-steel truffle slicer that I had scored at a local Village gourmet shop. I sliced several healthy paper-thin rounds of truffle on top of the steaming macaroni and cheese. I sampled it first. Then I handed the plate to Emil. He took a forkful, warily. "So?" I asked.

"Not bad," he said, characteristically. From Emil that was as good as a James Beard Award. The next evening we put Macaroni & Cheese with Shaved White Truffle on the specials menu at $55 a serving. For better or worse, our signature dish was born.

My haphazard culinary hybrid took on a life of its own. What I had intended as a fun dish to occasionally spruce up the daily specials became larger than life. People couldn't get enough of the stuff. I had to start stocking the ultra-expensive fungus, at enormous cost. The ceremony of shaving those tasty little morsels of white truffle often fell on me, which meant I found myself running out of the kitchen two dozen times a night to mingle with my truffle-struck guests, which struck me as rather odd. One night I did my truffle-shaving dance for a shapely, very young and insanely sexy woman who was at The Waverly no doubt on Daddy's black Amex. When I was done slicing the three curls of truffle on her bowl of steaming noodles she stood up and kissed me so hard on the lips that I nearly landed in the lap of the woman at the table behind me. I had never considered the aphrodisiacal qualities of the truffle. It seemed the oyster, lowly bivalve that it was, had newfound competition.

While fifty-five bucks for a plate of macaroni and cheese (give or take a hundred for market fluctuations) might seem extreme to the stroller set, in fact we were offering up a superb value. You could have your spaghetti with butter and truffles for north of a hundred dollars at any of a dozen places in the Village alone, and no one batted an eyelash. But our cozy, popular plate of Mac & Cheese had the press up in arms. *Entertainment Tonight* camped outside on Bank Street poking a microphone into the noses of our neighbors. "Tell us, sir, what do you think of paying fifty-five dollars for a plate of macaroni and cheese?" The *New York Times* did its usual, stately mocking of the new kid on the block's audacious offering. My cell phone number got leaked, and I found myself deleting furious messages, as if I had just poisoned the city's water supply. A food writer from the *Daily News* got ahold of me and asked for a reservation. We had a strict policy at The Waverly— everyone, including reviewers, paid their own tab. Mr. Food Journalist and his guest sat at the bar and each ordered up the Mac & Cheese in question. I noticed, even as the company credit card hit the table, that they had both cleaned their plates. This seemed a good sign.

The next day, as I'm reading along with three million of my fellow man-on-the-street New Yorkers, I open the review page to a three-inch blaring headline: MAC & JEEZ! I was cooked again. The media loved to hate us or perhaps hated to love us. For weeks you could not open the *Post*, *Daily News*, or *Times* and not read about our "overpriced" pasta. There was little I could do but grin and bear it and watch as we sold over thirty orders of the stuff a night, while the media howled in protest along the sidelines.

How *Not* to Hire a Chef

By Tim Carman

From the *Washington City Paper*

Running a successful kitchen is part art, part business, and part mind game—and at any new restaurant, the question is learning which percentage you'll need of each. *City Paper* food columnist Carman digs deep for the inside story behind one restaurant's revolving door of top chefs.

Near the tail end of his Southern road trip, Andy Shallal had come to a horrible realization: The winner of the *Top Chef*-like contest he'd staged wasn't the right man to lead the kitchen in his new restaurant after all. At the time of his epiphany in late March, Shallal and Chris Newsome, the lone chef standing after the grueling competition, were both silently milling around the New Orleans airport, fresh off a multiday tour of the South to sample the food that would define their project. Shallal, to be fair, wasn't the only one in crisis. Newsome had just learned that his elderly grandmother had died. Instead of catching a flight back to D.C. with Shallal, the chef was going to rent a car so he could drive to Birmingham, Ala., and attend the funeral of the woman who had influenced his love of food. Shallal, meanwhile, was stewing over recent events.

During the past few days, Shallal had been arguing with his new chef over what dishes to feature at Eatonville, the restaurant he was about to open across V Street NW from the restaurateur's first Busboys & Poets outlet in Shaw. Shallal, who was born in Iraq, wanted to limit the pork offerings. Newsome, an Alabama native, couldn't imagine a Southern restaurant without pig products.

As he stood there in the airport, Shallal simply couldn't fathom why his willful new hire thought so highly of himself. Had Newsome ever opened his own restaurant? Did he have any clue what middle-aged African-American women—Eatonville's targeted palate—really wanted to eat? Hell, as far as Shallal could determine, Newsome was a nobody. Shallal even had evidence: the lack of Google hits when the restaurateur searched on Newsome's name.

At some point—Newsome says it was after he learned about his grandmother's death, and Shallal says it was before—the owner finally spouted off to his chef. "You're interested in opening Chris Newsome's restaurant," Shallal told the toque. "Who the hell do you think you are?"

And with that, Shallal fired Newsome before the chef ever had a chance to cook a single meal at Eatonville.

It was an unpredictable ending to what had, just weeks earlier, all the signs of being a classic partnership. Back in February, Newsome was one of more than 200 people to submit résumés in hopes of landing the executive chef position at Eatonville, a gig with a $75,000 salary attached to it. Only 23 of those applicants, though, were called in for interviews. Newsome was one, and for good reason. He not only studied the culinary arts at Johnson & Wales University in Charleston, S.C., but had also worked for the James Beard Award–winning Bob Kinkead, first as a sous chef at Kinkead's and later as chef de cuisine at the now-shuttered Colvin Run Tavern.

Newsome's interview, however, started out on an odd note. Before even one question was posed, the job candidate was asked to sign a release so that videographers could record every word of his interview session. Newsome signed it and proceeded to spend the next 20 minutes or so fielding questions from Shallal and Carla Hall, the Wheaton-based caterer and former *Top Chef* finalist who was helping to weed through the candidates. The interviewers felt an instant connection to Newsome. "When he walked out of the room, we both had tears in our eyes," Hall said later. In a way, they felt as if they had already found their man. "This is our chef," Hall recalled thinking.

Because he was clearly partial to Newsome, Shallal admitted right after the contest that he was "a little harder on him from the beginning." You'd have a hard time proving that, though. Shallal checked only one of Newsome's references, and the chef all but breezed through the various rounds, each tied to some Southern ingredients or Southern dishes or the Southern strains of Zora Neale Hurston's novel *Their Eyes Were Watching God*, which is partially set in Eatonville, Fla., the writer's all-black hometown.

Then again, Newsome probably could have won this contest without a biased panel, which did include both Shallal and Hall as judges for the championship round. Newsome's final menu, after all, was a clever amalgam of food and Hurston biography. His "sweet and spicy" barbecued oysters, he told the judges, were inspired by Hurston's similarly "sweet and spicy" personality. His cornmeal-crusted flounder with tasso ham was a nod to Hurston's connection to the Southern coast, with its endless bounty of fresh fish. His gingerbread-scone dessert was even inspired by the character Tea Cake in *Their Eyes Were Watching God*.

The judges ate that treacly stuff up. Mike Curtin, CEO for D.C. Central Kitchen, felt that Newsome's approach showed the chef was putting the Eatonville concept before his own ego. "It's clear that [the chef] is cooking for this restaurant," Curtin said during the final challenge. "He's not cooking to show off." Curtin's assessment makes you wonder how, over the course of just a few weeks in March, Newsome could have shape-shifted from a thematically sensitive chef willing to sacrifice his ego in the name of Eatonville to an egomaniac willing to undermine his boss' very vision of the restaurant. The answer perhaps requires some background first.

To begin with, executive chefs typically aren't hired by means of a Food Network-esque contest designed to drum up public interest in a restaurant. No chef or restaurateur contacted for this story had ever heard of an executive chef hired via a competitive cook-off—save, of course, for those winners of reality shows such as *Hell's Kitchen*. Too much is at risk, most said, to hand over your multimillion-dollar restaurant to some chef who's only proven that he can cook a great meal.

A true executive chef, says Michael Babin, co-owner of the Neighborhood Restaurant Group, requires more skills than the ability to impress a random collection of judges who may not even understand your restaurant's concept. Chefs must also manage the motley crew of cooks who work under them. It takes someone with a big ego and a sense of humility. A chef must have the humility to accept feedback and to dish out 101 minor criticisms every day "without wiping out the people who work for them," Babin says. But a chef must also have an iron-will ego to prevent small compromises from creeping into the kitchen systems, the recipes, or whatever else might diminish the experience out in the dining room.

To find such a person, Babin will "use every means at [his] disposal." He'll interview the chef himself, then pass the potential hire to the director of operations, the manager of the restaurant, even to the public relations person for further questioning. Babin will also call everyone and anyone who might have an opinion on the chef, venturing far beyond the candidate's provided references. Babin wants to find out, among other things, if the chef is a screamer, a plate-thrower, or a bum who shows up late and leaves early, perhaps with a few tenderloins stuffed under his whites. Babin will, of course, also conduct a tasting or two with the chef. "It can be a long process," he says.

It's also a process with little guarantee for success, particularly for young cooks moving into the executive chef position for the first time. Babin believes such newbies succeed only about 30 percent of the time. The main problem with just about any hiring process is that you can only see how a chef works once he's in your kitchen for days and weeks. No exhaustive background check or interview session can tell you whether the chef has the necessary drive. Or if he's trustworthy. Or if he's philosophically aligned with the restaurant's mission.

But of all the analytical tools available to a restaurateur, a cooking contest is likely the least effective way to suss out a chef's real personality, says R.J. Cooper, the Beard Award–winning toque. At Cooper's Vidalia, cooks are almost always promoted from within once they've learned the restaurant's system and values. Even line cooks at Vidalia aren't hired until they make it through a brutal two-day ritual in which they must perform a wide variety of tasks, often under a number of different people. Cooper's trying to assess their dedication and determination. "You're not going to find that in a contest," he says. Andy Shallal will be the first to tell you that he doesn't kowtow to the cult of celebrity chefs—or even non-celebrity chefs. By his own recollection, he burned through three toques in three years at his last chef-driven restaurant, MiMi's American Bistro off Dupont Circle. After fighting over food costs, cleanliness, and basic kitchen management, Shallal told himself that "I'd never go down the chef route again."

And for years, he didn't. The model for his wildly successful Busboys & Poets chain doesn't include chefs. Instead, the restaurateur relies on kitchen managers to hire and train sous chefs and line cooks who, day in and day out, are content to execute a budget-minded menu of pizzas, burgers, sandwiches, salads, and a small number of entrees. In return, these kitchen drones receive a salary, benefits, health insurance, and paid vacations. "For my people, it's a job," Shallal says. "It's not about the showmanship."

But when it came time to develop Eatonville, Shallal realized he needed a fresh concept, particularly given the restaurant's proximity to the Busboys & Poets on 14th Street NW. "I can't do the same thing," Shallal notes. So he decided instead to build a chef-driven destination for "more foodie types."

It was Shallal's idea to turn his chef selection into a publicity stunt. His plan was both elaborate and sophisticated. He rented out CulinAerie, the new cooking school on 14th Street NW, to host the multi-day contest. He hired a team of videographers to capture every moment, from the initial interviews to the final cook-off. He paid the nine competitors after each stage of the competition, starting at $100 per chef for the first round and culminating at $1,000 per chef for the two finalists, Newsome and Rusty Holman, a North Carolina native who last cooked for the Young Republican crowd at the exclusive Rookery in the West End.

Shallal spent nearly $25,000 to stage the competition, but he hoped to reap the benefits in terms of press coverage and public excitement. His plan was to create a series of videos, which he would release over a period of weeks on the Eatonville Web site, concluding with one announcing the new chef just as the restaurant was set to open.

Complications arose from the day the contest started, at least for some of the chefs. The nine contestants had to elbow for room in CulinAerie's main instructional kitchen, which had a limited number of burners and ovens. In a way, the kitchen forced these competitors to act more like colleagues as they politely negotiated for space and open stoves. But on the second day of the contest, with six chefs remaining, each one required to make fried chicken, the contestants were confronted with an even bigger issue: no deep fryers at CulinAerie.

The chefs had to fall back on pan-frying techniques or had to improvise their own deep fryers on the stove top. This may explain why the judges weren't too impressed with the birds. "I'm an African-American," said E. Ethelbert Miller, a literary activist and editor of *Poet Lore* magazine, during the competition. "I've been eating chicken all my life . . . I didn't taste any chicken that I wanted to go back and eat some more."

A far more complicated problem, however, surfaced at the end of the fried-chicken round: The judges ultimately wanted to cut both of the African-American chefs, leaving only four white men for the remainder of the contest. Shallal balked at the idea. "We can't allow the process to be guided by race alone," the owner said. But "when I am honest, race plays a role." And with that remark, Shallal decided that five chefs would move into the next round, including Jacques Ford, one of the previously ousted toques.

The truth be told, the best chef—or at least the one with the most experience as executive chef—didn't win the contest. Trent Conry, previously head toque at both Ardeo and 701, was asked to leave in the semi-final round, a victim of his own refined skills. Conry prepared such dishes as a beet risotto, a potato cake topped with smothered onions and shiitake mushrooms, and a "coffee and doughnuts" dessert in which the drink was a multi-layered parfait-like creation with java-flavored granita in the middle.

"I'd say you're probably the most talented [chef] we had, but that's not all we're looking for," Shallal told Conry when he gave him the boot. "I'm not sure we're going to be a great fit, and that's why I think we need to move on." Minutes before he delivered the blow, though, Shallal told Conry one other thing: He thought the chef would be "a major challenge" to work with.

Shallal's comment, perhaps, should have been a warning sign to Chris Newsome. The Southern road trip was part of Shallal's master plan; he wanted his new chef to experience the real Eatonville, so that he could better understand the food and the culture that had shaped Hurston and, by extension, the new restaurant that pays homage to the writer. A number of people had told Shallal the trip was a bad idea.

Privately, Newsome didn't think much of the trip either. It's hard enough, he figured, traveling with friends and family, let alone traveling with three strangers—his new boss, Shallal's brother-in-law, and Brian Evans, an Eatonville manager. The chef's mood didn't improve any when Shallal allegedly told Newsome that he had never before visited the South, nor had he ever cracked open a Southern cookbook—aside, that is, from those by Vertamae Grosvenor, a culinary anthropologist who served as one of the Eatonville contest judges. (Shallal denies such remarks; he says he's visited the South repeatedly and has read a number of other cookbooks on Southern food.)

The 37-year-old Newsome, by contrast, has been steeped in Southern food and culture his entire life. He grew up on beans and corn and other crops pulled straight from his grandmother's Alabama farm; he started cooking professionally at age 19 at the Bottega Restaurant & Café in Birmingham, where he worked under the esteemed Southern chef Frank Stitt. To Newsome, it wasn't going to be easy to swallow lectures on Deep South cooking from an amateur.

Which may have been the crux of the problem when the foursome pulled into New Orleans. It was in Crescent City that Shallal delivered his speech to Newsome about Eatonville's target eater, that mythical middle-age African-American woman. Shallal said he knew from experience what such diners wanted, and it wasn't pork. Not long after the speech, as if on cue, Shallal and Newsome came across a 40-something black woman who admired the Busboys & Poets shirt that someone in their party was wearing. Shallal introduced himself and told the stranger about his new Eatonville venture. She wondered if he had hired a chef yet.

Shallal said the chef, in fact, was standing right here, pointing to Newsome. She then turned to Newsome and asked if he will have good things on his menu.

"If I'm allowed, I will," Newsome told the woman.

Shallal wasn't at all amused by the smartass remark. To the boss, it was just another sign of his new hire's misplaced arrogance.

For his part, Newsome doesn't deny that he's confident, a character trait that he believes stops well short of arrogance. It's a self-image that would appear to jibe with Babin's earlier description of a strong kitchen leader. Shallal, however, views Newsome's personality a different way. "He just had that way about him," the owner says. "He was resistant to any kind of criticism or change. . . . To be a good chef, you got to try to listen to comments from others."

When the ax finally fell on him at the airport, Newsome felt the decision was rash, perhaps based in part on the strain of the trip as well as Shallal's inability to clearly articulate his vision for the restaurant. Shallal, the chef said, wanted his restaurant to serve Southern cuisine, authentic Southern cuisine even, but wouldn't know the real stuff "if it was staring him in the face."

Shallal admits that Newsome was "probably right," that the owner never articulated a clear vision for Eatonville. "But I really wanted a collaborative process to take shape," he adds. The owner felt like Newsome had a clear idea for Eatonville—a sort of modern take on rustic Southern cuisine—and wouldn't budge from it.

Whatever the ultimate reason for the divorce, Newsome isn't holding any grudges against Shallal, though the chef does confess that he's "thrilled that I'm not" at Eatonville. Newsome says that even though he's still without a full-time gig.

As for Shallal, well, the show must go on. He ended up hiring Rusty Holman, the second-place finisher in the chef contest. "I remember [Holman] being good, kind of hit-or-miss good" during the competition, Shallal says. "But he's come through as being very good."

If you look at Eatonville's Web site today, you naturally won't find a word of this dust-up. Instead, you'll find an altered reality. The entire site has been designed completely around the competition; it features short descriptions of the competing chefs as well as the people who served as judges. The site, in fact, is so focused on the contest it doesn't even include a copy of Holman's opening menu.

But right there on the home page, the site boasts this bit of creative fiction, as fanciful as anything Hurston penned during her career:

"[Drum Roll] . . . The winner of our chef search is Mr. Rusty Holman!"

A Beautiful Mess

By Charles Montgomery

From *Gourmet*

Author of *The Shark God*, Canadian photojournalist Charles
Montgomery usually casts his literary adventure writing in
rugged locales like the Arctic, the Andes, and the South
Pacific. But sometimes adventure lies where you least expect
it—like in a Mexico City taqueria.

Dusk fell on Los Dorados de Durango. Flickering fluorescent lights glowed inside the restaurant's open windows. One by one, the bohemians and their sympathizers drifted
in from the darkened streets of Mexico City, past the flames of the
pastor spit and the bubbling pots of beans and spicy *caldo* and *mole*,
toward the table-size stage in the back room. First came the ancient cowboy with the pink electric guitar. Then the delicate
crooner in his starched shirt and tie. Then the señora of a certain
age with the wildly painted eyes and the gold fingernails.

Soon the first bars of a *ranchera* were echoing off the industrial-
orange walls. The señora wailed her sorrows to the ceiling in a
voice that sounded like it had been dragged along a gravel road.
She stabbed an imaginary knife into her heart. Just when it seemed
as though she would die from her wounds, she grinned, sashayed
over, and embraced me: "I won't forgive you!" she sang in my ear.

The sad songs kept coming. So did the rum. Beef fillets and
strips of nopal cactus sizzled on the grill. Waiters in baseball caps
charged back and forth with trays of *tacos al pastor*, tequila, and
rum. Telenovela beauties cursed each other on a wall-mounted TV.

Ciro Dominguez, the restaurant's proprietor, worked the room, waving his short arms, slamming the cash register, touching shoulders, breaking into a wide rascal's smile when his regular showed up. He treated his favorites to a firm handshake followed by a hearty, backslapping hug.

Finally, Don Ciro eyed the crowd, ran a thick hand through his graying hair, and deposited himself in a chair out in the front room, by the pop cooler. He pressed shreds of beef into his first tortilla, spooned in ripe crescents of avocado and a grilled green onion, then squeezed on lime. He paused, peered at his creation like an artist, then devoured it without a word. I wanted to talk to him, but this wasn't the time. His daughter Marisol leaned across the table toward me.

"I like to watch him eat," said Marisol. "It's the only time he really seems at peace."

"Come," he ordered me. "Sit. Eat."

I looked down at my hands, which were stained brick red. I had spent the day chopping chiles, pulling apart the soft flesh of cooked chicken, bathing pork fillets in *pastor* sauce and squeezing them onto the stainless-steel spit that now stood on the street. I would have done anything to win Don Ciro's approval. He knew it, and he seemed to take a perverse pleasure in it. "You owe me!" he had told me shortly after I arrived in Mexico City. "And you'll pay me through hard work—ha!"

I never quite knew when the guy was joking.

Don Ciro had been running this restaurant—essentially an outsize taqueria—in Colonia Roma, a neighborhood in the heart of the city, for more than three decades. His customers were mostly like him, country folk who had come to the megacity to make a buck and never left. The city had changed them all. They were rougher, louder, more aggressive, quicker on their feet. They were *chilangos*. He served them the dishes they knew from their villages: enchiladas drenched in black *mole*, *chilaquiles* heaped with green salsa and sour cream, and, of course, tacos stuffed with spiced pork or the thick stews, generously infused with chiles and garlic, known as *guisados*. He had the business figured out. But Don Ciro had other problems to deal with. For one thing, his son Omar had put down his dish rag a decade before and run off to Canada. Now Omar was back, with a boyfriend in tow. Me. There was no recipe for dealing with such a *locura*, such a craziness.

I followed Don Ciro around like an eager puppy, from the restaurant, through the streets and markets of Mexico City, even to the cornfields of his native Michoacán. At first I just wanted to win his respect. But as the weeks passed, the man and his taqueria became my window on the soul of Mexico City. Why did Don Ciro eat like it was an act of prayer? Where was the line between *alegría* and sorrow? Why was he happiest when surrounded by noise and haste? You could ask the same questions about the city itself.

I invited myself along on one of Don Ciro's biweekly trips to the market. I thought it would be a quaint excursion, but there is no such thing in Mexico City. We bounced across the south side, through a collage of Day-Glo painted signs, car wrecks, Jesus graffiti, juggling clowns, and blue fumes.

"What a mess we've made," Don Ciro boasted as he jerked his dusty pickup back and forth in the flow, waving jovially as he cut off trucks and boxy minibuses. Sometimes he hedged his bets, straddling lanes. Sometimes we didn't move at all. Many of his fellow *chilangos* commute for two hours every morning through this chaos. Don Ciro seemed to regard it with a transcendent sense of awe. "To be human in this city, you must be adaptable. You must stretch, you must contract—it's a marvelous thing!"

We pulled into Central de Abasto, the 750-acre wholesale market that supplies Mexico City with 30,000 tons of fresh fruits, vegetables, and meat every day. Thousands of bodegas lined a grid of hundreds of corridors, all linked by bridges and surrounded by stampeding tractor trailers. We hired a scruffy-looking porter and set off for the produce halls.

"Hurry up!" Don Ciro bellowed as he charged along, waving his clipboard, barking price inquiries, greetings, and flirtations as he went.

Soon our porter's cart was piled head-high with nopal cactus paddles, bundles of cilantro, crates of tomatoes and green tomatillos, a side of pork, and two sacks of onions. We coughed and sneezed our way through a gauntlet of stalls selling chiles—"It's the *manzano* chile that makes you cry," a vendor laughed, waving one at me like a hand grenade. We picked up dried *árbol* chiles for making the house salsa and meaty green poblanos for stuffing, then followed the sound of music into a cinder-block passageway with crates of limes stacked to the ceiling.

There, a pair of cowboys were launching into a ballad from Mexico's northern states. One strummed a guitar. The other squeezed a battered accordion. They wailed a tune so bittersweet that suddenly the lime vendor was dancing, our porter had dropped his load, and Ciro was howling along with the music.

My eyes still watery from chile fumes, it struck me that *chilangos* prefer their toil, tragedy, and joy all stirred together, like the meat and spice and fruits that Don Ciro's cooks stir into their *picadillo*, their pepper stuffing. This is the story of Mexico City, and especially the story of Ciro Dominguez.

DON CIRO WAS BORN amid the cornfields in the state of Michoacán, the sixteenth largest of Mexico's 31 states. We went there, Don Ciro, Omar, and I. After a day's bus ride, we pushed through a forest of tall corn, hopped a stone wall, then followed a trail up over rocky ground to the two-room adobe hut where Ciro had spent his first years. I watched him draw a weary hand across those crumbling mud bricks. He said he could see it all again, just like a movie.

It was the dry season, 1964. The boy was barely 12 years old. He woke up hungry. There was nothing to eat, said his mother, but a chile pepper and the tortillas she was flapping in her hands. So Ciro ate his tortilla and his chile, and as he walked through the fields crying from hunger, he told himself: "I've got to get out of here, *muy lejos*."

Like millions of Mexicans, Ciro headed for the capital to look for a way to escape the hunger and uncertainty of the countryside. No wonder he opened a restaurant.

I left Los Dorados for a few days in order to explore Mexico City. In the past decade, the city has experienced a renaissance, both on its streets and in its kitchens. The metropolis has exploded to a population of almost 20 million people. Splendid colonial plazas and pedestrian malls have been rebuilt in the Centro

Histórico. Lofts, hotels, and shopping arcades have sprouted on lots that had been derelict since the earthquakes of 1985. Some streets are converted into sandy "beaches" in the summer. In the winter, an ice rink appears on the Zócalo, the vast plaza in the center of the city.

Colonia Roma, Don Ciro's neighborhood, is being colonized by modern boutiques and espresso bars. Just down the Avenida Colima from Los Dorados, a sports-shoe boutique called Shelter displays $200 sneakers on glowing panels of translucent glass; kitschy Kong specializes in lowbrow art and design; and farther east, Tatei sells Hello Kitty-style clothes by Mexican designer Jaramara Mendoza.

It's enough to make one fear for the future of the humble taqueria, especially given the evolution of the taco itself. A new wave of chefs is laying claim to the traditional foods that restaurants like Los Dorados have served to working-class people for many years. I found beef tacos and corn soup on the menu at Izote, in the sophisticated neighborhood of Polanco, and bankers munching on tuna tostadas at Contramar, in trendy Colonia Condesa. I first set eyes on the Aztec specialty *escamoles* on a crisp white tablecloth at El Tajín.

"They are the Mexican caviar," my friend explained, as he insisted I try them. What arrived was a glistening heap of ant larvae. I was horrified until I actually tasted them. Sautéed in butter to a chewy texture, the larvae were surprisingly mild, with a lightly smoky aftertaste. We spooned them into handmade tortillas: *tacos con escamoles*.

When I returned to El Tajín the following week, I met Alicia Gironella De'Angeli, the godmother of *nueva cocina mexicana*. She is a stately woman with silver hair and a long, severe nose.

"A taco is a medium in which to eat anything," she explained. "There is no special recipe."

As laissez-faire as this may sound, Doña Alicia is a stickler for certain rules. I learned this firsthand when I used my index finger to sample the *chilmole* sauce that drenched the sea bass she served me. I parsed out burnt red chile, garlic, cloves, anise, coriander. . . .

"Don't use your finger for that!" she said sternly. "Use your tortilla."

The tortilla, she said, is the foundation of Mexican cuisine and should be respected as such. Tortillas must be served hot. And most importantly, they must be strong and pliable. She ordered a fresh plate and vigorously rolled and folded one of her own handmade tortillas. It survived. Then she did the same to a machine-made tortilla, which tore after a few tugs.

Taquerias like Los Dorados deserve to survive the gentrification of districts like Colonia Roma, she said—but only if their tortillas are worthy.

"You go back to Los Dorados and check and see if that tortilla is strong," she told me with the authority of the cooking teacher she was for many years. "You roll it. If it breaks, the place is no good. Okay?"

Doña Alicia's food was glorious. Her waiters were gracious. But after a few days of the white-tablecloth scene, I missed the flawed glory of Los Dorados: the racket, the Christmas lights, the telenovelas and rambunctious emotions that bounced off its very well-worn walls. And I missed Don Ciro.

I returned on a Friday evening, just as the bohemians were arriving. Smoke was billowing from the grill. Maura Gómez, the lady with the wild eyes and the gold fingernails, grabbed me by both hands. "Tonight," she said hoarsely, "I'm going to sing you *unas canciones chingonas*—some bloody great songs!"

And there was Don Ciro, finishing a plate of beef-tongue tacos. His granddaughter Fernanda sat at his side, coloring with crayons.

"Sit!" he ordered me.

"Bring it," he ordered the cooks.

He pushed his bare plate away and gazed at me. I pulled a warm tortilla from the basket in the middle of the table. As he spoke, I rolled it, folded it.

"You know, Chuck, I grew up here," he said. "I aged here, inside these walls. My liver is scrubbed on these walls. This is where I have known all my joy, my angers, and my deceptions."

I realized that to walk into Los Dorados is to inhabit the song of Don Ciro's own life, and now I had become a part of that song. Which is why I almost wept when my plate arrived: a plump green poblano chile drenched with almond cream sauce and sprinkled with red pomegranate seeds. The three colors of the Mexican flag made this *chiles en nogada* the most symbolic, and unsubtle, of dishes. You don't serve it to just anyone.

He watched me slice through the poblano. The *picadillo*, a blend of ground beef, pineapple, dates, pear, whole garlic, and gentle green chile, poured out. It smelled like Christmas cake and tasted like love.

The speakers in the back room crackled to life. Maura's gravelly lamentations issued from the speakers. "I have cried drops of blood," she howled. "Poor me!"

One after another, the bohemians gushed and wailed about the searing pain of life, of everything they had lost over the years, and it was a euphoric kind of sadness I'll never quite understand. The grill hissed and crackled, and the waiters passed around the tacos and tequila and rum. Fernanda tugged at Don Ciro's arms, but he was already on his feet.

He grabbed my hand. He shook it hard. Then he yanked me in for the backslap hug. One slap. Two slaps. The full embrace. He smiled his rascal's smile, and then he was off to the next table.

I looked down at my hand, and there was the tortilla: rolled, folded, crumpled, and gloriously intact.

BACK TO THE OLD WORLD, 1962–1967

By Marcella Hazan

From *Amarcord*

In this charming memoir, Hazan recounts how a brainy girl
from a village in Emilia-Romagna met and married a Jewish
ad man from New York, taught herself to cook, and became
the doyenne of traditional Italian cuisine in America.

I f Nero had lived here," I was saying to the real estate
agent, "he would have had a terrific view of Rome burning." We were on the *altana*—the roof terrace—of a Roman
palazzo, open to the four points of the compass and high enough
above the city to let one's eye wander over the cupolas, the rooftop
gardens, the parks, the Spanish Steps, the pattern of streets emptying into squares like so many streams spilling into ponds, which
form the most brilliant of urban tapestries. Stacked directly below
the *altana* were the other two tiers of the apartment that became
our Roman aerie.

Our new domicile had been carved out of the uppermost corner of Palazzo Ruspoli, a massive pile in the Florentine style
erected in the sixteenth century on the most central street corner
in Rome, one block down from Piazza di Spagna. The Ruspolis, a
large and princely Roman family, moved into it more than four
hundred years ago and have been living in it ever since. The
palazzo's celebrated architectural feature is a broad staircase of one
hundred steps, each one hewn from a single magnificent block of
marble. You breathe grandeur with every step you take. Victor liked
to climb it to the first landing and then take the candy box of an

elevator the rest of the way up to our apartment. He also enjoyed swinging open the enormous wooden front doors and driving his little Lancia into the old columned courtyard, where he had a reserved space alongside those of the princes.

We ate out often when we lived in Rome. The food was deeply satisfying; so was the check, and so was the social rhythm. It was not unusual for friends to organize a midnight *spaghettata*, straddling the end of one day and the beginning of another with bowls of *spaghetti alla puttanesca* or *alla carrettiera*, or more often perhaps, *bucatini all'Amatriciana*. The food I ate in Rome threw light on an inbred regional cooking style that was new to me. The difference from Milan was startling. Milan had opened its arms, or more precisely its workplaces, to immigrants from Italy's less industrious regions, as well as to professional people from over the border. Its own professional and entrepreneurial class traveled more than any other in the country. The city's approach to food was consequently cosmopolitan, easily drawn to traditions other than its own. Few were the restaurants where, aside from the ubiquitous risotto, osso buco, and breaded veal cutlet, you would be offered an excursion through the byways of domestic Milanese cuisine. The most popular establishments were Tuscan, while immigrants from the south were to open trattorias that featured the specialties of Apulia, Naples, and Sicily.

Even though Rome was the capital of the nation and the beneficiary of millennia of history, at the time we lived there it was essentially a glorious provincial town where the dishes of the restaurants—as well as the ingredients sold in its markets—were not radically different from those you might have found in the home kitchens of their patrons. We did have a few Tuscan trattorias—one of them, Fontanella Borghese, was down the street from the palazzo—but they did not rise to the level of those in Milan. And we had a few Bolognese restaurants, of which one, in Piazza del Popolo, was famous. But none of these stole the hearts, or rather the palates, of Roman eaters who knew that what they really wanted was the cooking on which they had been raised.

Once we had safely moved in, my first thought was to see what was in the food shops and the markets. Around the corner from the palazzo there was the kind of greengrocer we call a *primizaro*.

Primizie in Italian are the earliest, and by extension, the finest and sweetest-tasting fruits and vegetables. L'Ortolano, our Milanese greengrocer, had splendid produce, but that of the Roman *primizaro* surpassed it in appearance, in flavor, and by a vast margin, in price. It was worth it, however, and I regret that ill-placed frugality prevented me from getting more of my produce there.

We are hugely fond of good green beans. If they are at their best, I don't bother making a sauce. I just boil them until done, neither crunchy nor mushy, usually less than seven minutes, and toss them, while still warm, with red wine vinegar, then with salt and olive oil. I remember a time my mother had come to visit and I had bought a kilo of the *primizaro's* green beans. They were so fresh that they glistened and so firm, they snapped as sharply as dry twigs. They were perfectly formed and slender; a kilo of them made a daunting-looking mound on the kitchen table. "I have never seen such beautiful beans," said my mother. "Shall I trim them for you?" *"Grazie,"* I said, wondering whether she realized what she was letting herself in for. My mother was many endearing things, but long-suffering was not one of them. By the time she finished snapping off both ends of the last bean in that formidable heap, the drain on her patience had been such that her hands were shaking as though palsied, and so was her voice as she cried, *"Mai più!"* ("Never again!") "The next time you buy a kilo of such beans, get someone else to trim their little ends off!"

At my local Publix or Whole Foods now, when I feel the rock-hard peaches and pears, or I try to pick up a scent from the unforthcoming melons, when I bring home green beans or zucchini that have little more taste than the water with which they have been abundantly irrigated, not to mention the times that the musty smell of long storage forces me to discard what I have just bought, I think of the fragrance and juicy, sugary flesh of the *primizaro's* fruits, of the concentrated flavor of his vegetables, and I wonder why we in America can't have better-tasting produce. Why aren't we showing the people who raise our produce how to be better farmers? Not necessarily organic farmers, or more efficient farmers, just plain old cultivators of good food. If our vegetables had taste and cooks were shown what they need to do with them, which is very little, everyone would eat more vegetables. Italians don't eat as many as they do because a government agency or the press tells them how healthy it is for them. They eat them because they taste so good. It is through irresistibly good taste—never mind "organic" or other fashionable categories—that food makes people happy and healthy.

There was a small open-air market close to the river that I could easily walk to, and it filled most of my needs, but the market I remember most fondly was the one at Campo dei Fiori. Its name, until I first went there, led me to think it was a flower market. It was much too far for me to walk to, but I sometimes had a friend drive me, and when she couldn't, it was worth my taking a taxi. They were very cheap then, and no tipping was expected.

I have never received better or more desirable instruction about any subject than what I was taught about the Roman way of cooking vegetables at the Campo dei Fiori market. It was there that I became acquainted with *mammole*, the large, round-faced artichoke essential to two Roman preparations, *carciofi alla romana*, artichokes Roman style, and *carciofi alla giudia*, artichokes Jewish style. The woman selling them patiently showed me how to prepare both, and both techniques made themselves at home in my kitchen, eventually landing in my cookbook. For Roman style, the artichokes are trimmed of the tough part of the leaves, but the thick, long, meaty, virile-looking stem is left on. Only its leathery rind is peeled away. The whole artichoke, its stem thrusting upward, is braised in a tall saucepan in very little olive oil and water. "Cover the pan with a moist towel, to hold the moisture in, and put the lid over the towel," she told me. For *carciofi alla giudia*, Jewish style, the stem is sliced off, but it is not thrown away, because it is so good. It is reserved for use in a soup or a meat stew after the rind has been stripped from it. The head of the artichoke is here again trimmed of the tough, inedible portion of its leaves (Italians find it mystifying that others will cook something that they won't be able to eat), and it is fried in two successive batches of hot oil. A drizzle of water causes the second batch of oil to sizzle, and the leaves open, curl, and turn a golden brown. The finished artichoke resembles a chrysanthemum and is deliciously crisp.

Late in the fall, I had picked up a head of chicory to add to my purchases, intending to blanch it and sauté it, but the woman selling it, realizing that I didn't know what I had, took it from my hands and spread open the head to disclose a plump mass of twisting shoots. *"Sono le puntarelle,"* she said ("They are the chicory's shoots"). She cut them away and showed me that when she dropped them into a bowl of cold water they curled up. From her I learned to make what became our favorite salad that winter, *puntarelle* tossed with salt, vinegar, olive oil, garlic, black pepper, and anchovies. It is so good that I wanted it in one of my books, even though *puntarelle* rarely appear in a stateside market. I chose Belgian endive as an alternative. It doesn't curl up in ice water, but that aside, when it is treated to the *puntarelle* seasoning formula, it provides a reasonably tasty reminder of the original.

In the spring at Campo dei Fiori, I was introduced to what I believe to be the most ravishing of all vegetable dishes, *la vignarola*. I would even be prepared to omit the qualification "vegetable" as an unnecessary limitation. You must be there at just the one moment in the spring when baby fava beans, small rosebud artichokes, and very small peas, all at the same early stage of development, appear in the market at the identical time. If it should last more than two weeks, it is a lucky year; a month, a prodigy. You also need some *cipollotti*, young onions, and a small head of romaine lettuce. The onion is sliced and cooked in olive oil until it is very soft. You add the lettuce, the trimmed artichokes, the shelled beans and peas, and cook. The vegetables are so young that it doesn't take very long. When done, it doesn't look very presentable. It is a dark, mushy mass that you might think a careless cook had produced. But when you take a mouthful, it is as though spring itself in all its tenderness has been delivered in edible form.

Often after shopping, I would drag my packages over to one of the tables of a café in the Campo, where I would have an espresso or, if it was closer to lunch, a Campari soda. Other women would do the same and I would eavesdrop. They always talked about cooking. It is from such a group that I first heard about *coda alla vaccinara*, the iconic Roman dish. A tail butcher's style? What kind of a tail and what was butcher's style? I asked and they mentioned a restaurant whose specialty it was, which Victor and I promptly visited. Thereafter, I cooked oxtail several times in Rome, with the requisite jowl and celery, but less frequently later in New York, where celery was plentiful, but neither tail nor jowl was an every-day commodity at my butcher. What I most regretted having to give up in New York was *abbacchio*, milk-fed lamb, the whole lamb weighing just fourteen to fifteen pounds from its tail to its muzzle. The best parts were the tiny offal: the kidneys encased in fat, the sweetbreads, the delicate brains, the heart. Nor can one forget the *scottadito*, the miniature rib chops, cooked just long enough to "scald the fingers."

By the New Year, Victor could take me to Campo dei Fiori on any morning I wanted to go. The studio that had brought him to Rome had folded. Once again, Victor had no job, but it neither shocked nor worried him this time. Word spreads fast in the small world of advertising, and soon there were offers from Milan as well as from London and Munich. Munich was out of the question. Most of Victor's relatives had died in concentration camps. He could not bear to live in Germany. Nor was he willing to return to Milan. London we both loved, but the problem was that he didn't want to go back to advertising. That was a surprise for me.

"What is the matter with advertising?" I asked.

"It has come to a dead end for me. It makes me think of one of those slow emulsions photographers use to pull up and print the images they have shot, when inexplicably it stops short, and nothing comes up but a blur. If I go back, there will be no definition to my life; it too will be a blur."

"What are you—*we*—going to do?"

"I don't know yet."

It was the same phrase he had used when we had just come back to Italy.

"What would you *like* to do?"

"Ideally?"

"Yes, ideally."

I could guess what was coming.

WHAT WE HUNGER FOR

By Douglas Bauer

From *Tin House*

Over the years, M.F.K. Fisher has become the patron saint of food writers, her influence cited almost automatically. For those who actually knew her, however—and novelist Douglas Bauer was one—Fisher's approach to life was so much more than just words on paper.

I am, as often, tempted to start a personal book, mais a quoi bon? I think my present life is a strange, complicated, interesting one. But my deep distrust—or is it timidity, cowardice even?—of such self-revelations will, perhaps, always prevent me from thus relieving myself.

—M. F. K. Fisher, March 4, 1937

Mary Frances Kennedy Fisher died fifteen years ago last summer, in the bedroom of her small, graceful, white stone house tucked in a hillocky pasture in the Sonoma Valley, and I suppose it's that anniversary that has heightened my many memories of her. I'm thinking especially of the week when I first met her, and she showed me how to taste and savor life in ways I'd only started to sense I was hungry for; and also of the time, two decades later, when her life, as I saw it, was a vivid example of how to receive the meaner sustenance of age.

She was just twenty-eight years old when she wrote the entry in her journal I've quoted above. She'd left California the previous fall with her husband Al Fisher. The two planned to share a house in a vineyard above the Swiss village of Vevey with its owner, their friend, the painter Dillwyn Parrish, whom everyone called by his nickname, Timmy. And by the following early spring, when she made this entry, her marriage was ending and Al was returning to the States to teach at Smith. Mary Frances would return as well, but only briefly, to tell her parents she was divorcing Al Fisher and marrying Timmy Parrish and that the two of them would continue in Vevey. A strange, complicated, interesting life indeed.

Amid all the domestic turmoil, in 1937 she published her first book, *Serve It Forth*. Like the majority of Fisher's writing—more than twenty books, most of them devoted to "the art of eating," to borrow one of her titles—it speaks of cooking and dining and living, anecdotally reported within the context of her life at the time. And what makes the work unique—as her journal's early self-reflection foreshadows—was the way in which she shared that life so obliquely, the people and places in her world depicted for her readers with a beguiling incompleteness.

As, for instance, in a piece she wrote for *Holiday* in 1956: "Eating any meal with this family was fun. . . . It might be very simple . . . or it could be elaborate like the annual game dinner served on one occasion for three college presidents, a guru priest, a ship owner from the Islands and two movie belles."

Leaving us to ask: *Three* college presidents? A *guru*? To *whom*? *What* Islands? And *which* movie belles? None of which she answers.

And: "On that night I watched him sitting at a wobbly card table in my new apartment amidst a mess caused by the arrival of most everything I own from Aix-en-Provence, where I had stayed a year."

This just might be the prototypical Fisher sentence: its picture of her living modestly and making do with no apology, serving her guest at a wobbly card table, but also living an enviable, international, and—particularly to her readers in the forties and fifties and into the sixties—even fantastical life. And offering nothing further about her year in Aix, why Aix, why a year.

IN THE SPRING OF 1971 I was working as a lowly editor at *Playboy*, when the executive editor, a thin, perennially agitated man, called me into his office. He sat behind his desk, wreathed as always in a cirrus of cigarette smoke, and excitedly announced that M.F.K. Fisher was going to write a piece for the magazine on New Orleans food and restaurants. I hadn't heard of M.F.K. Fisher and he saved me from saying "Who's he?" by relaying her one demand. She'd explained that a woman dining anonymously and alone would always be given the worst table in the place. She needed a cohort, one who must be male. The editor laughed, adding, "She told me, 'I don't care what sex he is, as long as he wears pants.'"

I wore pants, and fairly expertly. And that was the sum and substance of my qualifications. I was a few months shy of twenty-six and I would bring to the task of dining partner no sophistication regarding food or anything else. Whenever I tell my story of meeting Mary Frances I inevitably cast myself as an extreme, a very extreme, example of how little of life any of us have lived at that age. And then I pause to think that I was then but two years younger than she was in 1937, when the first of her many books was being published and she was living her supremely complex life in Switzerland.

Which is to say, among other things, that she would bring to New Orleans more than enough sophisticated knowledge of food, and of the world, for both of us.

But she wore her sophistication lightly and offered it easily. As we greeted one another in the hotel lobby I instantly felt that lightness and ease and, with them, the invitation to be myself. She smiled and extended her hand and spoke in her breathy, girlish voice of the grand adventure ahead. She was a tall woman and, at sixty-two, somewhat stout. Pictures of her through the years show her gaining and losing weight, but the changing fullness of her beautiful face always conveys an open, welcoming curiosity. The moment we met I saw and sensed that welcoming.

SURELY OVER THE COURSE of those seven days I learned something about food and wine and dining. How could I have failed to? For with every dish of every meal, Mary Frances would look across the table and ask, her mood entirely professional, "What do you think? Tell me how it tastes." What an enormous act of charity that was, suggesting she actually valued my assessment. So I concentrated on what I was eating as I never had, chewing with the care of a

Fletcherite and trying to identify flavors as she furtively slipped her notebook out of her purse to jot things down.

Of course we did more that week than simply fulfill the splendid terms of our assignment. We walked, a lot, ambling among the tourists and past their debris on the narrow sidewalks of the French Quarter. Wherever we walked, whether to Preservation Hall to hear the geriatric jazz band or to the Café du Monde to eat its famous beignets, I got used to her coming to a dead stop when something caught her attention. She said she'd always been an unapologetic gawker. Often she stood for quite a long time, not ready to move on until she'd understood completely what she was looking at.

One night on Bourbon she came to a stop at the sight of a woman's legs swinging out into the night through a high open window of a strip club, then back inside again. Mary Frances watched the stripper on her swing for several seconds before saying, "How beautiful," her tone purely appreciative of those lovely white legs appearing and retreating in the night-lit sky.

She took in everything that way, all week long, ready simply to receive the sense of the experience, and I saw that the way to be curious about the life of a place is to wander and watch and to look with no apology for as long as it takes to get what you're seeing.

THE MORNING she was leaving, we walked through the waking Quarter to Felix's and the Acme, the city's celebrated oyster bars. We hadn't visited either one and she felt for the sake of her piece we should. When I told her I'd never eaten raw oysters she declared, "Then we must."

We stood at the counter of one of the bars—I don't remember which we tried first—and she instructed me to let the oyster slide down my gullet so that I would taste the sea. I did as I was told, savoring the briny freshness of flesh too ethereal to be called flesh. After a dozen at each place, we turned to leave. Just then Moran's, the restaurant directly across the street, was opening its doors for lunch. Whichever of us suggested a last Ramos gin fizz, the other quickly agreed. It was a drink she'd introduced me to at our hotel bar and we'd been sampling them all over town, searching in vain for the perfect one. Sometimes the citrus taste was too strong. Sometimes the concoction was shaken too vigorously for too long, resulting in a sweetish froth of cream and egg white and powdered sugar that hid the gin entirely.

We entered, ordered, watched the bartender's technique, sipped, and wordlessly assessed. Need I say we decided we tasted perfection at Moran's? The ingredients working in balanced harmony, the juniper of the gin like a breeze on the tongue. (And part of me knew even then that its excellence had mostly to do with the drama of when we drank it—just before she had to leave. We'd found gin-fizz perfection in the nick of time.)

We walked, triumphant, back out into a wet May heat. I waved down a cab and we hugged. A last slow stroll through the Quarter; my first raw oysters; the perfect Ramos gin fizz; and all before noon. It deserved a term of commemoration, I told her. What should we call it?

She smiled—I remember both affection and mischief in it—and said, "Breakfast, dear Doug. You should call it breakfast."

Of her gifts to me that week, this suggestion of permission— that life, if we let it, allows us to discover what we're hungry for and when we're hungry for it—is one of the two that stay most vivid. The other was a kind of validation that I still find remarkable. For again and again over the course of the days, I felt she was asking me, about life, what do you think? And, about mine, how does it taste? So prompted, I spoke at least as often about my untraveled life as she did about her incredibly eventful one. And when she did refer to a specific time, or someone vital to it, she did so with only a graceful allusion. In other words, she offered her life to me just as she did to her readers. And only much later did I see that week as my living in an M.F.K. Fisher essay, with its deftly placed ellipses, where food is the axis around which matters of deeper life revolve.

> I am sincere when I say this book is not for anybody. It is perhaps for myself—to read in ten or twenty years and wonder about.
> —June 27, 1934

Here, in the journal she always called "this book," was where she wrote of life's hungers directly, and not metaphorically through the art of eating. Here her writing made no graceful allusions for the reader to guess about. She was her reader, writing to and for herself, and so the motive of her prose was not to gloss intriguingly some social episode, but to make transparent sense of much harder stuff.

In Vevey, she and Parrish had nearly a year of idyllic life. He painted. She wrote. They ambitiously gardened. They entertained their rustic neighbors and loved doing so. It was a life that Mary Frances, just then turning thirty, embraced as one that helped to justify and verify her, well, her appetites. "My whole existence," she writes in the journal in February 1938, "has become more completely physical than ever before . . . I am completely absorbed in myself—but myself as seen through Timmy." (The ellipses, as one must especially note when quoting her, are mine.)

Then, the next summer, Parrish got sick with what proved to be Buerger's disease, a rare illness of the veins and arteries in the arms and legs. He was in great pain. A first operation made it greater, and a second, to amputate his left leg, left him suffering even more.

Their life became his pain and the efforts to solve it: clinics visited and medicines tried, punctuated by those rare hours when he could sleep and Mary Frances, who held him and bathed him and gave him his injections and listened to his primal moaning, could not. He had excited her passion as no one ever had, but now she was an invalid's lover. Their bodies' intimacy was the nurse's ministrations to her patient. What to do with those feelings of being completely physically absorbed in him? "Since I can remember," she writes in February 1937, "I've been very, very clean, but now I spend long serious minutes after my bath, drying each toe nail; I wash my navel or my ears as if they were Belleek china teacups; a tiny hangnail sends me hurrying for scissors, oil, all the minutiae of a complete manicure."

It seems to me a ritual both of generous alliance and of necessary self-reward.

The following year they moved back to California, to a crumbling house they named "Bareacres," on several acres of the Mojave Desert. The journal speaks of the barren beauty of the place and of plans for expanding the house. But still: "Behind all my pleasure and well-being about Bareacres is the miserable reality of his pain."

And then, scattered among descriptions of somehow enjoyable, mundane life, entries such as these begin to appear, incremental in their power, compelling in their eerie tranquility:

> May 7, 1940: I know that I could never blame T. for whatever he might feel that he must do to settle this problem that no one else seems able to settle for him. I am deadened by the very thought of it. And yet I must think of it with the same routine thoughtfulness that it takes to recognize hunger or peeing.
>
> May 30, 1940: Last night T. asked me to hide the .22 bullets. I do not mention this from any martyr complex. . . . Pity me, oh pity me . . . but because I think I had better. . . . Now I find that I have been living with the constant thought of suicide in my mind ever since September 1, 1938.
>
> June 18, 1940: Last night was a hard one for T. and he said once that he wanted to know where I had hidden the bullets. I told him I would tell him this morning. Finally he went to sleep.
>
> This morning we both woke rather early to a beautiful hot bright morning. . . . Finally, he said, "I . . . would like to see Mother, so I think when the next check comes we'd better get an Oldsmobile and drive east and maybe show you the Grand Canyon . . . and then come back and finish it up, after a really good time."
>
> Suddenly, talking so positively about killing himself in the morning, not during the night, made me sick.
>
> It's like the surrender of France or T.'s having his leg cut off. I know these things have happened, but I don't realize it. This morning, for just a minute, I realized T.'s possible escape from this business.

And they did make that trip, though by train, not in a new Oldsmobile, across the country to Parrish's family home in Delaware. They traveled elsewhere that year too, including a visit to the Mayo Clinic for tests that offered no more encouragement than they'd gotten elsewhere.

But the explicit subject of suicide fades from prominence in the journal, replaced in part by family letters reporting on their travels. Until September 3, 1941:

I drink a too-hot, too-strong toddy in bed, and if my luck holds I get to sleep after some dutiful trash reading (*Mystery of the Police, Death Holds the Cup*, et al.), and then in a while (I have no watch) I wake cold and sober and my unwilling minds leaps like a starved dog at the poisonous meaty thoughts. . . . Then, about one morning out of three or four, I sleep heavily until 8:00 or so without hearing the shot. I try to live (even asleep?) with what dignity I can muster, but I wonder if there is much in this abject procedure.

And six days later, on September 9: "It is four weeks and three days now. . . . Pretty soon I'll write about T.'s death, because I think I should. . . . There are too many things that I can't write yet. They're in my head, but I am afraid of writing them. It is as if they might make a little crack in me and let out some of all the howling, hideous, frightful grief."

HER YOUNGEST SISTER, Norah, wrote of her, "Mary Frances, of course, had to live on, day by day, after the loss of her love. Although she always considered herself a 'ghost' after Timmy's death, she was very much a person who continued to love and be loved during her long productive life." This wise valedictory concludes the introduction to *Stay Me, Oh Comfort Me: Journals and Stories, 1933–41*, the first of two books—*Last House: Reflections, Dreams, and Observations, 1943–91* was the other—published after her death.

In her last years she was increasingly crippled by arthritis and Parkinson's disease, her energy greatly compromised but her mind vigorously intact. Forced to dictate her thoughts, and wanting, perhaps more than ever, to speak to readers, she spent hours sorting through letters and notes, through bulging files and unpublished manuscripts. And also rereading, or having someone read to her, the journals she'd kept over the years, including the one I've quoted throughout, which became *Stay Me, Oh Comfort Me*. Finally she was ready to offer the world a personal book, and it was the very book in whose pages she'd once written that she was too timid or too cowardly ever to write one. But she was twenty-eight when she wrote that, and though—as the beauty of the language in what was then a journal shows—she already possessed the sensibility and wisdom to convey the hardest matters with a clean, brave grace, she was many years away from outliving her timidity or cowardice or whatever else fed her reticence to write fully for readers other than herself.

For the strength of its candor alone, never mind the language, *Stay Me, Oh Comfort Me* is, I think, her finest book. Like *Last House* and *Sister Age* (the last book she published while she was alive, a powerful collection whose stories blur memoir and fiction), *Stay Me* confronts and embraces and, in the best sense, exploits M. F. K. Fisher's true subject, which is another kind of hunger than that which she's best known for. It's the hunger to make meaning of one's days when age and illness loom and then descend. This is the hunger that moved her prose to a deep, delving, unfussy sensuousness that it never quite conveys when she speaks of food in adjectives surprisingly uninspired: "good" bread, a "good" olive oil, a "light, clean" wine. But food, the art of eating, was finally, for her, a literary figure, while age and steadily gathering illness were visceral, her ever more vital sensual companions. And I have to think she was mindful, constantly, of living her long and slowly declining life for Timmy as well, he who endured three brief, and endless, pain-wracked years and went from life into death in the time it took the bullet.

THE PASSAGE in *Stay Me, Oh Comfort Me* that most selfishly compels me was written as a letter to her mother from the New Monteleone Hotel, in New Orleans, on December 11, 1940, when she and Parrish were taking that last train journey across the country to Delaware:

> The New Monteleone is a typical convention hotel, complete with hordes of supercilious clerks, fat drunks with cigars and buttons saying, "Call me Joe—or Butch—or Gus." . . . However, the room is fairly quiet—and I doubt we could do better in "Nawlins," which after some six hours reminds me of a mixture of salesmen's conventions, the American Quarter in Paris in 1929 (full of shoddy bars and whiskey-voiced blond divorcées), and the brothel district of Colon.

We caused a minor revolution by refusing to go to Antoine's our first night here, and went instead to a fine place recommended by our cabby. . . . We'll remedy our heresy by going to Antoine's tomorrow night. We may even order oysters Rockefeller—but I'll be damned if I'll have crepes suzette, guidebooks or no guidebooks.

I've wondered so often whether, in the week I spent with her, she did make some oblique mention of this trip—the last they took that gave them any pleasure, the words of his surrender surely traveling with them. And just what she might have offered if I'd possessed her gawker's confidence, if I had come to a dead stop in the flow of conversation to "look" at what she'd told me and asked her to say more.

"Now and then," she wrote to me in April of 1972, "one meets a person who can last for two months or twenty years and suddenly be there and Time has done more good than harm. I think we are like that. I have a few friends like that in my life."

We stayed in touch over the years through a fitful correspondence, exchanges of notes and letters back and forth for a year, two years, then long lapses, and I visited her a few times in Sonoma in the early seventies.

Then, in the late eighties and early nineties, my wife and I began to cheat the end of the New England winter, renting places for a month or two in Northern California, and briefly, on a handful of occasions, I got to be in Mary Frances's life again.

On a warm September day, in 1988, I sat at her large round dining table with six or seven others, members of a television crew who'd come up from San Francisco to interview and film her for a documentary. Though she'd long been admired by an audience of readers, she became in her last years a kind of cult figure as well, both in the world of food and among a generation of women who saw her life as a model of courageous independence. Especially in California, the devotion of the foodies and the middle-aged feminists merged and it made her an icon. It was a status, I should say, that she was happy to accept.

We'd talked that morning and she'd invited me to lunch ("Don't bring any wine. I've got buckets of it") and now I sat in her huge sun-filled room with the television crew, sipping wine and joining the chatter and watching Mary Frances assemble a large tray of cheese and cold cuts. With the stiffness of her arthritis and her Parkinson's tremors, she was very slowly rolling the ham and the salami into tubes and fanning out the slices of cheese onto the platter. She was by then very thin and small, so much smaller than the tall, stout woman I'd met in New Orleans, and the penciled-in eyebrows she'd drawn with her unsteady hand rose like profit lines on a corporate graph almost to her temples.

She was mostly listening to the table talk. She'd been talking a lot for the interview and she needed to save what voice she had left. Her Parkinson's greatly weakened it and she often couldn't speak at all after early afternoon. But she was obviously monitoring the conversation keenly, smiling at a private thought sparked by something she'd overheard.

And then she slightly raised her index finger, as though signaling very subtly for a waiter's attention. Everyone paused.

"I want," she whispered hoarsely, "to talk about addictions." Who knew why, perhaps something one of us had said, though the subject seemed to me to have come purely from within her, whatever she'd been thinking or remembering or yearning for, and not from anything in the air. "Let's go around the table," she said, "and say what we're addicted to."

The mood among us had been chatty and relaxed, and whatever addictions were confessed to came from that same easy attitude.

I was sitting directly across from her. When it was my turn, I admitted that I really couldn't claim to have any interesting addictions.

"No," Mary Frances said. "I think that's right. I don't think you do."

"Routine, I guess," I said lamely. "I'm addicted to routine."

She smiled at that, and gave the slightest nod. Someone else confessed something safe—M&M's or junk TV—and someone else did too.

Until it came back around to her. She waited a moment, an exactly effective beat, her raconteur's timing as perfect as ever, and whispered, "I used to be addicted to sex." Another perfectly long beat. "Now," she added, smiling, "I'm addicted to breathing."

I SAW HER AGAIN in the spring of 1992, two months before she died. My wife and I were about to leave Sonoma, and I understood that it was surely the last time I would see her.

She was lying in her bedroom in the hospital bed that had been brought in for her. The nearness of death had made her incredibly tiny. What I remember noticing, as I sat down beside her, was her long, lovely nose in profile, still strong and now disproportionate on her small and withered face. That and her eyes, milky and searching, which seemed to be trying, as in New Orleans, to see and understand and hold in her memory whatever she was looking at.

She had only the faint breath of a voice left. I took her hand and told her not to try to talk, an instruction she didn't need or want, and weakly waved away. I remembered with her our last New Orleans breakfast. I suppose it's what one does, a sentimental instinct, summon the most memorable occasion. If so, she seemed happy to have it and lie with it a while. I watched her reach for a plastic glass, a kind of sippy cup, of pineapple juice and labor mightily to get some through a bent plastic straw. A perverse irony of her final days: she whose finest charm was conversation, whose livelihood was made by tasting food, lost not just her voice, but the ability to swallow.

Then she said, a slight exhale of infant sound, "We ate oysters, didn't we."

A short while later I could see that she was fighting sleep, and I got up and bent down to kiss her forehead.

At the door I stopped and looked back and I saw her hungrily, ravenously, breathing. In my mind's eye, there was something combative, carnal, something lustful, in her effort.

Dining Around

⚭

The Last Time I Saw Paris

By Ruth Reichl

From *Gourmet*

It's a treat for *Gourmet* readers when editor-in-chief Reichl—
former dining critic for the *New York Times* and food editor of
the *Los Angeles Times*—writes more than her usual one-page
editor's letter. Inspired by a nostalgic Parisian dine-around,
this essay goes well beyond mere restaurant reviewing.

Wandering around Paris in the '60s, I'd sit in the parks
eating bread and cheese, pretending that at any minute
I'd turn the corner and bump into F. Scott Fitzgerald. I'd walk
down the Rue Mouffetard to buy cheese at Androuët, yearning up
at the house where Hemingway once lived. I haunted Shakespeare
& Company, as if by staying long enough I might make Joyce or
Stein actually appear. It was a magical place, and I went back again
and again on cheap charter fares, wishing I could afford to live
there the way the writers of the '20s had. But everything was so
expensive! By staying in cheap pensions and eating dinner in
working-class cafés, I managed to get by on $3 a day. Still, as I sat
munching Brie in the Luxembourg Gardens, I always wished I had
been born earlier.

It never occurred to me that one day I would look back on
Paris in the '60s as its own magical time, an affordable feast of art
and culture where you woke up every morning convinced that an
eating adventure was waiting for you.

But those days are long gone. In the Paris of modern luxury,
with its three-star restaurants and five-star hotels, a person could
spend $5,000 a day without even trying. It is a lovely place, but not

exactly filled with surprises. Lately I've been wondering if, beneath all the glitter, the Paris of my past was still there.

And so I set off to find it. For one rainy spring week, travel editor Bill Sertl and I stayed in cheap hotels, wandered the streets, rode the *metro*, and attended free cultural events. Above all, we ate. What we discovered is that you can live stunningly well in Paris for very little money. Young chefs all over the city are serving thrillingly innovative food at remarkable affordable prices. And even with the dollar so low, if you are very careful (and, as you'll see, very lucky), you can stay in charming hotels that allow you to participate in the life of the city. I left luxury behind, but I have never eaten better or had as much fun doing it. Thanks to the new young chefs, Paris is reclaiming its title as food capital of the world, and I'm pretty sure that 30 years from now we'll all be looking back at this time with enormous nostalgia.

THE EUROSTAR TRAVELS from London to Paris in two hours and fifteen minutes, and I fretted about the hotel for the entire trip; what could I realistically expect for 80 euros? For the first couple of nights, I'd chosen a modest place at the very edge of the 5th arrondissement because of its proximity to the Rue Mouffetard. The bed might be lumpy, but I wouldn't go hungry.

Hôtel de L'Espérance turned out to be short on charm—the television in the lobby blared constantly—but the room was clean, comfortable, and larger than I had imagined. It had a desk, a TV, even an air conditioner. Dropping my bags, I headed out to eat, sniffing in at Androuët, the great cheese store, marveling at the size of the fat white asparagus, as big around as salamis, in the Mouffetard markets. By dinnertime, I was starving.

I was even hungrier by the time we reached Hier et Aujourd'hui, a serious hike from the nearest *metro* station. Happily, we had no sooner taken our seats than the waitress plunked a heavy terrine of pâté onto the table, along with a jar of crisp, home-cured cornichons and a basket of bread. "While you consider the menu," she murmured.

There was a lot to consider. The 28-euro menu is large, and it changes constantly, but every single thing we tried was superb. Franck Dervin has worked with both Alain Dutournier and Guy

Savoy, but his cooking is very much his own. His *pot de crème de foie gras* topped with a Port reduction was so extraordinarily seductive that we could tell who was eating it simply by listening for the moans. His tartare of beets looked like an adorable little bouquet topped with tiny leaves of spinach and infant anchovies. Its taste was equally attractive; with each bite, the layered sweet and salty flavors did enthusiastic somersaults in my mouth.

Parmentier of pig's foot is never pretty, but this deconstructed porcine hoof with its little hat of puréed potato was all texture and richness, and we wasted no time staring at it; in a flash, it was gone. So was a "risotto" of lentils topped with lobster.

We finished with a classic *baba* drenched in rum and a clean, fresh carpaccio of pineapple dotted with raspberries. With a bottle of 20-euro Côtes du Rhône, the meal was 76 euros for two, including tax and tip. "If this is what eating on a budget is all about," I said to Bill, "this is going to be a great week."

Under ordinary circumstances, we would not have even noticed Christophe. But the sign in the window offering a 12-euro lunch was irresistible; we walked right in. I immediately liked the modest little restaurant because the waitress was so sympathetic. When we said we'd be skipping wine in favor of a free carafe of water, she smiled and said, "You're right, it's too early for wine." And her pride in the chef, Christophe Philippe, was infectious. "Taste the compote of tomatoes on the side," she insisted as she set down plates of *accras de poisson*, airy little fish fritters. "It is homemade. Even the balsamic vinegar is *fait maison!*"

Were the portions so large because she thought we were poor and in need of a sturdy meal? Or is everyone served two hearty slabs of richly meaty hanger steak with piles of *panisses*, the chickpea fritters of Nice? Does the *cervelle de veau* always arrive as two fluffy clouds on a vivid heap of polenta? The brains hovered, as buoyant as air, anchored to the plate by polenta so fresh it tasted like biting into an ear of corn.

"Happy?" asked the waitress, picking up our shockingly empty plates. "Oh, yes," we sighed. She beamed. "Christophe seeks out his own special suppliers—he uses nothing but the best. You know, he used to work with Anne-Sophie Pic."

That night, at Le Beurre Noisette, a charmingly chic bistro in the 15th, the experience was much the same. We found ourselves in the hands of Thierry Blanqui, a talented young chef who had worked in the finest establishments (La Tour d'Argent, Ledoyen) before opening a modest restaurant of his own. Tired of cooking for rich tourists, these chefs are catering to true food lovers, and their clientele is primarily local. Eating here, you become an honorary Parisian.

I've never seen anything quite like Blanqui's carpaccio of pig's foot, a mosaic of flavor and texture in which each bite is slightly different, so that you keep eating, fascinated, until it is gone. Fat white asparagus came topped with an evanescent curl of foam, as if a wave had just crashed onto the plate. I took a bite, expecting brine, and experienced pure Parmigiano.

Robust *côte de porc* was served with a kind of *aligot*—deeply cheesy potatoes—and roasted lamb shoulder was imbued with the sunny taste of preserved lemon. But it was at the end, with the appearance of a huge, feathery *millefeuille* of strawberries, that I finally fell in love. A symphony of crunch, cream, and fruit, it was, hands down, the best dessert of the trip.

The bill? With a 14-euro bottle of Cahors, 78 euros for two.

I HAD BECOME COZY in my little room, and I was sad as I packed my bags the next morning to leave L'Espérance. But I was even sadder when I checked in to my new digs. The lobby was tricked out with fancy furniture, but the room I had rented for 90 euros was dark, dingy, and so small that the only way to open the closet was to balance the suitcase on the flimsy bed. On top of that, the minuscule bathroom was dank, with barely room for the tiny shower. I ran back outside, slamming the door and realizing how little I had appreciated my former fortune.

Disconsolate, I meandered slowly along the Seine, eventually meeting up with Bill. When we reached Lapérouse, I stopped to peer into the ancient restaurant, thinking it might cheer me up. The restaurant is fabulously old-fashioned, almost unchanged since the day it opened in 1766, and I've always loved the way it looks. And even though the restaurant's glory days are past, its Michelin stars long gone, the 35-euro lunch on the menu posted outside—wine included—seemed like a bargain. "How bad can it be?" said Bill, pushing me through the door.

We were dressed in jeans, but the maître d'hôtel welcomed us as if we were wearing black tie. "Would you like a *salle privée*?" he asked. Remnants of another time, these sexy rooms for two are little jewel boxes that afford total privacy. We settled into the velvet sofa while the very correct captain fussed in and out, eager for our happiness.

"Don't get too excited," I said to Bill. "This place is all about ambience. I haven't heard a word about the food in years." Indeed, the *amuse-bouche*, a dreadful thimble filled with purées of red and yellow peppers, confirmed all my fears; it was a clear sign of how far this once proud kitchen had plummeted.

So I was completely unprepared for the seriously wonderful mushroom soup garnished with a foie gras mousse that melted into a sensuous puddle. Asparagus, served in a perfect circle of interlocking green and white spears, was equally refined. Topped with a poached egg, it was gorgeous, elegant, utterly satisfying.

The main courses were even more pleasing. Veal breast arrived wearing a filigreed necklace, an intricate design composed of tiny rounds of crisped purple potatoes and baby romaine leaves. The meat was surrounded by gnocchi so light a passing breeze could have sent them soaring. *Maigre*, a firm-fleshed fish from Normandy, was delicious, too; the artichokes and tomatoes strewn across the top were an ideal counterpoint to the delicate flavor of the fillet.

Afterward, there was coffee served with plates of *mignardises*—*mascarons*, caramels, miniature homemade chocolate lollipops. It had been an amazing meal, both leisurely and luxurious, and I felt utterly restored. Emerging, we found that the sun had come out, making the world a much more cheerful place.

Walking away from the river, we followed the sound of birdsong and found ourselves in a small, enchanting garden. It belonged to a charming hotel, and as we took in the flowers around the cobbled walk, I began to feel as if we had conjured up Shangri-la.

It all seemed so magical that I was not surprised when the Hôtel des Grandes Écoles actually had a room available, and I was even less surprised that it was affordable (120 euros). It was so fresh and pretty, with a window opening right into the garden, that I danced all the way back up the street to get my suitcase from that other hotel. Unpacking, I felt nothing but lucky. I grabbed a book, went out into the garden, threw back my head, and basked in the sun.

I COULD HARDLY BEAR to leave my bit of paradise for dinner. Fortunately, Ribouldingue was only a short walk away. Like so many of the great new Parisian places, it was started by veterans of Yves Camdeborde's La Régalade. And like so many of those places, it is run by two extremely hardworking people. Nadège Varigny oversees the not-small dining room by herself, and with astonishing efficiency. Her eyes swept the room constantly as she opened wine, took orders, delivered food, and bused tables. The only time I saw her falter was when someone on the other end of the phone apparently refused to believe that there were no available seats.

The lovely room with its butter-colored walls was, indeed, packed to the rafters. We seemed to be the only Americans, and one glance at the menu told me why: If you don't eat offal, then Ribouldingue is definitely not for you.

But if you are ever going to be tempted to try pigs' head cheese, cows' udders, or veal kidneys, this is the place. The chef cooks with subtle assurance, and his lamb brains are soft, sweet little puffs dotted with gently roasted garlic and pungent whole caper berries. His salad of shredded pig's ear is a textbook on the nature of crispness. The beef cheeks cooked in red wine are gently enticing, and the wine list is filled with bargains.

Walking back to the hotel, we were still savoring the desserts— lemon curd and rhubarb compote, both topped with billows of whipped cream—as we nibbled the chocolate-covered almonds that arrived with the bill. It was an amazing meal for 27 euros each. Strolling through the garden to my room at midnight, I could have sworn the birds were still up, singing.

We had been eating almost all our meals in restaurants run by the new guard of Paris chefs, and it had been exciting to see how their casual attitude and experimental style are restoring Paris to greatness. But I woke up with a sudden yearning for a longtime favorite. I first went to Robert et Louise in the '70s, loving it because Robert cooked his great haunches of beef right in the old fireplace.

The air was always fragrant, the ancient beams above the long tables black with the smoke of ages. I'd heard that he had passed away, and now I wondered what had become of the restaurant.

The door creaked authentically when I peeked in, which I took as a good sign. The beams were blacker, but nothing else seemed to have changed; over by the fireplace, a man in an apron was cooking meat. Robert's daughter Pascale has taken over, and she continues to offer wonderfully old-fashioned food at wonderfully old-fashioned prices.

Settling in with a glass of wine, a huge, charred pork chop, a salad, and a pile of potatoes, I listened to the badinage between Pascale and her customers. I was so lost in Paris past that I was stunned to find that my bill for this feast was 12 euros, rather than francs. Watching Pascale carve off a *côte de boeuf* (40 euros for two people and easily enough to feed a normal person for a week), I smiled. The Paris I once knew is still here, waiting right behind this door.

ON OUR FINAL DAY in Paris, we hoped for one last memorable meal. A little research revealed that if we were willing to splurge, the best deal at a great restaurant was the 55-euro lunch (wine included) at La Table de Joël Robuchon.

When the doors slid silently open, we found ourselves basking in the splendor of France in an elegant (dare I say stuffy?) gold and black room. The service was so achingly correct that the captain looked positively offended when we asked for a carafe of water. Tap water? Please! (The bottle of Evian was included.)

The meal began with a dreamy foam-topped *crème de foie gras*, a fantastic contrast between the sheer richness of the one and the ephemeral lightness of the other. A *millefeuille* of anchovies with *tomates confites* and a *méli-mélo* of little spring vegetables—the most delicate salad ever created—was equally impressive. It was followed by farm chicken and asparagus, along with a little pot of the "famous *pommes purée de Joël Robuchon*."

The wine was just a country white, but it was poured with a generous hand from an endless bottle. The bread was impeccable, the cheese perfectly à point. Dessert, a lemon mousse hiding a few perfect berries, was a dream. Afterward, there were tiny bitter espressos and plates of chocolates. A bit of luxury can be a lovely thing, and we floated out the door.

There are now hundreds of amazing places to eat affordably in Paris—and I recommend all the restaurants in this issue. But when I dream about the city, it is my final meal I think of. L'Ami Jean reminds me of everything I love about modern Paris.

This small, bustling, rollicking restaurant is pure fun. It is what I imagine L'Ami Louis must once have been like. Customers—older aristocrats in gorgeous clothes, students from the Sorbonne, accountants who live in the neighborhood—crowd together at the narrow tables, talking to each other because the food is so joyfully wonderful.

"Don't miss the *boudin noir*," said the man next to us, passing over a forkful of the dense, black blood sausage on his plate. With its intense porkiness, it was, without question, the best I've ever tasted. "But what about the scallops?" I protested. "Those, too," he said, watching the progress of the shells sizzling their way to my neighbor on the right, sending out fragrant billows of butter, bacon, garlic, and thyme. In the end, I opted for cannelloni of oxtail, slowly eating the robust layering of meat and pasta, wishing it would never end.

But after that came duck breast, a richly mineral slab of bird, as bloody as the rarest steak, whose flavor sang in my veins all night. You don't get duck like that in the States. It is why you go to France, and I hold it in my memory so that, even now, if I close my eyes and think very hard, I can still taste it.

Finally, there was rice pudding, buckets of it, served on a wooden board. So thick that the wooden spoon stood upright in the bowl, it was served with *confiture de lait*, nuts, dried fruit, bits of praline. As I finished eating, I had a brief fantasy of moving in and eating every meal here for the rest of my life.

The chef, Stéphane Jégo, was at La Régalade for ten years before setting up on his own. He has a knack for treating the rustic food of France with enormous respect. But more than that, he knows how to make people happy. L'Ami Jean is the perfect ending to a Paris vacation because you walk out with an overwhelming desire to return.

Very soon.

ENGLISH OYSTER CULT

By Robb Walsh

From *Sex, Death & Oysters*

It began as a single feature story (included in 2004's *Best Food
Writing*) for Robb Walsh's home paper, the weekly *Houston
Press*. But Walsh's quest eventually took him around the world,
hunting for succulent oysters, sustainable oystering practices,
and the briny pleasures of the oyster bar.

Martinis and oysters are a natural combination, especially
in London where people love gin," the bartender at J.
Sheekey in Covent Garden told me as he set my martini down in
front of me. It was a Beefeater martini, dry with a twist of lemon. I
asked him to shake it hard and make it slushy, but he refused. Shaking bruises the liquor and dilutes the cocktail too much—a martini should be stirred, not shaken, he said. And he wasn't kidding.

I couldn't get a reservation at J. Sheekey—it's considered the top
fish restaurant in London—but I found an open seat at their oyster bar
at around three on a Saturday afternoon. The bartender at Sheekey's
recommended a half dozen No. 2 Mersea *(O. edulis)* oysters.

Sheekey's Mersea oysters were pretty impressive. The combination of the oysters and the icy martini, with its herbal aroma and
the hint of lemon, was sublime. The bartender was waiting for a reaction, but my mouth was full. I made a grateful groaning sound to
show my approval.

"Gin and oysters—it's just like vodka and caviar," the bartender
said with satisfaction.

My plan had been to spend a weekend in London touring the
city's famous oyster bars. The martini part of my oyster-and-
martini weekend came about by accident.

On Friday night, after I arrived from Colchester, the first oysters I came across were at an oyster stall out in front of Bibendum Oyster Bar in the Chelsea neighborhood near my hotel. It looked just like the oyster stands you see in front of restaurants in Paris. So I went inside and sat down at a table.

Eavesdropping on the other tables, I surmised my fellow patrons weren't British. There was an Italian couple, a French couple, and a Japanese guy with several Asian women. All of them had wine bottles in ice buckets.

I really didn't want to drink a whole bottle of wine by myself, and the waiter indignantly told me they didn't serve beer. I ordered the national cocktail, a gin martini. And so my first oyster-and-martini pairing came about by accident. But I liked it—a whole lot. While martinis might overpower more delicate oysters, they went perfectly with the *(O. edulis)* natives. The cold fire of a gin martini, with its juniper berry and botanical aroma, stands up to the briny "licking the bottom of a boat" flavor of the natives like nothing else I've tried. And it cleanses the palate brilliantly. I had that first one with an olive.

As for Bibendum's oysters, they were shucked in the French style, with the bottom foot still attached. The half dozen Belons I sampled were shriveled up; I suspected they had been shucked hours ago. If a half dozen sounds conservative, consider that six oysters along with one martini set me back more than $50. Sad, when you consider that in 1864, laborers in London were buying four oysters for a penny.

J. Sheekey's was the one London restaurant I would most like to visit again. A warren of booths and snugs furnished in dark wood paneling and decorated with black-and-white photos of old London, the restaurant is charming but utterly unpretentious.

Sheekey's got started in 1896, when Lord Salisbury made a deal with a Covent Garden fish stall operator. Josef Sheekey would open an oyster bar in Lord Salisbury's building at a favorable rent, provided he supplied the Lord's private theater parties with the very choicest oysters in London.

AFTER I LEFT J. Sheekey's in Covent Garden, I walked to an even older restaurant located nearby. Rules on Maiden Lane is said to be the oldest restaurant in London. It was opened as an oyster bar in 1798 by a playboy named Thomas Rule, who had promised his parents he would abandon his dissolute life and run a proper oyster bar.

Over the years, the restaurant has hosted such literary luminaries as Charles Dickens, H. G. Wells, and William Makepeace Thackeray. It is decorated with hundreds of cartoons and artworks hung on the walls by patrons.

Rules is still quite proud of its oysters. The menu features Lindisfarne rock *(C. gigas)* oysters from Northumberland and Strangford Lough *(O. edulis)* from Ireland. When I visited, six oysters on the half shell were £10.95 for rock oysters, and a comparatively reasonable £13.50 for the Irish natives. I got six of each.

They were brought to the table on a large, round tray of ice with a stand placed underneath, much the way pizzas are served at some Italian restaurants in the States. The ice was garnished with seaweed. Mignonette was served in a little steel cup in the middle of the platter, flanked by two half lemons with sprigs of parsley on top.

Tucked under the platter were salt, pepper, Tabasco sauce, and a shaker bottle of red wine vinegar with mixed peppercorns soaking in it. The table was set with lots of silver, linen, and bread and butter.

The rock oysters had a very salty flavor. I sprinkled a little of the peppercorn vinegar on some and doused others with the mignonette, which made for an interesting variation. The natives were chewy and sweet. I was pleasantly surprised by how diluted the Rules martini tasted. Is it possible the bartender at the oldest restaurant in London is shaking the martinis instead of stirring them?

THE NEXT DAY, I made my way to Harrods Department Store. At Harrods seafood counter, the oysters were displayed neatly in a bed of crushed ice, in perfect rows and columns with their pointy ends sticking up. Colchester natives went for £2 apiece, while rock oysters were seventy-five pence (the exchange rate was roughly $2 to the pound then.) I got six Colchester natives, which were served at the bar with toast points, vinegar, and shallots. There weren't any martinis available, so I had a London Pride beer.

The oysters were exceptionally sweet, but utterly brineless. There was no hint of salt in the flavor whatsoever. Looking back at the seafood counter, I realized that while the display looked impressive, sticking the oysters in ice sharp end up was probably responsible for the loss of brine. The little card stuck in the ice beside them said "Natives, Catchment Area: Colchester." "Where exactly are these oysters from?" I asked the seafood manager.

"All I know is that they are from somewhere in the Essex estuary," she said. "They are actually oysters that are harvested in Ireland and deposited in the Colchester area," she told me.

Irish oysters? In Colchester?

At Bentley's, one of the toniest oyster bars of the West End, they serve only Irish oysters. Which is ironic since Bentley's was opened in 1916 by the Bentley family, who made their fortune selling Colchester oysters.

"We don't serve Colchester oysters anymore. It's Grade B water. It's a compromise," the bartender at Bentley's told me. "We serve only Strangford Loughs."

Doubts about the cleanliness of Colchester waters began to arise in the 1890s. Thanks to the Industrial Revolution, the population of London was increasing rapidly at that time, and so was the amount of sewage being dumped into the Thames Estuary. A report titled "On Oyster Cultivation in Relation to Disease," issued in 1896, identified four different places where oyster beds were exposed to sewage outflows.

Oystermen ridiculed the alarmist report. Then, six years later, in 1902, the Dean of Winchester and several other people died of typhoid from contaminated Brightlingsea oysters served at a public banquet. A systematic study of water quality ensued, but oysters had gained a dangerous reputation. In 1930, a sanitizing facility was built to purify oysters taken from Colchester's "Grade B" waters. Colchester oysters still must be treated before they can be served.

The bartender at Bentley's explained that Irish oysters were the only ones in Great Britain that came from Grade A waters. I found his honesty refreshing. But then again, Bentley's was owned by Richard Corrigan, a famous Irish chef.

Sitting at Bentley's lustrous marble bar, I ordered three No. 1 and three No. 2 Strangford Loughs and a martini. I was promptly set up with a dark green and gold placemat, a napkin, silverware, a bread plate, an oyster plate, some fresh bread, a plate of deep yellow butter rounds, vinegar, red pepper, Tabasco sauce, and a saucer full of lemons wrapped in cheesecloth. Bentley's is a very serious oyster bar.

When the bartender asked me if I wanted olives or a twist, I asked him which garnish he liked better with oysters. He recommended both. I had never seen both garnishes served together, but he told me he combined them all the time. When he served me the cocktail, there was a toothpick loaded with olives and a piece of lemon peel in it.

Like all the martinis I drank in London, Bentley's was much more potent than the more diluted style of martini we drink in America and not quite as cold. The V-on-a-stem martini glass was small, and it was chilled by being filled with ice water for a few minutes, not stored in the freezer like my martini glasses at home. The lemon and olives did go well together, and they tasted great with the oysters too.

Bentley's was the only place I remember seeing oysters Rockefeller on the menu; six went for £18.50, five or six times what they sell for in New Orleans. A half dozen Irish (O. edulis) native No. 1 oysters on the half shell were £18.50 at Bentley's, while a half dozen No. 2s went for £16.50. I decided to compare the No. 1s and No. 2s, so they kindly made up a plate with three of each.

The texture of the No. 1 oysters was very different from the smaller oysters. As I bit into them, they came apart in pieces in my mouth, like a big bite of scrambled eggs. Some of the firmer pieces required more chewing than others. The big oysters were salty, with lots of marine and mineral flavors. I sat back and savored the last oyster, the dregs of my martini, and the olives.

"I MAKE THE BEST MARTINI you will ever drink," the bartender at Green's Restaurant and Oyster Bar, a short walk from Bentley's, told me. He pooh-poohed my usual choice of Beefeater and recommended I go with the bar gin, which was Tanqueray. His preparations—chilling the glass, carving and trimming a large hunk of fresh lemon peel—were quite elaborate. But then again, I was the only customer at three in the afternoon.

Green's is located in such an exclusive neighborhood, it is sometimes given the title "Green's of Duke Street, St. James." The restaurant feels more like an exclusive men's club than the sort of oyster saloons we have in Texas. It was founded in 1982 by Simon Parker Bowles, the brother-in-law of Camilla Parker Bowles (now better known as HRH the Duchess of Cornwall, second wife of Prince Charles). Along with the best martini-maker in London, Green's also employs the city's best oyster shucker. Or so he says, anyway.

Shucker Jack Pasinski moved to London from Poland, where he was trained as a chef. He had been shucking oysters for six years in London, four of them at Green's. When I spoke with Pasinski, he said that, in his opinion, No. 1s were too big and too chewy. They were also thirty-five percent more expensive. Colchester No. 2s were his recommendation. A half dozen Colchester *(O. edulis)* natives went for £15.50.

The oysters were perfectly shucked and daintily presented with a profusion of silverware, linen, and china. They tasted sweet and a tad salty. The martini tasted quite different from the others I had been drinking, owing mainly to the difference in gin. Tanqueray is heavier on the juniper than most other gins, while Beefeater has a bit of coriander in the nose. The bartender gave me the oft-repeated bit about stirring rather than shaking so as not to bruise the liquor.

The contention that shaking "bruises the gin" is so rampant among London bartenders that you have to wonder what's behind it. A martini-loving scientist once wrote a treatise that theorizes that shaking causes the aldehyde molecules in the alcohol to bond with more oxygen, resulting in a nasty oxidized taste. I think he was spoofing us. I prefer W. Somerset Maugham's explanation: "Martinis should always be stirred, not shaken, so that the molecules lie sensuously one on top of the other."

For whatever reason, the martini I drank at Green's was distinctive. "What is the secret of your martini?" I asked the bartender.

"It's love," he said with a smile.

Tokyo, Cocktail Capital of the World

By Hugh Garvey

From *Bon Appetit*

Though he's now the features editor at *Bon Appetit*, Hugh
Garvey formerly chronicled the rebirth of cocktail culture in
his "Liquid City" column for the *Village Voice*. Here he takes a
tour of Tokyo's glam cocktail bars, a scintillating window into
Japanese mod culture.

I'm hungover in Tokyo, trying to remember how many
drinks I had the night before. *Does the beer at the yakitori
place count?* The backlit shelves of shrunken liquor bottles in my
hotel mini bar give me flashbacks. *Did I actually finish that precisely
mixed Sidecar?* Below the airplane bottles is a shelf of elegantly pro-
portioned highballs and lowballs. *That was cask-strength Scotch bottled specially for Ginza; 110 proof. Suntory time, indeed.* Midway
through a weeklong high-end bar crawl, I'm learning that this city
takes its drinking very seriously. In Tokyo, the mini bars actually
look like miniature bars.

My friend Shinji Nohara calls up from the lobby. He was out
with me until two in the morning, yet claims he feels tip-top. When
he says we should go for tempura, I know he's lying. A fried-food
lunch is international code for "I'm hungover." Two bottles of Kirin
and a hundred dollars' worth of fried fish later, we feel better and
plan that evening's tour: First, the place that only serves drinks in
Baccarat crystal, then the spot that specializes in *shochu* infused with
seasonal fruit, then the lounge presided over by an up-and-coming
female bartender. Followed by the inevitable tempura lunch. Such

are the hazards of researching a story about a city of countless hidden speakeasies, impossibly artistic mixology, and infinite drinks. Welcome to Tokyo, cocktail capital of the world.

I'M HERE BECAUSE I've heard from professional foodies, itinerant bartenders, and other bibulous travelers that Tokyo was besting New York and London at the cocktail game. Mixologists from Sydney to San Juan were returning from pilgrimages and breathlessly describing their experiences as epiphanic. Bartenders were attending traveling seminars to learn Japanese technique. So, armed with a sheaf of recommendations and my friend Shinji as translator and guide, I hit the streets, subbasements, and skyscrapers of Tokyo to experience this cocktail revolution firsthand.

In that sparkling, sprawling metropolis of 12.8 million people, there is as structured and codified a drinking culture as any in the world: At *izakayas* (Japanese pubs), salarymen are allowed to criticize their managers under the cover of alcohol. *Sake* and *shochu* are sold in vending machines on street corners. And as the evening draws to a close, it's not uncommon to see salarymen stumbling for the trains and taxis. Drinking is a culturally accepted form of extreme relaxation in an otherwise excessively civilized city.

I fill up with a defensive meal of yakitori beneath the Yurakucho Station train tracks and watch the city transition out of its workday and into its nightlife. Here, on the edge of Ginza, salarymen eat grilled chicken and drink beer before heading home or out for the night. Here is where mixology first took hold in the cafés nearly 100 years ago, and where legendary Tokyo bartender Kazuo Uyeda practices his craft today. To get to Tender Bar, you take an elevator to the fifth floor of an office building. If you see a salon with geishas getting their hair coiffed, you're on the right floor.

Uyeda is slim and dapper in his white dinner jacket and wire-rimmed aviators. He has invented some of Japan's cocktail canon: the Pure Love, made with gin, framboise, lime juice, and ginger ale, and the Shungyo, made of *sake*, vodka, green tea liqueur, and salted cherry blossom. Both were invented in the early '80s, when in America a margarita made with fresh lime and real tequila was still a rarity. As his assistant bartenders prepare for the evening rush by hand-carving ice cubes, Uyeda tells me how, over the decades,

Japanese bartenders preserved the American art of the cocktail while American bartenders neglected it. "The difference is that American bartenders aren't thinking enough about the customer," he says.

It's a bold statement, but compared to how Uyeda thinks about the art of bartending, it's true. Uyeda says that his approach to cocktail-making is grounded in the Japanese tea ceremony. It is an "adoration of the beautiful among the sordid facts of everyday existence. It inculcates purity and harmony, the mystery of mutual charity, the romanticism of the social order." Which is a pretty accurate description of how it feels to be in his elegant little bar, having white-jacketed bartenders mix perfect drinks while men in slim suits and women in wrap dresses and beehive hairdos chat quietly over cocktails with names like M–30 Rain and Tokio.

I learned about Uyeda through the online writings of Stanislav Vadrna, a Slovakian bartender who apprenticed under Uyeda. Vadrna teaches classes in Japanese bartending and has become a missionary of sorts, preaching the gospel of the "hard shake," Uyeda's signature technique, which purportedly produces a drink a full ten degrees colder than a standard shake does.

To see the hard shake in action, I order a gimlet and witness for the first time a precision that will be repeated at all the bars I visit in Tokyo: Uyeda lines up the bottles on the bar, labels facing the customer. With a single, quick twist he opens them and fills the shaker, which he shakes in a rapid-fire serpentine fashion that decelerates to a slow trot and then a standstill. "The gin is broken out," Uyeda says, "then comes back together, smoother, softer." Indeed, the drink contains a profusion of fine ice shards, and the acid from the lime and the alcohol in the gin have both mellowed. It's a bit light for my taste. Not a bad thing, given the night I have ahead of me.

OUTSIDE, TOKYO is in full swing, the streets crowded with students and salarymen. Two geishas gently help a drunken patron into a taxi, while the driver patiently waits, behaving as if the impeccable white lace doilies in the backseat aren't in peril. We turn off onto a side street, into an office building, and head two stories underground to Little Smith, where more white-jacketed bartenders stand behind a striking oval-shape, hand-hewn wooden bar. I say "omakase" to one, who smiles instantly. The phrase is usually spoken to sushi chefs when you want them to devise a special tasting menu. It means "I trust you." He instantly earns my trust by muddling Ukrainian chile-pepper vodka and a whole cooked tomato into an artisanal Bloody Mary.

Then it's on to Star Bar Ginza, where I have seven of the best drinks of my trip. Hidetsugu Ueno, the head bartender there, is so obsessive about his craft that he even makes his own bar snacks. He cures his own Japanese version of Spanish-style *jamón* in the mountains of the Akita Prefecture because he finds the traditional stuff too salty to serve with single malt Scotch. And Ueno's care with the bar snacks is just the beginning: When he stirs a Martini (and it will most definitely be stirred, not shaken), he uses a combination of chilled and room-temperature gin to achieve the proper viscosity. He shakes certain cocktails in a soft-sided plastic container to keep the ice from chipping too much. His ever-evolving drink menu is beyond seasonal: In winter it might be Champagne mixed with pomelo, but only during that citrus fruit's fleeting two-week season. In summer, rum is paired with ripe Okinawa mango.

It's autumn, so we have pear gin and tonics. And then fresh grape Tom Collinses. And then Gaja grappa. And then Madeira from 1968. "My birth year," says Ueno. We have Sidecars, which are perfectly balanced. He carves us a perfectly spherical ice diamond with no fewer than 14 facets. And over the ice goes Scotch. My final memory of the night is Shinji shaking my hand, expressing his eternal gratitude for showing him something so transcendent in his hometown. I don't know which of the drinks is talking, but I do know it's breakfast time in the U.S. and bedtime in Tokyo.

I BLAME A BAR back in New York for the headache I have here in Tokyo the next day. At Angel's Share in Manhattan's East Village, I first became fascinated with Japanese-style bartending. The bartenders were Japanese and wore bow ties and crisp white shirts and shook textbook-perfect classic cocktails in gleaming vintage shakers. It was the coolest, old-schoolest, Jazz Age mixological marvel I'd ever seen. Influential bartenders, like Sasha Petraskse of the New York neo-speakeasy Milk & Honey, credit Angel's Share as inspiration.

To put this all in perspective—and to take a much-needed break—I visit Tokyo's Meiji Jingu shrine, on the edge of the Harujuku neighborhood, home to fashion boutiques and Tokyo's wild teenage street style. On the path leading to the shrine, I pass through a canyon of alcohol. On one side of the path is a 20-foot wall of *sake* barrels. Across from that is a rack of 50 barrels of exceptional Bordeaux. These are offerings to the temple spirits and a symbol of the Japanese tradition of cross-cultural exchange. This tradition was first ushered in by Emperor Meiji in the late 19th century, the era in which the Savile Row suit became the standard uniform of the Japanese salaryman and French food became all the rage.

The Meiji period also just happened to coincide with the golden age of the cocktail in Europe and America. During the Meiji period, the first cocktails were served in Tokyo in Ginza cafés like Café Printemps and Café Lion, which employed bartenders who'd learned the craft at the luxury hotels of Asia. They made the Bamboo and the Million Dollar and the Singapore Sling, cocktails served at The Grand Hotel in Yokohama and Raffles Hotel Singapore. Tokyo café society embraced these cocktails and the Japanese fascination with cocktails was born.

On my last night in Tokyo, at Peter, a bar at the top of the brand-new Peninsula Tokyo hotel, I realize that the city's most skilled bartenders are modern-day practitioners of the Meiji-era tradition: taking the West and East and fusing the two with the utmost respect. I'm there with Shinji and he can barely read the names of the drinks, which are written in a form of the kanji script usually reserved for writing haiku. "I haven't had to read this since grade school," he says. We order drinks that are inspired by and named for the seasons.

The walls of Peter are computerized. Guests appear to walk amid the Tokyo skyline that is projected onto the wall; as it morphs electronically, digitalized leaves follow in the wake of diners heading to their tables. Shinji and I debate where to go next: Tokyo Kaikan, where the late, great Mr. Martini schooled Kazuo Uyeda? To the Imperial Hotel, where the Frank Lloyd Wright-designed bar is perfectly preserved? We think better of it. We've had enough for the night, and decide to toast the city. And here's where all the revelations of a cocktail tour of Tokyo cease to surprise. It comes down to the drink at hand and to living in the moment. And whether you're in an old *izakaya*, in a Ginza cocktail bar, or at the top of the newest luxury skyscraper hotel, that toast would still be "Kanpai."

ETERNAL CITY

By Josh Ozersky

From *Saveur*

Josh Ozersky—author of *Meat Me in Manhattan* and
The Hamburger: A History—edits the online gazette *The Feedbag*,
where he blogs with gusto about eateries high and low. This
colorful memoir of his Atlantic City boyhood takes us to the
old-school off-boardwalk restaurants that first trained his
palate.

I didn't think there was anything strange, really, about sitting
around in the Superstar Theater dressing room in Atlantic
City, New Jersey, eating from Rip Taylor's pupu platter. The Ripper, as my father and all the other Resorts International Casino
stagehands called the comedian, had put on his shaggy blond stage
wit and was munching egg rolls, sent down as part of a preposter-
ously overloaded catering spread from a low-end eatery at the re-
sort called Café Casino.

"Take something," he said to me, gesturing to the plate of
spareribs.

I looked at them pensively. "They do look good," I said and
shrugged. "And they're free."

"You're LEARNing!" he yelled, reverting to his queeny, outsize
stage manner. I took a sparerib. Then I took two more and
wrapped them up in a cocktail napkin, for later.

I didn't know the Ripper well, though I had seen his act something like 50 times. This was 1989, and in the 11 years since my
dad had started working at the casino, I had spent thousands of
lonely hours in the light booth or at the back of the house, watching the likes of Buddy Hackett, Lola Falana, and the Ripper do

their thing. On this night, though, I was there only to borrow $40 from my father; I had a big date and didn't want to be caught short. It was to be one of the first happy experiences I'd had since moving to Atlantic City. I took the girl to Angelo's Fairmount Tavern for veal and homemade red wine and then pushed her around in a shopping cart in the lot of ShopRite before taking her back home and losing my virginity. I was 20.

Rip Taylor was the last thing on my mind that night, but I knew his act, one of the great ones, down to the last piece of thrown confetti. His best joke, told about two minutes in, was delivered in what sounded like a single breath:

"I went down to Café Casino and ordered a hamburger and a hot dog, and the waitress came back with a hamburger under her arm, and I said, 'What's that hamburger doing under your arm,' and she said, 'I'm defrosting it.' And I said, "CANCEL the HOT DOG!'"

This was during Merv Griffin's brief ownership of Resorts International—Merv being the only casino owner in the history of Atlantic City who was more interested in the talent than in the gaming. For my family, the casino was salvation. We had moved to Atlantic City in 1979 from Miami, where my mother had worked in a Coral Gables boutique and my father, a struggling abstract expressionist painter, earned a living in his family's hardware store; when it closed, my uncle got Dad a job as a stage technician in Atlantic City's first casino, which had opened the year before. It wasn't an easy transition. Mom, Dad, and I were exiles in a strange world, a semi-abandoned city by the sea that had lost its luster and was hoping to gain it back with old celebrities and new slot machines.

We cheered ourselves up with food. My father worked until nine or ten o'clock each night, and I remember waiting up for him to return with spareribs from China Land or strombolis from Mama Tucci's. When my mom died, three years after we'd moved to Atlantic City, those late-night meals and dining with Dad at our favorite haunts became a comforting routine. The city that adopted us was a ghost town, the boardwalk a monument, but the old Italian-American restaurants, the sub shops, the taverns, producing in that elegant squalor the same satisfying dishes over and over again, gave me a love of Atlantic City's food that has never left me.

Atlantic City had a few puffed-up Italian places—restaurants like Chef Vola's, located in the Chelsea neighborhood, and Scannicchio's, on California Avenue—known for serving foods like lobster tails and buffalo milk mozzarella, items as alien to the city's workaday menus as fugu. But the stagehands at Resorts were more likely to repair to places like the Lighthouse Tavern, long since demolished, renowned for its roast beef sandwiches (though my dad and I could never figure out why). Or Angelo's Fairmount Tavern, with its veal scallopine and baked manicotti and homemade wine. Or Tony's Baltimore Grill, a pizzeria that sat a block from the boardwalk, unchanged since the beginning of time.

While Philadelphia day-trippers would flock to the White House, the famous sub shop that branded itself an institution, my father invariably favored places like Tony's and Angelo's. Maybe he recognized that, amid the proliferation of hotels and tourist traps, those relics, with their comforting insularity and fixedness, were among the few remaining vessels for the city's soul.

THE UNREMODELED ANGELO'S of my father's era set like a citadel in the middle of Ducktown, a mostly black neighborhood in the center of Atlantic City, now largely razed and rebuilt, that had earlier been an Italian-American enclave. I often wonder whether my father, a generally tolerant man, ever felt ill at ease among the Angelo's regulars, who had a reputation for being hostile to the local black residents who occasionally came in for a meal; if he was, he didn't show it. For him, the 18-seat dining room and comfortably worn bar were a solace.

The wine flowed freely at Angelo's, and the veal parmesan was dense and luscious, a thing to dream of all through a work shift. Framed eight-by-tens of baseball players lined the walls, along with movie stills from *The Godfather* and hagiographic images of Frank Sinatra and Dean Martin. On the floor, writ in black and white tiles, were the words ANGELO'S FAIRMOUNT TAVERN, EST. 1936. Those faded photos of East Coast baseball clubs, their players now old or dead, would never fail to send my father into sentimental reveries, activated by red wine and loss.

And yet, for my father, Atlantic City wasn't the stuff of early memories and vanished time; it was the cultural slag heap on which his misfortunes had placed him. I never went a day without hearing, at some point, about the small-mindedness and suffocating quality of AC. His discovery, to cite one of a million instances, that American cheese was known locally as "square cheese" was as damning in his eyes as a DNA test. "Square cheese! Could there possibly be a more unimaginative term than that? Where else would they think to call it square cheese?"

That said, the parochialism that he so despised had a way of growing on him. I seldom saw him happier than at Tony's Baltimore Grill. The squat white building, with fewer windows than an adult bookstore, served little pizzas that came in a small pan and were topped with a sweet red sauce, greasy cheese, and irregular chunks of sweet Italian sausage made by an old man named Bongiovanni up the street on Atlantic Avenue. My father used to go to Tony's with the other stagehands, and I would come along, a miniature adult being indoctrinated in both the local culture and my father's half-hearted repudiation of it. He loved those pizzas even as he disparaged them. By the time he died, in 1998, my father had taken to speaking of what the sausage was like "back when Bongiovanni was still making it." It was accepted as gospel truth by Tony's regulars that, after Bongiovanni retired, the secret sausage recipe had been conveyed, presumably by armored car, to the Delaware Food Market, a grocery and meat store in neighboring Ventnor City, but somehow it just wasn't the same. Even my father had to admit it.

Tony's is still there, and I go back often. It now stands in the shadow of the immense Tropicana hotel and casino, but as far as I'm concerned, the place hasn't changed a bit. The portly waitresses in their red shirts and black pants are just as I remember them; so are the tiny, laminated menus advertising pizza, spaghetti with meatballs, fried fish platters, and open-face white-bread sandwiches of roast beef. These days, the individual jukeboxes that still furnish the booths are filled with the likes of Kelly Clarkson and Justin Timberlake, but you can always find, as inviolate as the baseball photos in Angelo's bar, Sinatra's "My Way." I can barely hear the song without wanting to cry; it makes me think of Dad sitting there in his black work clothes with three other identically dressed stagehands, telling his favorite Sinatra story over a plate of pizza crusts.

"This was in 1979," he'd begin, "before 'New York, New York' came out, and Frank was still closing with 'My Way.' Frank likes to play with the microphone cable while he's singing, so I was supposed to be paying out the cord, making sure that there was enough slack, but not so much that Frank might trip. I also had to keep the flashlight on his feet when he left the stage, so he could see where he was going. I had just started, and I was trying to do both at the same time. Frank finished up and walked toward me, and I had forgotten to move. And"—the story continued to its practiced climax—"Frank pointed at me and sang, 'Get out of MYYYY WAAAAY!'"

I think of the story whenever I'm at Tony's. And I think of how, even a mere two or three years into our stay in Atlantic City, we became tethered to oft-told anecdotes, fixed reference points, thousand-pound anchors of time and place. It seemed to us then that Atlantic City could never change. Of course, it has, as dozens of towering casinos and sleek restaurants have opened over the years. But, at least in a few poignant pockets, everything is unchanged.

Bridging the Chasm

By John T. Edge

From the *Oxford American*

The quintessential social historian as food writer, John T.
Edge always captures the human interest angle, whether in his
"Local Fare" column for the *Oxford American* or the write-ups
in his guidebook, *Southern Belly*. Director of the Southern
Foodways Alliance, he lives in Oxford, Mississippi.

New Orleans is a great restaurant town. On that we can
agree. (In the U.S., only New York City and San Francisco are rivals.) Measures of that greatness, however, are arguable.

Iconic dishes, standard-bearer restaurateurs, and residents who
know and defend the culinary canon are a given. But two contrar-
ian measures are, in my book, defining:

1) A great restaurant town boasts eating places where, during
time spent at table, diners bridge, if only briefly, the chasms of class
and race that segregate citizens. Taking into account economic and
social matters, such commingling rarely happens in white tablecloth restaurants.

In New Orleans, on the high end, regulars revere (and aspirants
fetishize) temples of Creole cookery, among them, Galatoire's and
Commander's Palace. But the low end is where locals of all stripes
commune.

At back-of-town spots like Parasol's, in the Irish Channel, where
they gob roast beef poboys with garlicky-brown gravy. And Willie
Mae's Scotch House, in Treme, where the white beans with pickled
pork rival the crackle-and-snap drumsticks. And Two Sisters, down
on Derbigny, where gumbos often bob with turkey necks.

In those joints, the twain of New Orleans meet. There, community is fostered and greatness achieved.

2) Any good restaurant town claims a core of old-guard restaurants, worthy of devoted patronage. But a great one excels at the
fringes, too. At restaurants off the so-called row. At joints set beyond the back-of-beyond. At liminal eating halls that are both *of
the city* and *beyond the city*.

New Orleans boasts, among others, Mosca's, an Italian-Creole
roadhouse. Family-run, the fifty-plus-year-old restaurant is famous
for garlic-punched and olive oil-drenched oysters and chicken,
dishes so good they compel otherwise sane eaters to leave the city
and negotiate a white-knuckle drive of thirty minutes, over the
shimmying Huey P. Long Bridge, through a phalanx of strip malls,
and past a freight terminal, into Avondale, an almost rural precinct
where my friend Pableaux recently saw a wild boar rooting in the
gravel parking lot.

New Orleans also claims Middendorf's. Forty-odd miles north
of the city, hard by the I-55 off-ramp, it's a side-of-the-swamp destination restaurant, doing business on the narrow isthmus that separates Lake Maurepas and Lake Pontchartrain.

(Pangs of anxiety always precede my arrival in New Orleans.
Meals *count* down here and I don't want to squander an opportunity. So after years of scrambling to find the right place to eat upon
crossing the Orleans Parish line, I've begun stopping on the way
in, at Middendorf's.)

At Middendorf's, in the ragtag settlement of Manchac, roadhouse food reaches its apogee and New Orleans defines its hinter-
land. It's the place where, for three generations, women have
worked with cutlass-tipped knives, shaving fish into vellum filets
that, after a soak in salt water, a roll in cream meal, and a dip in
popping cottonseed oil, emerge from the fry vats looking like
crumpled yellow tissues and tasting like the lovely and raspy off-
spring of a bag of Lays and a net of channel cats.

PERCHED AT the southernmost point in Tangipahoa Parish, at water's edge, Middendorf's is within sight of five bridge spans, three
of which are still functional. The view from the interstate high-top

offers no clues about what transpires below, down at swamp level, among the bald cypress and tupelo, where egrets jackknife and cranes belly flop.

The approach, along Old Highway 51, is forlorn. Tourists do drive-bys of a nearby market, snapping cellphone pictures of a sandwich-board advertisement for fresh coon. Locals, in search of crappie and crab, cast off from a swamp bank, piloting flat-bottoms through the scrub and around concrete pilings.

Middendorf's is not merely a restaurant. It's a complex of buildings, a veritable municipality of catfish and commerce. At its heart is a double-arched dining hall, built in the early years of the twentieth century atop the swamp muck on a raft of timbers. Next door is an aluminum-sided overflow dining room, put to good use during Middendorf's high holy occasions, Mother's Day and Father's Day.

To the rear of the parking lot, in front of the railroad tracks that snake north toward Chicago and the levee that girds the lakes, stands a Tangipahoa Parish Sheriff substation that resembles nothing so much as a rabbit hutch. Next door is a coop, framed by a picket fence, bursting at the seams with an ark's-worth of creatures, among them a flock of frizzle chickens. Alongside that is the proprietor's residence, a white clapboard bungalow. Its proximity to the restaurant calls to mind the customary distance between a Baptist church and the preacher's parsonage.

Towering above all is a skyscraping sign, stacked with block letters that spell out the surname of the man who, on July 4, 1934, leveraged a $500 military-pension payout to install his wife, Josie Middendorf, at a six-burner stove. For the next thirty years, she fried chicken and fish in cast-iron skillets, while Louis Middendorf made supply runs to New Orleans and sold beer from the bar.

UNTIL VERY RECENTLY, Susie Lamonte, granddaughter of Josie, ran the restaurant with her husband, Joey Lamonte. Susie, blonde and garrulous, was the chief of operations. Joey, more cautious, more angular, did the books. But in the wake of Hurricane Katrina, when so much about New Orleans and the Gulf South changed, the ownership of Middendorf's changed.

I learn that, and many other things from Susie, as I sit at the dining-room table of her ranch house, in a Ponchatoula suburb, trying not to stare at the oil paintings that blanket the walls. In the corner is a Rembrandt self-portrait, one of a dozen or more masterwork knockoffs, all painted by Susie. (A cursory glance reveals that Joey posed for her, that he's the beret-wearing young artist.)

We talk fish-cutting technique and restaurant history. I learn that, in the early years, her grandmother called their signature dish of thinner-than-thin catfish the "Middendorf's Special." "Catfish was poor folks' food," Susie says. "And my grandmother had a lot of New Orleans customers. They were Gulf-fish people, coming to the lake. They wanted fried catfish, but we knew not to offend their delicate sensibilities, so we didn't use the name."

And I learn that the true secret of their thin catfish—the lusciousness and the thinness of which is imponderable unless experienced firsthand—is stored in the muscle memory of the women, starting with Josie Middendorf, continuing through the present slicer-in-charge, Ann Curb, who know the exact leverage to exert, as they press a filet down on the cutting board and saw laterally through the flesh, before lifting clear a catfish cutlet.

"We tried a slicing machine once," Susie says. "Everybody always said to us that we had to be using a machine to get it that thin, so we decided to try one. We went up to Massachusetts for a tryout on this German machine that cost seventy thousand dollars—and that was way back when. It worked on their smoked salmon but it tore up our catfish, just shredded it. Fresh, frozen, it didn't matter. We decided to stick with the local ladies."

I ask Susie to describe the crew who cuts and fries and serves, telling her that I understand the import of technique, but I want to know about personality and temperament, too. "My grandmother would say that you had to be nervous to work at Middendorf's," Susie says, recalling, by extension, her own three decades of service, beginning in 1967, when she was still in high school. "I think she meant you had to be high-strung, you had to be high-energy, to keep up. And we found lots of people like that. In the kitchen. Out front, on the floor, too."

HORST PFEIFER looks nervous. A native of Germany, he, along with his rail-thin, Texas-born wife, Karen, bought Middendorf's in April of 2007. Prior to Katrina, they had been proprietors of Bella Luna, a French Quarter restaurant of the Beautiful View School.

After Katrina, they counted their losses—which Horst estimates at a million or more dollars—and opted for the stability that a restaurant in business for nearly three-quarters of a century offers. Or, as Karen puts it, "I always wanted to own a place with laminated menus."

A classically trained chef, Horst has close-shorn gray hair and pinball eyes that carom across a room. He's a restaurant lifer, the sort of guy who lives for the adrenaline rush of service. But it's not the stress of running a restaurant that makes him nervous; it's measuring up to the expectations of the regulars he inherited.

(That confounding situation is, in and of itself, a New Orleans tradition. Just ask Melvin Rodrigue, who, after taking over daily operations of Galatoire's, reaped a whirlwind of criticism for, among other changes, futzing with the restaurant's four-finger cocktails and replacing hand-chipped ice with cubed ice.)

Regulars know the Middendorf's way of doing things. They know that Heinz is the only acceptable ketchup, and that reserve supplies of said ketchup should be stacked like cordwood in a cypress cubby in the front dining room. They noticed when Horst switched from the stubby, bubble-lipped beer glasses, which were a Middendorf's trademark, to what you might recognize as an iced-tea glass.

Some customers scoff when Horst, doing his best imitation of an on-message politician, tells them, "Change is not part of our vocabulary. We don't talk about change. Improvement, yes, but not change."

No matter the rhetoric, regulars acknowledge, at least on some level, that change has long been a constant at Middendorf's. In the 1930s, fried chicken was as popular as catfish. And born-to-the-manor pilgrims from Uptown New Orleans, as well as gun rack Republicans from Hammond remember the old days, before Susie and Joey switched to frozen and bagged fries.

Back then, before pond-raised catfish was the norm, Dennis Rottman—a local monger who also made a market in turtle meat—

sourced Middendorf's fish from local men, who earned their living while working the waters of Maurepas and Pontchartrain. Back then, the lone things green on the menu were a monkey bowl of coleslaw and maybe an iceberg salad drenched in olive salad.

REGULARS CAN TELL you the story of the fire that engulfed the main dining room, back in 1947. In conversation, they will pretend to know the name of the nameless carpenter who, during the rebuild, lined the front dining room with cypress paneling, stained the wood a sort of drawing-room brown, and installed a line of coat hooks, crafted from polished cypress knees.

What they won't tell you is that, like any restaurant, Middendorf's is built upon various conceits, both small and large. Resistance to change is one. Another is the restaurant's iconography, specifically the trademark coat-of-arms, mounted on the wall in the front dining room and reproduced on the cover of Karen's yellow laminate menu.

The crest looks almost regal. As if it was designed for a lodge full of Masons who moonlight as restaurateurs. There's a catfish at top left. A crab at top right. Along the bottom are a shrimp, a smiling chef with a poofy toque, and a scroll, inscribed with the restaurant's natal year.

Staring at it, I'm filled with the sense of belonging, and the belief that each time I take a seat at Middendorf's, I pledge my troth to the role of the restaurant in the American experience. But then I recall the story that Susie told me, about how the coat-of-arms was the creation of a New Orleans interior decorator. "She came up with the idea and the design," Susie said. "My father thought it looked classy."

(Dedicated patrons, it seems, often ascribe an inappropriate significance to such restaurant trappings. Sharing such delusional tendencies are literary theorists who read too much into the omnipresence of mules in Faulkner's Yoknapatawpha and Dylan fabulists who overanalyze the geologic composition of his rolling stone.)

IF MIDDENDORF'S still matters to the next generation of New Orleanians, if it remains a place of pilgrimage, if it still serves as a culinary way station for the likes of me, Horst and Karen will get the credit. And they'll deserve it. So far they have managed changes that neither threaten their regulars nor hamstring their employees.

Catch Horst with his guard down, get him excited about the possibilities, and he'll take you over to his newly built deck annex, where he has installed a brace of misters and a frozen-drink machine. And he'll start talking about converting his used fry grease into bio-diesel for the maintenance truck. He'll talk about the monstrous broilers, which rage day and night, waiting for a cook to shove a butter-swabbed flounder underneath. He'll tell you that he wants to replace the broilers with a kind of instant-on cooking apparatus—powered by an electromagnetic reactor—called an induction broiler.

Get him really going and Horse will rave about turbines as power sources, about how the wind coming off the lakes promises an off-the-grid future for the restaurant.

In the kitchen, a bunker of a space set behind the main dining room, a squadron of black cooks, most of whom are related, roll and fry fish, while white waitresses, wearing sensible shoes and short-sleeve white blouses, ferry top-heavy plates from the fryer bank to the tables. The work is intense. And owing to the close confines of the kitchen, not to mention the ever-present threat of roiling grease, it's balletic.

Horst gives them a wide berth. "I try and support my ladies," he tells me. "But mostly I stay out of their way. Same deal with my fish cutters. They know what they're doing. I just sharpen their knives."

Fewer than two years ago, Horst Pfeifer was a certified, beurre noisette-making New Orleans chef. Now he's a knife sharpener, charged with carrying forward the traditions of a beloved institution. Ask him what it feels like to bear that responsibility on his shoulders and he'll take you to a cinder-block building, two doors down from the chicken coop, alongside the sheriff's substation, where, for seven or eight hours each workday, Ann Curb, age thirty-one, stands at a stainless-steel table, heaped with tubs of catfish filets, wielding a white-handled knife with a long, thin, newly sharpened blade.

Ann lives up the road in Natalbany. Her aunt and her mother preceded her here at Middendorf's. Her two sisters now work here, too, frying the fish that she cuts. As she plows her way through a tub of fish, trimming fat from filets, shaving them down into what some on the crew call "chips," I watch Horst watch her. His gaze remains fixed on Ann's nimble black hands. And his eyes are wide.

FoiX GraX

By Mark Caro

From *The Foie Gras Wars*

A routine assignment sent *Chicago Tribune* entertainment
reporter Mark Caro to interview two local restaurateurs
feuding over goose liver pâté. Caught in the crossfire
between animal rights protesters and gourmands, Caro was
soon investigating a surreal culture war with dimensions
he never expected.

If you didn't want to drive to the suburbs or to decipher
which Chicago restaurants would serve you forbidden
foie, another option to satisfy your liver jones was to go the outlaw
route. You're seeking illegal product, after all, so you might as well
feel like a danger-courting, authority-defying, organ-munching
rebel as you covertly slip into one of the growing number of secret
roaming supper clubs cropping up around town. The culinary underground had embraced foie gras, thus spawning the phenomenon referred to as "quackeasys." Through my *Tribune* food-writing
colleague/friend Monica Eng, I heard about one such dinner, a
BYOB "FoiX GraX Feast" that would highlight the banned liver
in all four courses, including dessert. I signed up and paid my $75
online and waited for the e-mail telling me where it would take
place. (Gotta prevent The Man from finding out, after all.)

The chef was a 30-year-old named Efrain Cuevas, a Mexican-
American who grew up in Aurora (Illinois's second-largest city,
most famous as the setting for *Wayne's World*). He'd recently moved
back to Chicago after living for two years in Oakland, California,
where he prepared underground dinners with a "wandering supper club" called the Ghetto Gourmet. He'd hosted some of the

group's dinners in Chicago, too, but, he said, when they balked at his plan to produce a Ghetto Gourmet foie gras meal in defiance of the ban, he broke ranks to launch his own new supper club, 24Below. (Foie gras's illegality sorta-kinda should be beside the point given that these dinners were being hosted without proper licenses, hence their "underground" status.)

Cuevas was no foie gras veteran. He'd tasted it for the first time in 2006 at an Oakland underground dinner, and at that point he knew nothing of how it was produced or of the controversy surrounding it. All he knew was that he found it delicious, even though he'd tried it in a form that sounds, let's say, unconventional. "This guy made buckwheat waffles and melted the foie gras into the waffles, cut them up, put it inside quail and roasted the quail," he recalled. "It was really good." The meal prompted Cuevas to do a little research. He watched horrific animal-rights videos ("I was like, Wow, this is pretty bad") and a sunnier one from the pro side ("The ducks were so happy: 'Oh, yes, stick a pipe down my throat. I love it.'") and finally decided to explore the issue in the way he knew best: by cooking.

"To Foie Gras or Not to Foie Gras?" read the headline on his 24Below blog as he announced the October 14, 2007, "FoiX GraX" dinner. "I consider myself a very responsible, sensitive, and socially conscious individual," he wrote. "I'm the guy that brings canvas bags to the market, gets on everybody's case about recycling, and saves up for a biodiesel car. I eat cage-free egg omelets, and I even like cats, a lot. But I also like the Foie Gras, and I appreciate the right to eat it and especially to serve it." His hope was that by serving up a lavish meal featuring the yummy livers, he would inspire his guests to weigh the pros and cons of force-feeding birds. "I've bought all this foie gras," he told me a few days before the event. "I've prepared the menu. I'm going to cook it. The question I have to ask myself next week is was it worth it?"

Accompanying me into the culinary underground was Michaela DeSoucey, a 29-year-old Northwestern University PhD student writing her sociology dissertation on the contentious moral and cultural politics surrounding foie gras in the United States and France. (Michaela and I had met at a local food conference, and each of us was amazed to find a kindred foie gras obsessive.) After arriving in a warehousey area of Chicago wedged among Chinatown, the white working-class Bridgeport and the Mexican Pilsen, we entered a large art-filled loft apartment. The kitchen wasn't particularly updated, but it offered plenty of room for Cuevas and several volunteer assistants, whom he'd found on Craigslist, to roll out gnocchi and to grill tomato slices. The chef, an easygoing guy with a soul patch, was happy to chat as he pulled out a pan of foie gras slices for searing, and I was curious to learn how preparing a four-course meal might possibly affect how he weighs the underlying ethical issues.

"Does how it tastes make a difference to you as to whether it's OK?" I asked him.

"Yeah," he replied. "That's actually the biggest reason, because where is there a substitute if I want that kind of flavor, if I want that kind of ingredient?"

"So," I continued, "you think a certain amount of suffering is justified if something tastes really good?"

"Yes. Yes. But it's not like a big yes or 100 percent yes. It's like 60/40. It's hard to say. But then again it's either all or nothing."

Clearly, this chef was joining the ranks of those who have stumbled down this slippery slope. I gave him another nudge:

"So if you had the most delicious food in the world, but the only way to get it would be to take kitty cats and hang them on hooks until they bled to death, would that be OK?"

"See, that's different," he said. "That's different."

"The most delicious food in the world," I persisted.

"Another thing is the tradition, the history of the ingredient," Cuevas said. "If it's something they were doing for a long, long time—like you're saying, oh, a kitten and hanging and suffering. Well, that's just something you just threw at me. But if it was something that had been done for such a long time, I'm not that sensitive to it because it's accepted by some culture."

"Slavery was accepted for a long time," I said, employing a common animal-rights argument.

"That's true."

"There could be some secret society where they discovered that the secretions of the kittens turned the cat into the most delicious meat ever." I was officially getting carried away. "And say that in

Mongolia they have this 5,000-year-old tradition of torturing cats and eating their kidneys, and it's the most delicious food anyone's ever had."

"I guess I would have to try it in that case," Cuevas admitted, finally hitting the base of the slippery slope. "I would be curious about it. I was in China last summer, and there was a dog restaurant. My co-worker was like, 'Look, there's a dog restaurant. Let's go try it.' So I'll try stuff like that."

"How was the dog?"

"It tasted a little beefy, a little porkish."

"But if it had tasted really great, would you want to go down to the Anti-Cruelty Society and pick up an unwanted dog?"

"And kill it and cook it? No."

"So there's no level of deliciousness that would have you kill a dog to eat it?"

"There is. I think there is." *Ding!* "It's like an equation: The degree of suffering plus the historic nature, the tradition of it, you sum it all up, and you have to really factor those things if you want to keep serving it. That's kind of how I am."

For this meal, Cuevas had gotten his livers from Sonoma Foie Gras, some that were shipped and some that he'd carried onto a plane from the Bay Area. "They asked what was in the box, and I just said it was chocolate. I didn't want to take any chances because I spent a lot of money on it." Most of the 20 or so people at the dinner were the chef's friends (or friends' friends), and it was a laid-back crowd without many strict foodie expectations. Before service began, Cuevas offered his quick take on the controversy and encouraged everyone to check out an animal-rights video that he'd posted on his Web site. As for the foie itself, "we're going to try it out tonight," he said as the Bee Gees' "How Can You Mend a Broken Heart?" played in the background. "I want you guys to talk about it, see what you think."

Aside from the ethical/taste issue, another question mark was hanging over this dinner, one not acknowledged or perhaps even realized by our host. Foie gras tends to be the domain of chefs who have received some classical French training or at least have engaged in a long, careful courtship of this precious product. Foie gras is a roll-out-the-red-carpet delicacy; you wouldn't use it in the kitchen like an everyday ingredient any more than you would toss white truffles into a vat of chili.

But Cuevas had no practical history with foie gras. He'd cooked with it for the first time the previous week as a practice round and was surprised that his foie gras slices had reduced to half their size when he seared them for, he realized, too long over too low heat. For the dessert, he planned to adapt a foie gras mousse recipe that he'd seen executed on the Bravo TV show *Top Chef*. With other courses he was more or less playing Iron Chef, winging it in a calculated way. His pasta course would be a gnocchi in which he substituted a whole lobe of foie gras for the ricotta cheese that his recipe originally called for. As a dessert garnish, he planned to serve a foie gras cotton candy even though he'd never made any kind of cotton candy before; in fact, the machine was still sealed in the box as dinner got under way. Cuevas may have intended this meal as a sort of referendum on whether the experience of cooking and eating foie gras transcends the accompanying ethical issues, but it also served as a culinary test of foie gras's being cooked in a way that's pretty much divorced from tradition or widely accepted ways of handling the ingredient.

The first course was a seared foie gras slice laid atop a bed of red lentils, flash-sautéed zucchini and grilled tomato. This was an unusual accompaniment, especially given that the lentils were flavored with an aggressive, Middle Eastern spice mixture that led with cumin and crushed red pepper. Seared foie gras usually is paired with some sort of fruit preparation to get that mouth-tingling sweet-savory contrast going on, the fruit gently caressing the liver and bringing out its deep yet delicate flavor. The spiced lentils here simply overpowered the foie; you could barely taste the liver for all of that cumin-and-pepper zing. Plus, Cuevas had cooked the slices on an electric skillet, and the sear didn't create any kind of crust; the foie just came out with an almost-uniform gray color. Without the dark, hard sear, you lost that sublime contrast of the crispy outside and gelatinous inside. Greg Christian, a Cuevas friend as well as a chef who specializes in working with local, organic ingredients, termed this preparation "flaccid foie."

"And when it's flaccid foie—which is mostly what people serve, even people that know how to cook—it's not that good," he told a veteran local TV producer sitting next to him. "There's really only one way to cook foie gras, and that's in a hot pan in butter, fast." (When I later mentioned this bit of wisdom to Ariane Daguin, she was appalled. "I don't know any chef, sous chef or dishwasher who would put butter in the pan," she said. "The butter is going to burn before the foie gras is going to cook. And why do you need butter? The foie gras is going to lose fat anyway. This is so not possible. He cannot be a chef saying that. The secret is hot, that's all." However, Michael Lachowicz at his three-star suburban Chicago restaurant, Michael, demonstrated to me how he places the foie slice into a freezer for a bit, dusts it with flour and then sears it at a high temperature with, yes, a bit of butter for an excellent preparation.)

Next up was the gnocchi, with the foie gras "mushed in there with the potatoes and flour," as Cuevas described it. The pasta was topped with pancetta, Manchego cheese and a variation on a traditional brown-butter sauce that actually was a half stick of melted butter combined with a cup and a half of the rendered fat that came from the seared foie gras. (Ariane Daguin also said never to use the rendered fat from searing because it's burnt—though maybe Cuevas's was OK because the searing heat wasn't so high.) He'd cooked the pancetta in this foie gras fat as well. The result was a nice gnocchi, rich yet not heavy feeling, but I'll be damned if I could taste the foie gras. My tablemates agreed; they'd never have known that the fat liver (or liver fat) was in the dish without the advance warning.

The table conversation, no surprise, veered toward Chicago's ban of the ingredient we'd all been consuming. Christian, a leading figure in bringing organic foods to Chicago's public schools, deemed the controversy "a silly argument" given how relatively few people it affects. "In the Chicago public schools, we feed 400,000 kids dog food every day for lunch, so I wasn't willing to have much of an opinion about the foie gras controversy." He was more concerned over how many miles an average ingredient in Trotter's or Tramonto's kitchen was traveling or how many millions of chickens were being slaughtered on industrial chicken farms.

"I really think it's a function of people's unwillingness to look at their unconscious guilt around the bigger things that are happening in life," he said. "Instead of looking at things that are really overwhelming, things that are really much more serious, they'll try and change this because that's what they can get their head around. In Chicago 50 or 75 people eat foie gras in a night, right? And there's probably a million people a night eating beef that's raised really inhumanely."

"OK," I said, "but does that mean the ducks don't suffer?"

"I've actually been thinking about that," Christian said. "It's hard for me to say that's OK. I'm mostly a vegetarian. This will be the most meat I've eaten in the last four months, by far. I eat mostly vegetables, mostly vegan, almost exclusively, 99.9 percent. So it is kind of awful the way they're treated. But, I think . . . I don't know." Christian said he'd come to the dinner because Monica had invited him, and he wanted to support his friend Efrain. "This is the first time he's ever cooked foie. I said, 'What are you doing?' I offered to show him. I talked to him about it for like 20 minutes, but talking for 20 minutes is different from cooking foie gras for 25 years like me."

"So are you dubious about the foie cotton candy then?"

"Yeah," he laughed.

Cuevas came out to introduce the third course: a wild-boar roast with a rub of brown sugar, black pepper, red pepper and coriander and a red-wine reduction sauce made with carrots and a pound of foie gras that "just kind of melted and disintegrated" into it. This deeply orange sauce was a rich, complementary accompaniment to the boar, though, again, it didn't taste a lot like foie gras unless you happened to come across a stray liver niblet. So although this was a perfectly fine course, it would be hard to make the argument that the foie gras surpassed Cuevas's threshold of being absolutely necessary here.

Over in the kitchen, the chef and his volunteers were prepping dessert. "I'm getting a little nervous," Monica said with a laugh, "because Efrain's just reading the directions for the cotton candy machine right now."

Monica and I got up to take a closer look. As his helpers cut out circles of a hazelnut cake using the top of an empty organic tomatoes can, Cuevas contemplated the white cotton candy machine spinning atop the counter as he clutched a stainless steel bowl filled with a yellowish, damp sugar. "It's sugar and melted foie gras," he explained, "and then I'll just run it through the cotton candy machine."

"Will that work?" Monica asked.

The machine kept spinning. "Let's just see what happens," he finally said and dropped a bit of the sugar in there. Immediately, his black shirt looked like it was coated with dandruff. He added more of the foie sugar and waited. And waited.

A 10-year-old boy named Willie Wagner approached and peered inside. "It might be too wet," he told Cuevas. "If any of the sugar gets wet, you have to throw it all out."

The boy's father, also named Willie Wagner (and owner of Honky Tonk Barbeque in Pilsen), explained that little Willie used to make cotton candy at a circus. Cuevas grimaced. The machine kept spinning without producing any wispy threads. Cuevas took the rest of the foie sugar and stuck it in the freezer. A few minutes later he removed it and dumped it all into a sauté pan on the stove, where it began to melt. Meanwhile, he cleaned out the cotton candy machine and tried again with some regular, dry, liver-free sugar. Sure enough, the sugary threads started accumulating along the inside.

"Efrain!" cried out a female volunteer. The foie gras sugar was bubbling over the stove. Cuevas dashed over and turned down the heat. One of the volunteers poured the molten foie sugar into a plastic squirt bottle. Cuevas squirted out some of the contents onto a baking sheet to create hard, candy-like strands. They tasted like caramelized sugar, not so much like foie gras.

"Change of plans," he announced, emptying the squirt bottle back into the sauté pan. I'm going to make foie gras caramel." He added whipping cream and a balsamic vanilla reduction to the mixture and stirred. The dessert wound up being hazelnut cake and figs topped by a foie gras mousse (made with egg yolks, whipped cream, honey and melted liver) with the foie gras caramel drizzled on top and around, and a puff of white cotton candy as a "texture garnish." In this case you really could taste the foie gras in the mousse, not so much in the caramel. Foie gras and figs play well together, so the dish didn't taste as weird as it might sound. Most folks cleaned their plates.

As people finished their dinners, I asked Efrain whether he was more of a foie gras fan now than before the meal. "I am," he replied. "Yeah, everything was really good. I was a little bit put out by the dessert with the cotton candy, but it worked out fine."

His biggest surprise had been how much the foie gras slices again reduced upon searing, but he was glad that the rendered fat came in handy. "What I really liked about doing this four-course menu was I actually used everything. The fat from the first course, I used for the second course, and then whatever I had left over there, I even threw some into the sauce for the wild boar. Everything got used, the fat and the liver."

He agreed with me that the foie gras was most prominent in the first and last courses, but he wasn't bothered that it wasn't so noticeable in the gnocchi or wild boar because he liked how those courses came out. "Do you think the foie gras was indispensable for each of the dishes?" I asked.

"Yes."

The other diners were enthusiastic; certainly none of them expressed qualms about having eaten foie gras. Cuevas was intrigued enough by the experience that he tried again two months later at another underground dinner, dubbed "Fxxx Gxxx in West Town." This time he paired his seared foie gras with something sweet: seared apple slices infused with lavender honey, plus sour cherry compote. Other courses included leek and endive soup with a foie gras crouton and Gruyère; braised pork shoulder roast with purple yams and rutabaga, cognac and foie gras caramel (yes!); and Viognier-poached pears filled with fuyu persimmon custard plus pistachio ice cream with vanilla foie caramel (again!).

When I was in France weeks later, I mentioned Cuevas's foie gras gnocchi and cotton candy to André Daguin, Ariane's famous father. He gave a deep laugh and pronounced, "If he comes here and does that, he will be in the river!"

OTHER CHICAGO RESTAURANTS hosted their own secret foie gras dinners, and more new supper clubs emerged. One, organized by the local wine distributor H2Vino, was dubbed Turtle Soup, and it had a novel concept. Not only would a different restaurant present each month's multicourse foie gras dinner—which cost $99 including wine pairings, tax and tip—but at the end of the meal you'd receive two business cards with "The Turtle Soup Club" printed above the line "Saving the turtles, eat more foie" and an illustration of a happy turtle lying on its back with a bowl of something hot atop its tummy. The back of the card listed five Chicago restaurants—including Cyrano's Bistrot and Bin 36—and the instruction, "Present this card to your server at any of the restaurants below for a special turtle soup appetizer."

Yes, "turtle soup" was code, and the card was the equivalent of a secret handshake to get a foie gras appetizer delivered surreptitiously to your table. The first Turtle Soup dinner was at Copperblue in early 2008, and Tsonton's training with the ingredient was evident in his variety of cold and hot preparations, including a foie gras mousse, rice croquettes with "yummy foie gras middles," a foie gras terrine, seared foie gras in a rich risotto, and roasted foie gras with cocoa nibs alongside duck leg confit and a breast roulade. Tsonton introduced the meal to the 40 or so diners with his typical off-the-cuff enthusiasm, but he was a bit chagrined; he'd just received his second warning letter from the city for selling foie gras. (Like at Hot Doug's, his first warning letter was displayed at the restaurant's entrance, next to a basket of "Quack If You Like Foie Gras" buttons on sale for five dollars to support Chicago Chefs for Choice.) One of Tsonton's regular clients had asked him to host a private, fancy lunch for 12 staffers at the restaurant, so he offered a foie gras terrine as one of the appetizer options. Almost immediately afterward, Copperblue received the city's warning with a notation of when the complaint had been filed. "The person called at 12:10 in the afternoon," Tsonton told the group. "The lunch started at 11:45. So they were on their phone calling the city narking on me on a private lunch."

A few weeks after the Turtle Soup dinner, my curiosity about the card got the better of me. Would it really work? Did all of those listed restaurants actually keep foie gras on the premises just in case someone walked in and slipped them one of these babies? I figured Cyrano's, Bin 36 and Copperblue probably had foie gras in the kitchen, but I wasn't so sure about the other two listed restaurants: the Italian wine bar Enoteca Piattini or the French-Vietnamese restaurant Le Lan. I'd been meaning to try Le Lan anyway—in fact,

I'd met its chef, Bill Kim, when he was still working in Trotter's kitchen—so Michaela and I headed out there on a Thursday night.

We perused the menu, and when our server—an appropriately refined fellow befitting the restaurant's quiet elegance—came by, I smoothly handed him the Turtle Soup card and said *sotto voce*, "I hope you'll be able to honor this."

He nodded, politely smiled and tried not to look like he'd just been handed something written in Sanskrit. Soon he and the restaurant's manager were exchanging puzzled expressions in a corner by the kitchen. When we finally ordered our meals, the server said he hadn't yet had a chance to discuss the card with the chef. But soon he returned to inform us: "We shall be able to honor your request."

Eventually, the server delivered two plates sporting lovely foie gras terrine slices. They were, as expected, tasty. "This is very similar to Michael Tsonton's preparation," Michaela noted, perceptively.

After the meal, Chef Kim visited from the kitchen, and we commended him on a wonderful meal. I told him, "I was surprised that the Turtle Soup card worked. I didn't imagine that people from that dinner had been making a run on the restaurant with those cards."

"I gotta tell you," he said with a sigh, "we don't keep foie gras in the kitchen." In fact, he explained, my request had thrown the restaurant into a tizzy. Up to that point, Kim's involvement in Turtle Soup had been to agree to host a dinner (the second one, it turned out), but he'd never seen one of those cards before and didn't know what to do. The restaurant's manager tracked down Michael Tsonton on his cell phone, and Tsonton, who was at a Chicago Bulls game that evening, informed him that he had some foie gras terrines in the Copperblue walk-in refrigerator. Le Lan's owner then drove to Copperblue, picked up one of Tsonton's terrines and delivered it to the Le Lan kitchen, where Kim plated the disk.

That was one powerful card.

Eat Your Damn Dessert

By Scott Hocker

From *San Francisco Magazine*

As senior editor of this San Francisco weekly entertainment
magazine, Scott Hocker noticed one thing missing from many
of the city's most renowned restaurants—and a new crop of
star pastry chefs angling to fill the vacuum.

Two hours before the doors open on what promises to be
another busy Friday night in September at Candybar,
the first self-proclaimed dessert lounge in San Francisco, chef Boris
Portnoy is deconstructing a lit cigarette. Standing in the restaurant's kitchen, he removes a plastic container filled with beige
cream from the fridge, peels off the lid, dips in a spoon, and tastes.
"Hmmm," he mutters, moving the cream around in his mouth.
"This one's better." He then has his sous-chef, Kyle Caporicci, try
some. Caporicci nods. "Yeah, it's not as sharp."

The liquid in question is the duo's fourth attempt at infusing
the flavor of blond tobacco into cream. Bizarre, yes. Almost as
strange as putting icing on pea soup, some might say. But Portnoy
was convinced that a hint of smoky tobacco would add an unexpected savory note alongside the other four elements of a dessert
he calls Before and After 8. To achieve the perfect amount of tobacco flavor—sharp enough, but without the acridness of actual
cigarette smoke—Portnoy and Caporicci tried more than 16 techniques, including steeping the dried leaves in hot cream (too intense), blanching the tobacco before infusing it (too mild), and
using carbon dioxide to lighten the infused cream and quicken the
process (a critical step, they learned). The ideal method turns out

to involve a combination of the first and third: steeping dried tobacco in a mixture of cold milk and cream, then adding a bit of carbon dioxide.

When dinner service begins, the cream will be piped into a rice-paper cylinder, then wrapped in a chocolate shell. Across the tiny workspace for Portnoy, Caporicci is spreading a layer of sweetened red pepper pulp between sheets of silicon. When it sets, the pulp will resemble an enormous Fruit Roll-Up. After being broken into small pieces, the pulp, standing in for the embers at the end of a Marlboro, will be affixed to the tobacco-cream "cigarette," as Portnoy calls it. On the plate, the cigarette will be strewn with "ash" made from almond flour and coffee grounds and accompanied by a quenelle of coffee ice cream. Coffee and cigarettes—already a fine pairing in their traditional incarnations—have never been so well matched.

PORTNOY'S SUGAR-FUELED reverie may be an extreme example, but it's a delicious response to an unsavory Bay Area problem. He and a band of like-minded pastry chefs are trying to breathe new life into a neglected corner of the local restaurant scene: dessert. It may be going unnoticed by all but die-hard dining enthusiasts, but in one of the country's culinary epicenters, the last course has become an afterthought. Imagine, if you will, a recent meal at one of the region's cherished restaurants: You've already enjoyed an inventive first course of prawns with watermelon and lemongrass, or red abalone with pork belly and artichokes. The excitement continued with grilled pork loin with faro and borage, or foie gras—stuffed quail with cabbage and huckleberries. Now, you're anticipating something equally inspired for dessert. But the menu arrives, and déjà vu strikes—hard—with a lineup of usual suspects: a fruit tart, maybe apple, maybe peach, with a scoop of vanilla ice cream; a lovely but uninspired crème brûlée; and chocolate cake, probably warm, surrounded by caramel sauce or crème anglaise. In my five years reviewing restaurants for this magazine, it's disheartening how regularly I've experienced this kind of letdown. The bitter truth is, dessert in this food mecca has become a broken record. And the lyrics to the tune on constant repeat are "boring and—worse still—bad."

It's not as if Bay Area diners don't sometimes exhibit a more discerning sweet tooth. Consider the proliferation of artisan ice cream shops like Berkeley's Sketch and Ici, and Bi-Rite Creamery and the highly anticipated Humphry Slocombe, both in the Mission; bakeries like Tartine; our panoply of boutique chocolatiers; and even the new, high-end Dynamo Donut. But compared with that of other major cities, our restaurant dessert culture is downright backwoods. In New York, chefs like Alex Stupak, at WD-50, are wowing diners with desserts such as grapefruit curd with nasturtium ice cream, or a disassembled cornbread pudding with lemongrass and prunes. Likewise, Ramon Perez, at Sona, in Los Angeles—a city known more for counting calories than for enjoying them—pairs caramelized Satsuma oranges with black-sesame ice cream and almond-miso biscuits, and everyone's asking for more.

Here in San Francisco, the heroes are few and far between—and too often unappreciated. It's unclear whether lack of demand is driving the lack of supply, or vice versa, but either way, dessert sales are down. "Only 35 to 40 percent of our customers order dessert," says Charlie Hallowell, chef-owner of Pizzaiolo, in Oakland. Elisabeth Pruiett, co-owner of Bar Tartine, in the Mission, clocks the number even lower: The restaurant's association with the bakery of the same name notwithstanding, only 30 percent of dinners at Bar Tartine end with dessert. Compare that with New York, where, according to a longtime Bay Area pastry chef who's done an informal survey of his Big Apple peers, up to 80 percent of diners insist on finishing on a sweet note.

Portnoy and a group of fellow iconoclasts are poised to change that—not by throwing tradition to the wind or being innovative for innovation's sake, but by striving to create what could best be called "smart desserts." This means desserts that are surprising and new but are designed, above all, to taste great. At the most avant-garde end of the spectrum is Orson's Luis Villavelazquez, a renegade with matching male and female skull tattoos on his hands who's as comfortable with microwaved cakes discharged from a siphon as he is with simple poached figs. On the more traditional front, we find Range's Michelle Polzine, an ex-no-wave rock musician with serious bangs and horn-rimmed glasses. She bakes like a grandma running a chemistry lab, turning out the smoothest blackberry ice cream and flakiest tart dough while creating quietly subversive flavor combinations, like apple and rosemary. Somewhere in the middle is Nicole Krasinski, formerly of the shuttered Rubicon, who comes at dessert like a savory chef on holiday, finishing a plate of cocoa custard with honey-lard granola and lard-accented pumpkin-seed shortbread.

Unfortunately, in the current restaurant climate, talent isn't always a recipe for success. Portnoy, for example, lost his post at Candybar in mid-September. The owners told him, he says, that they wanted to head in a "different direction"—one leading toward brownies and chocolate mousse. This means one of the most innovative pastry chefs in town is now without a job. No offense to Portnoy's replacement, who's doing good work with his limited options, but interesting desserts clearly face an uphill battle in the Bay Area. Portnoy worries that perhaps he's just "not a good fit for people's tastes right now." So why, exactly, did the sweet life go so sour—and can Portnoy and his compatriots once again whip dessert into the knockout way to end a meal?

IT SEEMS TO NEVER END, the crediting of Chez Panisse for local restaurant culture as we know it. But our dessert story, for better and for worse, also starts on Shattuck Avenue. From the time Lindsey Shere debuted there as the pastry chef in 1971 until now, with Mia Ponce and Stacie Pierce jointly running the department, there has been an unwavering through line: pristine ingredients treated simply and reverently. Start with perfect, locally grown strawberries. Showcase them in a sorbet or an impeccably executed, butter-laden crust—and don't get too fancy. "You have to know when to leave something be," says Mary Jo Thoresen, who worked at Chez Panisse for 12 years and is now pastry chef and co-owner of Jojo, in Oakland, where she continues to turn out exquisite desserts in the Shere tradition. Like a dropped scoop of mulberry ice cream spreading across the sidewalk on a balmy day, the iconic restaurant's dessert menu has led to a multitude of imitators. Notice an Autumn Flame peach tart on a buttery bed of short-crust dough, accompanied by a scoop of vanilla-bean ice cream, at your neighborhood restaurant last night: You have Ms. Shere and company to thank.

And thank them you should. Before Shere's purity-first mindset swept across the pastry landscape, desserts here were typically copycat renditions of French classics, like crème caramel and pastry cream-filled napoleons with out-of-season fruit. So the turn toward fresh ingredients treated with respect was a welcome change. But almost 40 years have ticked by since the launch of Chez Panisse, and the Shere dessert ethic hasn't always weathered well. When it's done right, the perfect peach tart is still a marvel—but it requires flawless technique (it just looks simple), and there's less of that to go around these days.

"I meet these people who call themselves pastry chefs who've only been out of culinary school for eight months," says William Werner, a pastry chef and consultant who has worked at the Ritz-Carlton, Half Moon Bay. "I try to talk to them about tempering chocolate, and they look at me like I have three heads." Werner, by contrast, has been working in pastry for more than a decade and began his career at the bottom of the sugar barrel, training under Stéphane Ghéramy at the Ritz-Carlton in Sarasota, Florida. "I worked for free, 12 hours a day. After showing me how to make bonbons, he would leave, and I would clean his tools and polish the whole kitchen. I didn't care; I was there to learn," Werner recalls. Others, including Shuna Lydon, founder of the blog Eggbeater and a pastry chef at large who has worked at the French Laundry and Aziza and in the lauded pastry department at New York's Gramercy Tavern, tell similar stories. Even Villavelazquez, who at 24 is one of San Francisco's youngest pastry chefs, began his career at 18 in the kitchen at Citizen Cake but acquired his title only when Orson opened this past February.

Of course, considering how little most pastry chef jobs in the Bay Area pay, it's no wonder the slots are being filled by underbaked culinary-school graduates. "I've been let go by restaurants and replaced by people making $23,000 a year," says Lydon, who last month moved to London for a better-paying job. Compare that with places like New York and Las Vegas, where, Werner notes, it's possible—even likely—for professionals in his field to make a decent living. "I'm getting calls from headhunters, and they're offering jobs in Vegas that pay six figures," he says. Some argue that the local stinginess might be misguided, because an excellent pastry chef can actually be a good investment. The better the desserts, this line of thought goes, the more people order them and the less that's thrown out at the end of the night. But at a time when the economics of running a restaurant are tighter than ever (reminder: San Francisco restaurants are now struggling with the costs of mandatory sick pay, a higher minimum wage, and universal health-care), pastry chefs are often the first to feel the vise.

Some places simply can't afford to pay someone to make dessert—particularly neighborhood restaurants, where Bay Area folks do the bulk of their dining. And those that do have one often give that person the short end of the whisk. The pastry chef at Pizzaiolo, for instance, has a makeshift hallway station on the way to the bathroom. Even Boulevard, one of the busiest restaurants in town, with one of the largest pastry departments, doesn't give its dessert staff adequate real estate, says Lydon. "You should see where the pastry people have to work," she says. "They share the entire space with the rest of the cooks." Another problem: The dessert chef often has to share equipment with the savory department. In one case, an entire batch of panna cotta had to be thrown out after being tainted by garlic residue. The media certainly doesn't help the situation, either: In an August review of Coi in the *San Francisco Chronicle*, in which the restaurant was upgraded to four-star status, only four words were devoted to the tasting menu's two desserts, and there was no mention of Carlos Salgado, who masterminded them.

BEYOND LESS-THAN-SWEET economics, the stumbling dessert culture reflects the Bay Area's fine-dining priorities. For starters, many people around here are just too health-obsessed to care much about dessert. If diners are going to consume sweet calories, says Portnoy, they often do so at the beginning of the meal, in the form of one of the area's typically sugar-heavy cocktails. Portion sizing is another culprit. While working other jobs before opening Citizen Cake and Orson, Elizabeth Falkner was flabbergasted by the amount of food coming out of the kitchen. "I'd think, 'You guys are killing me! We're never going to sell dessert if people eat that much short ribs and mashed potatoes.'" At Citizen Cake and Orson, she aims for a better balance. "I want people to have an appetizer, an entrée, and dessert and not feel like a pig when they leave."

Even when local diners do order dessert, they tend to gravitate toward the familiar. "When I was at Mecca, the servers would always tell me to make gooey, sticky desserts, because they sell better," recalls Eric Shelton, co-owner of Sketch with his wife, Ruthie Planas-Shelton. Some of that knee-jerk desire for pure sweetness may be a biological inheritance that even the most adventuresome diners—the type who go for the nine-course tasting menu at the French Laundry—are powerless to resist. As Harold McGee notes in his seminal tome, *On Food and Cooking*, studies indicate that of the four basic taste sensations, "only sweetness is innately preferred." Our fondness for sugar, he posits, most likely stems from our history of eating nutrient-rich, glucose-filled plants; as a result, sweetness began to equal sustenance.

This biological push helps to explain why it's more work to develop a smart sweet tooth than a smart savory tooth. "People want comfort-food favorites for dessert," says Kara Nielsen, a trend analyst at the Center for Culinary Development and a former pastry chef. Hence the profusion of s'mores, brownie sundaes, and root-beer floats on many local menus. Even food writer Alan Richman, who is fond of extolling the virtues of such gastronomic destinations as New York's seafood temple, Le Bernardin, and Spain's molecular-gastronomy mecca, El Bulli, regresses when writing about the subject, as he did in the July 2008 issue of *GQ*. "I am no longer eight years old, but I feel that way whenever I order dessert," he wrote. (The finest candy is See's California Brittle, he says, and his holy grail is an over-the-top sundae called Pig's Dinner.) Locally, an institution as beloved as Tartine Bakery isn't immune to diners' often hide-bound dessert needs. A few years ago, co-owner Pruiett made blancmange (a simple almond-flavored dessert much like panna cotta) and served it with fresh cherries. The bakery's customers would have none of it. "But we can't sell enough chocolate pudding," she says.

For Portnoy, chocolate pudding was never an option. He discovered early in his career that he wanted to make food that was complex and exciting, even if it meant guiding wary diners by the fork. Indeed, many a night at Candybar found him stepping out of the kitchen to walk guests through his unusual offerings. The week he was serving milk-chocolate fingers with celery-licorice sorbet, for example, he had to explain that the sorbet didn't have a heavy celery taste; the vegetable simply added a bright note to the rich chocolate.

Portnoy's dessert philosophy is rooted in one main idea: creating a well-tuned interplay among disparate elements, some of which may not seem to belong in a dessert. His Before and After 8, for example, somehow balances sweetness, acidity, smoke, texture, and salt. Sure, tobacco in cream might be considered a stretch—but that improbable combination is really only the extension of a dessert tradition many of us have already begun to embrace in the Bay Area. (Even undaring diners expand their horizons, given enough time.)

Take salted caramel. The flavor combination had an underground following, thanks to such chocolatiers as Recchiuti—but some traditionalists still couldn't wrap their heads around it. Now it's the Bi-Rite Creamery's top-selling flavor, and it's turning up in candy and ice cream all over the Bay Area. Likewise, Falkner touts the success of her Peruvian-corn ice cream. "When we first put it on the menu, people would scratch their heads," she recalls. "But we kept pushing people to taste it, and now when they don't see it on the menu, they say, 'Oh, I really miss that corn ice cream!'" In Portnoy's world, it's not such a great leap from savory caramel and vegetables in ice cream to olive cream piped into a chocolate cannellone.

The key is finding the right balance, which, you could say, Portnoy's entire career has been training him to do. At his first restaurant job, at the classically French Deux Cheminées, in Philadelphia (a land of pork medallions, marsala, and napoleons with brûléed bananas and pastry cream), Portnoy worked under chef Fritz Blank, who was once a microbiologist. Blank approached savory food with a scientific precision usually reserved for baking, regularly sending Portnoy to one of the restaurant's 10,000 culinary texts for answers to gastronomic questions. Portnoy then helped open the restaurant Salt (also in Philadelphia) with Vernon Morales, an intrepid chef who had worked at New York's four-star, haute-French Daniel and at some of Spain's most cutting-edge restaurants. At Salt, Morales bolstered Portnoy's education in molecular gastronomy, the current movement that relies on unconventional techniques and additives to alter the shape and texture of food.

Portnoy continued his avant-garde schooling at Mugaritz, in Spain's Basque country, where the cooks would forage for herbs every morning. After a stint in New York, he came west with Morales to open Winterland, a short-lived Pacific Heights restaurant that was one of the first local practitioners in the culinary vanguard. When Winterland closed, Portnoy landed at Campton Place, where he introduced curious diners to dishes like cauliflower mousse ringed with milk chocolate and swathed in a mixture of reduced carrot juice and briny sea urchin that had been thickened with xanthan gum and albumen, then aerated with an immersion blender.

Portnoy's work at Candybar was similarly innovative, but in a casual environment. Now that he's no longer there, he is consulting for the California Walnut Marketing Board and launching a food zine, *Paper Napkin*. He's uncertain about the future, but it's hard to imagine he won't land in a restaurant kitchen again soon; in fact, rumor has it that he'll be spearheading the pastry department of a splashy restaurant due to open next year. (Portnoy confirmed the rumor, but wouldn't offer any details.) Anyone who wants to be a "purveyor of ideas," as he calls himself, is bound to rebound.

The future is similarly ambiguous for Nicole Krasinski. She and her longtime co-chef and partner, Stuart Brioza, no longer have full-time jobs, since Rubicon closed its doors in August after 14 years (for financial reasons, according to proprietor Drew Nieporent). So there's currently no place to sample her frozen Earl Grey mousse, topped with a buckwheat tuile cookie and paired with a compote made from Mutsu apples and umeboshi (pickled Japanese apricots), or her plum financier with olive-oil ice cream and shaved Sardinian pecorino. Over the years, she and Brioza gained a loyal following. Luckily for locals, they plan to stay in the Bay Area and open their own place.

Two of Portnoy and Krasinski's standout peers are (thankfully) still employed. The shelves behind the dessert-plating station at Orson, where Villavelazquez runs the show, teem with many of the tools of the culinary cutting edge that Portnoy has employed:

Kelcogel (a gelling agent), carbon dioxide chargers for creating foams, and intriguing flavorings, such as Douglas fir-tip tea. But Villavelazquez is also deeply in touch with the current dicta of Bay Area cooking. In the fall, his ingenious dessert the Swift Strike starred seasonal black Mission figs poached in the Italian liqueur Fernet-Branca—an herbaceous spirit that is drunk more in San Francisco than anywhere else in the country. But he took it a step further by adding black-pepper granola and pine nut-caramel ice cream to the plate; these disparate components seem odd only until you taste them together.

Polzine, on the other hand, is devoted to reinvigorating dessert at the neighborhood-restaurant level. This generally entails turning out sweets that are exquisitely executed and slightly offbeat, but not as overtly edgy as what you'd find at Orson. At Range, you'll find soufflés, crêpes, turnovers, upside-down cakes, and even fruit tarts— but ones unlike those made by her peers. Polzine's flawless chocolate crêpes come with grapefruit segments and pink-peppercorn ice cream. Her ridiculously creamy butterscotch pudding is made from real butter, brown sugar, and rum—not melted synthetic butterscotch chips—and accompanied by three freshly baked vanilla wafers shot through with real vanilla-bean seeds. And her impossibly flaky tarte tatin, featuring apples and quince, is finished with quince syrup and rosemary ice cream. This is dining at its best, where dessert completes the arc of the meal by complementing what came before, sending you home with equal parts contentment and pleasant surprise.

In the end, that is the goal of every member of this band of committed pastry chefs. We dine in restaurants to be coddled and cared for, but also to eat food that challenges us—sometimes on the smallest of scales—even as it satisfies. After all, if we weren't interested in food that surpasses our expectations or skills as home cooks, wouldn't we just stay home?

The shaky economy certainly won't make this sugary march forward any easier. During tough times, diners tend to gravitate toward the familiar—and money troubles for restaurants could make talented pastry chefs all the more dispensable. Still, food is a primal comfort, and a taste of sweetness can be a salve like little else. And this is the Bay Area, where diners' devotion to great restaurants is unlikely to waver. So while we continue to champion the ice cream parlors, bakeries, chocolatiers, and doughnut shops that have recently turned sweet snacking into a high art, let's also embrace the pear tart with cardamom ice cream, or the pumpkin custard with brown-butter streusel and root-beer maple syrup, at the end of a restaurant meal. We can have that salted-caramel ice cream and eat our microwaved walnut cake, too.

SHOULD FINE DINING DIE?

By Anya von Bremzen

From *Food & Wine*

Born in Russia, award-winning cookbook writer Anya von
Bremzen lives today in Queens, in between globe-trotting
assignments for *Food & Wine* and *Travel & Leisure*. Years of
international dining more than qualify her to wonder: Have
we lost the point of haute cuisine?

While scanning the Russian press a while back, I came
across an interview with Anatoly Komm, the country's
top chef. Komm is famous for the dazzling avant-garde riffs on
black bread and borscht at his Moscow restaurant Varvary. Asked
why people need haute cuisine these days, Komm had this to say:
"Why go to the opera when you can buy a CD? If I don't wow
and regale diners with totally new sensations, I have wasted their
money and failed as a chef!"

Of course, as a former Muscovite, I chuckled at Komm's bluster.
But then I couldn't get his words out of my mind. As customers
around the world abandon white-tablecloth restaurants, haute dining rooms have begun to feel like an endangered species. America's
most elite chefs, like Daniel Boulud, are opening beer halls, and
Thomas Keller dreams of launching a burger place. Their disciples,
meanwhile, have swapped foie gras for chicken livers at the neighborhood bistros where they cook now. Fed up with elaborate four-
hour, three-figure meals, diners aren't opting for the new
sensations that Komm reveres; they would rather go to their local
gastropub and order heritage pork belly.

After eating countless multi-starred meals around the world, I share—in spades—this aversion to the contrived *amuse-gueules*-to-petits-fours rigmarole known as fine dining. Yet there I was recently, nearly weeping into my lobster bisque at the unabashedly haute L_2O restaurant in Chicago. Why? Well, for starters, the bisque was extraordinary. A pool of decadent chestnut puree surrounding sweet, succulent nuggets of lobster meat (vacuum-cooked in a fancy gadget called a Gastrovac), it had an opulence you just can't find in a dish that's ever been described as "yummy." And in a clever conceptual gambit, chef Laurent Gras served the bisque as a nod to his classic French training—a stark contrast to the rest of his ultramodern tasting menu featuring sometimes-esoteric fish, much of it flown in from Japan. But there was more to my revelatory experience at L_2O than simply the food.

Opened last year by the burningly talented Gras (an *F&W* Best New Chef 2002), L_2O is a seriously luxe seafood restaurant, with the grand gestures of French haute cuisine carefully refined for 21st-century Chicago. "In France, three-star dining can feel like going to church," declared Gras, who himself trained with Michelin-starred chefs like Alain Ducasse before making a name for himself at San Francisco's Fifth Floor. "For American diners, you need a much more relaxing environment." For L_2O's serene open space, which references Chicago's glorious mid-century modernism, Gras opted for bare tables of expensive but understated ebony wood, exquisite pure-white German china and service with genuine warmth. In a great restaurant, details are crucial: They add up to what my boyfriend, wryly invoking composer Richard Wagner, calls a *gesamtkunstwerk*—a complete artwork on all fronts. And, from the first bite of Japanese snapper smoked over cherrywood to the ethereal salt-cod parfait, everything about the dinner reminded me of what a first-class meal can achieve. The refinement, the rigor, the setting—they deliver a fully articulated aesthetic vision that elevates the restaurant experience to something transcendent.

We left L_2O with a kind of post-opera glow, back into the real world of stress and uncertainty. I flashed back to Komm and then thought, Do I really want to see such restaurants disappear?

WHENEVER I TALK to critics and chefs, they mostly blame France for our current fine-dining phobia. The Gauls did invent haute cuisine—and the restaurant proper—but these days, their Gilded Age model is seen as an elitist, over-codified relic that doesn't reflect what we now appreciate most in a restaurant: hospitality and human connection. If you pay an arm and a leg for a meal, shouldn't it have an emotional resonance and a value that represents something more than the sum of the food and the plush upholstered chairs and the designer-clad waitstaff? No wonder French chefs are sending back their Michelin stars, while the world has firmly embraced Spain's alternative paradigm. Even at the fanciest Spanish places, the experience never feels redundant or fusty, thanks to the immediacy and excitement that Spain's avant-garde chefs have brought to their food. Dissatisfied with the label "molecular gastronomy," the country's most famous cook, Ferran Adrià, prefers to call Spain's futuristic cuisine "techno-emotional," emphasizing the sense of connection, of diners' engagement. At its very best, an avant-garde Spanish meal is a piece of whimsical, interactive performance art.

And yet. Why sink fortunes into a degustation menu from a multistarred chef, whether he's from Spain or not? Why not enjoy downsized versions of those same dishes cooked by the chef's disciple at a convivial tapas bar? Recently I suggested to Adrià that the future of Spanish cuisine might not lie with his restaurant El Bulli, located outside Barcelona, but rather with Barcelona's new wave of casual gastro-bistros—pared-down storefront restaurants where young chefs are channeling cutting-edge inspirations into earthy, affordable food.

"Oh yeah?" Adrià replied, cocking an eyebrow. "And who supplies them with their ideas?"

That was Gras's line, too. Top-end restaurants, he insisted, are like creative laboratories; from them, experimental ideas trickle down to more casual places. Case in point: my lunch in Chicago the day after my L_2O meal. The place was Urban Belly, a hipster noodle joint opened recently on a very small budget by Korean-American chef Bill Kim. After working with some of the country's fanciest chefs, like Charlie Trotter and David Bouley, Kim decided, like most of us, that four-star dining wasn't his thing. His amazing, labor-intensive seven-buck dumplings, however, tell a different story—delicate squash pouches, for instance, with intricate background accents of kaffir lime and passion fruit. Would this sophisticated layering of flavors be possible without Kim's training? No more than a $60 Zara knockoff of Prada could exist without Prada. Thanks to such trickle-down effects, the salmon on the crostini at Spur gastropub in Seattle is cooked sous vide for ultimate silkiness, while the fried chicken at Washington, D.C.'s' Art and Soul undergoes two complex stages of brining—that "simple" bird takes two days to prepare.

Intellectually, then, I conceded the need for serious restaurants. But I still wasn't sure (L_2O notwithstanding) that a dazzling dish really requires a setting to match. To expand my research, I went to Corton in New York City, which ace restaurateur Drew Nieporent recently opened to rave reviews. The minimalist, stunningly comfortable all-white room won me over the minute I walked in. Twenty-four years ago, Nieporent took the pretension out of linen-tablecloth dining with his groundbreaking Montrachet. Having recently revived the space as Corton, he has reenergized the allure of fine dining. No fan of what he calls "carpetbagger" Continental-style imports, Nieporent, like Gras, stresses the need to redefine haute cuisine for specific times and places. "I wanted my restaurant to feel right for downtown New York today," he insists. As I scanned the room, I could see what he meant about the "subliminal luxury" he was after. The banquettes' perfect curves, the flattering lighting—you can't get that carefully streamlined vision of downtown chic at a Michelin-all-star-Euro-chef franchise. And I'll certainly miss it the next time I fight for an uncomfortable stool in the sonic blast of a gastropub.

The food at Corton does its part, too, of course. Nieporent has smartly installed British-born wunderkind chef Paul Liebrandt at the stoves. Liebrandt is the kind of chef who will accent the saline twang of an oyster with the earthy crunch of toasted buckwheat and a hint of nutmeg oil—a dish with mysterious layers of flavor that unfold, evoking a dozen different taste memories. He brilliantly smokes—smokes!—the flour for pasta, which he then accentuates with dusky slices of black truffle and the barest suggestion of Gouda cheese. And he gives a classic foie gras tor-chon a haute-couture twist with a gorgeous pink gelée of hibiscus and beet. Personally, I don't need those totemic luxury food-stuffs—truffles, foie gras—but indisputably, Liebrandt's playful, sometimes challenging riffs lend a sexy frisson to the stylish room. (Imagine a killingly glamorous supper club where Miles Davis might play.) Is fine dining dead? Not at Corton. The place does al-most a hundred covers a night with a $79 three-course prix fixe.

I BEGAN TO WONDER if haute cuisine *done right* was the answer. I be-came convinced of it the following week, when I dined at Coi in San Francisco. This subtly experimental 29-seat restaurant is pow-ered by the passion, intelligence and disarming humility of chef-owner Daniel Patterson (an *F&W* Best New Chef 1997). If for Liebrandt, beet is an accessory to foie gras, Northern California chef Patterson brilliantly spotlights the actual vegetable. The beets were presented on a plate like three small M&M's. My first reac-tion—ingredient worship—gave way to the childish pleasure of popping the delicious, vibrantly colored root-vegetable "candies" into my mouth. Later I learned that the beets, topped with shiny jellies made from a blend of their roasted juices and citrus oil, took Patterson hours of intense work to prepare. "It's an idealization of a beet," he explained, then added, "And who's to say that beets can't be as valuable and exciting as caviar?" Not I.

Similar thought and exquisite craftsmanship went into the rest of my meal at Coi. A dish called Abstraction of a Garden in Win-ter combined local, seasonal root vegetables, aromatic herbs, cocoa nibs and smoked oil in a dark still life that evoked a barren cold-weather landscape. There was supernally buttery beef from a bou-tique ranch that supplies loins almost exclusively to Patterson, paired with a classic wild mushroom duxelle and gently transmo-grified roasted bone marrow. Liquefied and re-formed into its natural shape with gellan (a gelatin that can withstand heat), the marrow tasted like a delicate yet luscious distillation of offal, jolting my complacent taste buds, which had been numbed by a gastropub-pork-belly overdose.

The entire meal at Coi bridged nature and culture, past and fu-ture, while the intimate service, the idiosyncratic wine list and the tactile, slightly irregular handmade ceramics on the table all brought home the idea—again—that a great restaurant is a total environment. Best of all, like Corton and L$_2$O, Coi spoke to its time and location, delivering that crucial sense of emotional authenticity. If this is the haute cuisine of the future, we'd be mad to abandon it.

After I finished my meal I needed no reassurances, but I asked Patterson anyway why he thought fine dining mattered. "Because a great restaurant," he replied, "creates an illusion of a life where everyone is happy to see us, every need is met and everything tastes better. And we need this now more than ever." Knock off the very top level, he went on, and the next level down becomes the top. Keep "democratizing" like that, and eventually, a five-buck burrito will be the new standard.

So what would be lost then? I asked Patterson before I left.

"Risk-taking, inspiration, the sense of discovery." In short: the transformative power of cooking.

The Family Table

The Grapes of Wrath, in Three Episodes

By Steven Shaw

From eGullet.org

eGullet founder Steven Shaw was one of the Internet's
pioneer food bloggers, winning mainstream credibility with
his site fatguy.com. He later deconstructed the Manhattan
restaurant biz in his absorbing book *Turning the Tables*. And
like most food writers, he has a family story to tell.

Episode One:
The International Grape Boycott of 1969

I was born on June 10, 1969.

May 10, 1969, was International Grape Boycott Day.

During her ninth month of pregnancy, my mother was craving
grapes.

César Chávez and his National Farm Workers Association
(NFWA, later the United Farm Workers) had been supporting
boycotts of California table grapes and picketing growers since
1965. Protests aimed at the Schenley Vineyards Corporation in
1965 and Di Giorgio Fruit Corporation in 1966 had drawn national attention (not least for Chávez's legendary 25-day, 340-mile
march from Delano to Sacramento, where he arrived with 10,000
followers) and earned the admiration of Robert F. Kennedy and
Martin Luther King, Jr.

But while those early disputes had been resolved by contract
negotiations, the 1967 attempt to take on the Giumarra Vineyards

Corporation, the largest producer of table grapes in the U.S., was not going as well. Giumarra turned out to be a truculent adversary, printing fraudulent labels to disguise its grapes as produce from other companies, and using intimidation and violence against the pickets. In 1968, Chávez went on a 25-day hunger strike. The NFWA finally declared International Grape Boycott Day on May 10, 1969. The flow of grapes to the major U.S. and Canadian cities was cut off overnight.

On May 11, 1969, my father went in search of grapes. He found them to be in good supply at the Pioneer supermarket on 75th Street and Columbus Avenue (it's still there) near our apartment on the Upper West Side of Manhattan. But, the produce manager warned my father, whatever inventory the store had was all that would be available for the foreseeable future. My father sheepishly carried two brown-paper shopping bags full of grapes down the leftist gauntlet of Columbus Avenue, carefully evading detection by packing bunches of carrots on top of the grapes.

Five days later, when my mother had consumed all the grapes, my father went farther afield, first to the A&P in the West 90s and then pushing up into Harlem. Eventually, with two weeks left to go in the pregnancy, the grape supply in Manhattan had been exhausted. Near our country house upstate in Rhinebeck, New York, there were grapes aplenty being grown but the vines would not bear fruit for a couple of more months. The only grapelike fruit available that weekend in the countryside was a bag of frozen elderberries from the previous season, which my mother rejected because she thought they tasted like rhubarb.

Back in Manhattan, my father was dispatched to Chock full o'Nuts. Those who grew up elsewhere in the U.S. know of Chock full o'Nuts as a brand of canned coffee sold in supermarkets. In the New York City of the 1960s and 1970s, however, Chock full o'Nuts cafes were nearly as prevalent as Starbucks stores today. The signature food item at Chock full o'Nuts was a sandwich consisting of cream cheese on date-nut bread. The date component of the bread was raisin-like and raisins are made from grapes, so it took some of the edge off my mother's craving. My father absolutely hated making these trips to the nearby Chock full o'Nuts, which was frequented by a motley crew of drunkards, fugitives and other marginal characters. But he'd do anything for my mother.

On July 29, 1970, after five years, the protests against the California grape growers officially ended when Giumarra Vineyards Corporation agreed to Chávez's terms.

Episode Two: The Great Grape Disaster of 1978

Previously, I alluded to our country house in Rhinebeck, New York.

My parents were city kids. They both grew up in Queens. Their rural experiences were limited to beach adventures on Fire Island, where they met as teenagers while employed as counselors at the local summer camp. Like many city folk, they had a certain idealized image of rural life. One day, as married adults, they decided to bring that fantasy to life.

Two teachers' salaries couldn't buy much of a country house, even in the 1960s, so they expanded their search farther and farther north from the city (Rhinebeck is about a two-hour drive, if you're lucky). Every house they'd looked at in their price range was minuscule, but finally in Rhinebeck they stumbled across the mother lode: a rambling old house, formerly a boarding house, with 12 bedrooms, two gigantic institutional kitchens, a barn, a pond and five acres of wooded land. For cheap.

It was the Titanic of country houses. The house spent the entire time my family owned it slowly falling apart. But it gave my father the opportunity to do all the country stuff he'd fantasized about: mow the lawn on a mini-tractor, adopt two cats to battle the mice, fix the roof time and again, engage in extreme gardening and get to know our country neighbors.

My father must have had a mental checklist of country things he aspired to do, because one day he announced that we'd be picking grapes and making grape jelly. A great deal of grape jelly. Given the size of our kitchen—either kitchen—we never cooked anything small.

We drove the old blue Chrysler station wagon to a pick-your-own vineyard my father had learned about, likely through a conversation with a local cop or auto mechanic. My older sister and I were each given a metal bucket and instructed to pick grapes.

The temperature was in the 90s, the humidity was in the 100s and the ground was wet from the last night's rain. The Concord grapes we were picking had unpleasant, leathery skins and their flesh tasted as though it had been rejected by Manischewitz for being too cloying. Each time we filled a bucket, we were given another to fill. At age nine, I didn't know who César Chávez was, but I sensed I needed his help.

We arrived back at the country house with a station-wagon full of grapes. It was time to make jelly. My mother hauled out two 20-quart stockpots, which we filled with grapes after washing them in freezing-cold water that numbed my hands and then crushing them in a bowl with a potato masher. As the grapes cooked down, we added more. The stockpots seemed to be able to accommodate several times their apparent volume in grapes, and we kept them filled to the very top. The straining operation required the manpower of the Works Progress Administration.

The grapes were already sweet, but the jelly-making instructions we had called for half a cup of sugar per pound of grapes. We had no idea how many pounds of grapes we'd picked, but my father came up with a theory—right or wrong—for estimating it. He went into the pantry to get the sugar and emerged with what looked like a small garbage can full of the stuff. He poured something like 10 pounds in each stockpot, where it was hungrily absorbed by the grape juice. Pectin also came into the picture at some point.

As my mother prepared the jars for canning, my father declared that it was time for us to taste our creation. He distributed spoons full of grapey fluid to me, my sister and himself. We tasted.

We spit it out. It was inedible. It tasted overwhelmingly . . . salty. Forensic investigation by my mother revealed that the white substance my father had retrieved from the pantry was not granulated sugar but iodized salt.

Our day's labor was poured down the drain, and we stuck with Welch's from there on in.

Years later, we sold the country house to a family with seven children. When they renovated the house, they made it smaller by removing one kitchen, a dining room and several bedrooms.

Episode Three: The Hoboken Grape Operation of 2005

Our son, PJ, was born on August 17, 2005.

In her ninth month of pregnancy, my wife was craving grapes.

There must be something about the male genetic makeup in my lineage that triggers grape cravings in expecting mothers, because my wife was at that time completely unaware of my mother's past pregnancy cravings. The cravings were slightly different: my mother was partial to green seedless table grapes; my wife insisted on seeded red globe grapes exclusively. But it can't have been coincidental.

Ellen had been eating red globe grapes throughout her pregnancy, but as she came closer to term she became increasingly insistent that grapes always be on the premises. Not just any old red globe grapes would do. They couldn't be too pale (because the pale ones aren't sweet and flavorful enough) or too deep purple (overripe with tough skins), and with each passing trimester the acceptable color spectrum narrowed to a range barely discernible by the male human eye. They also had to be in about the 90th percentile of size for red globe grapes. She never expected diamonds or other finery, as many women do. All she wanted in return for bearing our firstborn son was those colossal red globe grapes.

In modern times, table grapes are grown at various latitudes, ensuring a steady supply during most of the year. But for some reason, in July of 2005, there was a break in the chain of supply of red globe grapes. There was not a red globe grape to be had in all of Manhattan, not at Fairway, not at any regular supermarket, not even at Dean & DeLuca where they always have everything.

This is not exactly the kind of news you can bring back to a woman who's nine months pregnant and craving grapes. And given that, in the summer of 2005, we were being treated to a steady diet of news stories about June and July being the hottest on record in cities across the Northeast, I felt it was my husbandly duty to locate grapes. Although I was unaware of the family history with respect to grape cravings–I only learned about that the next summer, while visiting my sister on Cape Cod–every facet of my moral education and my spiritual connection to my late father compelled me to do so.

So I started to work the phones. I called places in Queens. Nothing. The Bronx. Nothing. Finally, in a last-ditch grape-locating effort, I called Han Ah Reum, the Korean mega-market in Hackensack, New Jersey. The first three people I spoke to didn't have enough English to answer my question, but finally I got "Eddie" on the phone. "Red globe grape? Yeah I got like a million pounds just come in on a BIG TRUCK!"

I bolted out the door. It was 9:15 p.m. Han Ah Reum was to close at 10 p.m. Under ideal driving conditions, it's possible to get from our home on the Upper East Side of Manhattan, across Central Park to the West Side Highway, over the George Washington Bridge and out Route 46 to Han Ah Reum in about 35 minutes.

Ideal driving conditions, needless to say, have rarely occurred in the history of New York City. I got to the West Side Highway and there was standstill traffic, so I diverted to Riverside Drive. The upper level of the George Washington Bridge, according to 1010 WINS radio's "jam cam," had a tractor-trailer blocking one lane, so I took the lower level. The traffic circle where Route 46 intersects the Bergen Turnpike—the last obstacle on the trip—was a mess. The red and black signage of Han Ah Reum was in view across the traffic circle and I wasn't moving. I watched the minutes elapse on the dashboard clock.

I finally pulled in to a parking space in the nearly empty Han Ah Reum lot at 9:58 p.m. I barged into the store past a Korean lady scolding me, insisting that they were closing imminently. Over the loudspeaker an announcement in Korean blared, which I imagine was saying the same thing. I wheeled around the corner into the produce area, almost knocking over a display of Hello Kitty merchandise with my shopping cart, and stopped dead in my tracks.

There, before me, was a mountain of pristine red globe grapes higher than my head. They were the most gorgeous red globe grapes I'd ever seen, each one the size of a small plum and possessing the ideal garnet hue. And they were on sale. I loaded bunch after bunch of the grapes into my shopping cart and made a bee-line for the checkout. Nobody was happy about my late checkout but I was allowed to pay and leave.

By the time I got home and parked, it was 11 p.m. Ellen was sound asleep.

The next morning, a switch had flipped in Ellen's brain. She had no interest whatsoever in grapes. The grapes sat, unconsumed, filling most of the available space in the refrigerator for several days until she announced that she would no longer be eating grapes.

For the next week, anybody visiting our apartment was required to take home a pound of grapes.

To be continued . . .

PICKY-PICKY

By Matthew Amster-Burton
From *Hungry Monkey*

As a stay-at-home dad with adventurous appetites and culinary
chops, Seattle food writer Amster-Burton saw a unique
opportunity to form his toddler daughter's palate—and to blog
proudly about it on his Web site, www.rootsandgrub.com. Ah, the
best-laid plans . . .

When Iris was about nine months old, I bragged that she
showed signs of being an adventurous eater. She
packed away pad Thai and spicy enchiladas, spinach and Brussels
sprouts. I did my best to imply that this was because of my skills in
the kitchen and my no-compromises approach to child-feeding.

The nonparents who heard my boasts were impressed. The parents were not, because they knew a secret: All two-year-olds are
pickier than all one-year-olds, and three-year-olds are even worse.
The average one-year-old is as discriminating as a goat, still drunk
on the knowledge that there is a whole class of things she can put
into her mouth without her parents screaming and yanking them
back out.

Don't believe me? Listen to this. Just before Iris turned two, we
took a family trip to Vancouver, British Columbia, and had dinner
at Vij's Rangoli, an incredible Indian restaurant. We ordered spicy
salmon cakes, pork curry, and vegetable pakoras. Iris gobbled
everything with gusto.

We had so much fun in Vancouver that we went back a year
later and rented an apartment with a kitchen. I got enough takeout
from Rangoli for three meals. There were chickpea curries, meat

curries, spicy green beans, and dal. This, with basmati rice, was our Christmas dinner. I'd been looking forward to it for a year. Iris, now almost three, ate the rice and possibly half a chunk of pork.

This progression from omnivorous to "Ewww!" was not at all what I expected. I figured most kids started out picky and steadily learned to like new foods. I didn't realize Iris would gobble a huge plate of Brussels sprouts one day and then decide two days later that Brussels sprouts were grown in Hell and sent up via dumb-waiter to torment her.

It's hard not to take this personally, since Brussels sprouts are my favorite vegetable and I write about food for a living. There are, no doubt, some three-year-olds who are truly adventurous eaters. But I haven't met any. Children of chefs? Hardly. I talked to one ac-claimed Seattle chef who admitted that his five-year-old son likes to eat Trader Joe's frozen cheese pizza, *still frozen.* Another chef said of his three-year-old, "Once in a while we can get him to eat a lit-tle bit of broccoli, but it's pretty hit and miss right now." The chef with the young broccoliphobe makes some of the best vegetable dishes in town. We took Iris to his restaurant one night, and while Laurie and I moaned over a creamy Swiss chard gratin, Iris ate some noodles and a bunch of chocolate madeleines.

Kids love ketchup, right? Not all kids. At age two, Iris suddenly stopped liking all condiments other than soy sauce—even syrup—and has only partially recovered. I must have passed down an anti-condiment gene, because the same thing happened to me at around the same age. I ate plain burgers for many years. Plain as in bun, meat, bun. I've come around, sort of: instead of ketchup or mustard, I prefer A1, barbecue, or HP sauce. (HP sauce is really just the English version of A1, but don't tell the English I said that.) There's something awfully toddlerish about this preference. Down with your mainstream condiments! Give me extremely similar condiments with different names! I'm in charge of this burger, not some parent or corporate goon.

One of my clearest memories from the early 1980s is of a Saturday-morning public service ad starring a tiny lifeguard who rescues a po-tato from drowning in too much sour cream and sings a jingle entitled "Don't Drown Your Food." Really, there was a TV commercial warning kids not to overuse condiments. Maybe I wasn't picky, just overly influenced by TV.

When I saw Iris slipping down the same long, lonely road I once traveled, I thought maybe I could fend off her condimento-phobia by setting her loose on a choice of sauces. She was excited about HP sauce for about a week but has taken her burgers plain since then, disassembling them and eating the meat and bun sepa-rately. (I'm pretty sure this is how Takeru Kobayashi, the tiny Japanese guy who can eat fifty-three hot dogs in twelve minutes, eats *his* burgers.) Lately, we're seeing signs of progress: sometimes Iris requests a dot of sauce on her plate and eats it with her finger, making sure that none of it defiles the rest of the food. And the other day at a restaurant, I saw her dip her French fry in ketchup. She looked around to make sure no one was watching, extended her tongue, licked a tiny dot of ketchup, and smiled.

HERE'S THE BIG QUESTION: What should I do about this?

Not a month goes by without an article about picky eating in one of the glossy parenting magazines. The advice hasn't changed since the days of canned peas:

1. Present new foods alongside old favorites.

2. Sneak vegetables into pasta sauce or other foods.

3. Threaten to withhold dessert.

4. Be persistent: It may take ten or twelve tries before they learn to like a new food. (Every time someone mentions this, the number seems to change; I've seen it as seven tries, fifteen tries. I haven't yet seen "seven hundred tries," but that's about how many times we've served Iris Brussels sprouts.)

Sometimes I wonder whether anyone associated with those mag-azines even has kids, because none of these things works. There is a solution to picky eating, but you may not like it: it's recognizing that it isn't a problem. Kids are not dropping dead of scurvy. Oh, I know what they say next: lifelong eating habits are formed at a young age.

As I heard one mom (Georgia Orcutt, author of *How to Feed a Teenage Boy*) say on the radio, "When they turn twenty, they're not suddenly going to discover spinach and Brussels sprouts."

I discovered Brussels sprouts at a restaurant in my twenties and have been cooking them once a week ever since. For that matter, think of all the newly minted college vegetarians who will discover all-you-can-eat salad at the dining hall this fall.

The adult palate isn't simply made up of childhood preferences that have hardened into prejudices. I didn't grow up eating sushi. Once I was forced to try it on a fourth-grade field trip and almost puked. (Yes, I went to a school so upper-crusty that it force-fed sushi to kids.)

Then, when I was in my early twenties, I noticed many of my friends speaking in near sexual terms about their experiences with a platter of raw fish. I got myself invited along on a sushi excursion and was hooked (sorry) immediately. Now I take Iris to a place where you pick your sushi from a conveyor belt. I choose the salmon skin roll, the mackerel, and the spicy tuna, while Iris takes the potstickers and the cream puff.

I didn't start liking sushi because I was won over by the ocean-fresh flavors. It was because I was won over by the idea, and I had to mull it over for a while before I worked up the guts to give it another try. I already knew I was going to like it before I tasted it. (Another possibility is that the fourth grade sushi gave me a brain parasite that slowly reprogrammed me into a sushi lover.)

Another way of saying this is, yeah, it's possible to know you won't like something when you haven't even tried it. The MIT professor Dan Ariely even performed an ingenious experiment that confirms this.

For the study, Ariely and his colleagues used a foodstuff popular among college students: beer. They had no trouble recruiting subjects. The subjects tasted two beers: one glass of Sam Adams and one of "MIT Brew," which was just Sam Adams adulterated with a few drops of balsamic vinegar.

Most subjects who were not told about the secret ingredient liked the MIT Brew better than the regular. When subjects were told about the vinegar before drinking, they thought the vinegar-spiked brew was gross. No surprise there.

But when subjects were told about the vinegar after drinking, few changed their minds about it. That is, they said they still liked the MIT Brew—who cares if it's made with vinegar?—and would drink it again.

I don't have to explain how this generalizes to kids and new foods, because Ariely's paper did it for me:

> Our mothers often used creative labeling to trick us into eating something they knew we would otherwise oppose (e.g., by calling crab cakes "sea hamburgers"). They knew such deception was required to gain our consent, but that they need not maintain the lie *after* we had consumed the foods, and would often debrief us afterward, with smug satisfaction ("By the way, son, in case you were wondering, 'sea' means 'crab.'")

Another way to put this: if you think you're not going to like a new food, that's a self-fulfilling prophecy. In my career as a food critic, I've had a few experiences where I thought I would like something and didn't (sea urchin comes to mind, although I intend to give it a few more chances), but I can't recall ever thinking I wasn't going to like something and then being pleasantly surprised. Seriously, have you ever seen a kid whine because he didn't want to try broccoli, then take a bite and say, "Hey, this is pretty good!" Have you ever seen the Easter Bunny? Cold fusion?

Iris knows that tastes change over time, or at least she knows how to placate me. When I served salmon for dinner one night, Iris pushed hers around on the plate and sighed, "Iris *can't* like that." She came around on salmon and now eats tons of it, which is a good thing, because otherwise the Seattle authorities were going to take her into custody. Another time, Iris peered into a bowl of tamarind dipping sauce and said, "That looks *good*. And I don't want any." Recently she told me, "When I'm bigger, I'm going to like spicy foods. Tomatillo sauce, pickled jalapeños . . . what else am I going to like?"

Like most four-year-olds, Iris spends a mind-boggling amount of time pretending to do things—perform surgery, cook dinner, drive a truck. (For a while, she was so into the truck-driving idea that when she was accepted to preschool and I told her, "Iris, you're going to go to school this fall!" she replied, "Truck-driving school?") And in her imagination, she eats plenty of things that would never actually pass her lips—even pickled jalapeños. She does this even when she's playing alone in her room and thinks I'm not listening.

I'm sure it would be possible to get Iris to choke down some vegetables through a regime of bribes, but that would be like insisting that she enjoy all my favorite bands. I admit it—it was a thrill when Iris gorged herself on that plate of Brussels sprouts. I had a similar shiver of victory when she became obsessed with the indie rocker John Vanderslice. But you can't hang your happiness on this kind of rare event. Sure enough, Brussels sprouts were just a phase, and while Iris can still handle indie rock, she prefers show tunes and songs like "Here We Go Round the Mulberry Bush" as performed by some kids who sound like eunuchs on Zoloft. (Now she's into the Shins. Is that cool or uncool?)

How we handle picky eating is so simple that I call it the Second Rule of Baby Food (not that I invented this one, either; Ellyn Satter calls it "the division of responsibility"). The rule is, when I put the food down in front of Iris, my job is done. I don't also hold myself responsible for making sure it gets into her mouth—no cajoling, no airplane game. I have been known to say things like, "Iris, this kale is awesome," but I say that to everyone.

The Second Rule is appealingly simple but hard to implement in practice. I find it difficult to keep my mouth shut, not because I'm worried about Iris's nutrition, but because I'm like chef Dan Barber of Blue Hill in New York.

That is, like Barber, I have my own farm upstate where I . . . Wait, that's not it. Like Barber, when I cook for someone, I want to see them eat with gusto, clean their plate, wipe the plate with a piece of bread or their finger to get every last morsel, unsnap their pants, and sigh contentedly. Or, as he puts it:

Clean plates don't lie. That's what I say when waiters at my restaurant, Blue Hill, ask me why I insist on examining every plate that returns to the kitchen with the slightest bit of food on it. The waiters think I'm intrusive. They also think I'm neurotic and insecure, but like most neurotic and insecure chefs, I don't quite agree. I tell them that a clean plate is proof of a perfect meal.

Iris offers a different indication of a perfect meal. She winks one eye and gives a thumbs-up. I'm not sure where she learned this. But I'll take it.

WATCHING IRIS pull all of the soft crumb out of her bread for dinner one night, I wondered: Could she possibly be getting all the nutrients she needs from what appears to be a very limited diet?

I relaxed after reading a 2000 article entitled *Revisiting the Picky Eater Phenomenon: Neophobic Behaviors of Young Children*. As you might guess, this article did not appear in *Parenting* magazine; it was in the *Journal of the American College of Nutrition*. I only read it for the articles.

The authors, who are professors of nutrition at the University of Tennessee, followed seventy children from ages two to seven. Based on questionnaires filled out by the children's mothers, researchers divided the kids into two groups: picky and nonpicky. (Even the "nonpicky" kids were still pickier than most one-year-olds or adults, I'd wager.) Then they did a long-term analysis of the children's diets. The moms were right: The picky eaters ate a smaller variety of foods and were much more resistant to trying new foods. Some of the phrases used by the mothers of picky eaters were:

- "Eats maybe ten things; all others she finds repulsive."

- "Won't eat anything green."

- "'Mommy, I don't like it'—she hasn't even tried it!"

Presumably this sounds familiar. But there's a punch line. A nutritional analysis found that the picky eaters got just as many nutrients from their diet as the nonpicky eaters, and there was no difference in height and weight between the two groups. In other words, picky eating may be annoying, but it's not a medical problem.

Now, forget the academics. For a personal perspective, I called up one of the world's foremost experts on picky eating: my mother, Judy Amster, who raised three exceedingly picky boys.

"You did all the classic things," Mom sighed. "You didn't like anything, and you had no appetite. And that went on for a long time."

So what *did* I eat?

"You ate dry Cheerios without milk. You ate macaroni and cheese, and you ate pizza. But everything had to be separate. We started using those portioned-out plastic dishes. And you really, really didn't ever want to try anything new. One of the only things that I could guarantee you would eat was cut up white meat chicken, in small pieces, not touching anything."

This went on for *seven years*, from age three to ten. (Neophobic behaviors of young children, indeed.) "It was torture sending lunch to school for you," said Mom. "By then, the only things that you would eat besides cookies, which I did put in because I wanted you to not fall down starving, was a PB&J on white bread, cut in half vertically. Then you would take the sandwich apart, take one half-circle bite in each of them and put them back together, and not eat anything else because you didn't want to spoil the circle."

Apparently I was not just picky, but borderline OCD. So what broke the cycle? Yep, old-fashioned peer pressure. In fourth grade, I started at a new school and made a new friend, Alex, whose mother was Japanese. "When you went home with him for dinner," Mom remembered, "you came home every time and said, 'How come we never have fish?' And I would say, 'Matthew, you threatened to move out if I brought fish into the house.' 'How come you never make curry?' 'Matthew, you don't want anything touching, no sauces, no gravies.' This went on with about twelve different things."

Alex and his family also took me out to a (sadly defunct) Chinese restaurant in Portland called Potstickers & Sizzling Rice Soup. "And you came home and asked about potstickers, and I said, 'Matthew, when we've taken you to a Chinese restaurant, the only thing you would eat was rice.'"

See, your kid isn't as bad as I was. And just like the kids in the study, I was completely normal in terms of growth. I did not collapse on the playground. And now I'll eat *anything*. Well, not tuna salad or egg salad, because those things are nasty. But anything else.

So PICKY EATING isn't a health problem. Big deal. It's still not a whole lot of fun to have dinner with a family member who'd rather throw peas than eat them. I don't want to soft-pedal this. I'm frequently frustrated when I want to make something for dinner that is hard to adapt to Iris's palate. The most annoying example is Thai curry. I love Thai curry and even have one of those green Thai mortar and pestles, as seen on Jamie Oliver's show, for making curry pastes. But the most important ingredient in Thai curry is lots of chiles. There's no way to make a good Thai curry that isn't spicy, and Iris isn't into spicy these days. So for now, I mostly eat Thai curry when I take myself out for lunch.

At the same time, I've learned to savor the rare appearances of Future Iris, the one who is partial to tomatillo sauce and other strange foods.

One night I made roasted stuffed trout for dinner. "And will the trout get very, very big when you stuff it?" Iris asked. She helped me stuff the trout with fennel, bacon, red onion, and fresh herbs.

Stuffed trout is easier to make than it is to eat, because you want to just cut off a hunk with stuffing sandwiched between two pieces of boneless fish, but there are many bones in the way of this noble intention. For this reason and because Iris is frequently more enthusiastic about cooking than eating, I figured she would forget about the trout by the time it hit the table and concentrate on the hash browns I served with it.

Wrong. Iris ate the fish, the bacon, the vegetables, the potatoes, and even, well . . .

To say that she was undeterred by the fact that the fish's head was there on the platter would be an understatement. "There's the head!" she exclaimed. I found a piece of cheek meat and ate it, and Iris said, "I want to eat some cheek."

I said okay and rooted around for another piece. "There's some cheek," Iris said, pointing.

"No, that's the eyeball."

"I want to eat the eyeball."

"Seriously?"

"Yes." She took a bite. "It's gooey! Why is it gooey?"

"Eyeballs are just like that," said Laurie.

Iris thought about this, then requested and ate *the other eyeball*.

IN CASE YOU were wondering why there are no soup recipes in this book . . .

It's November. A week ago, Laurie sent me to the store with a sacred mission: bring back half a spiral-sliced ham. I agreed to lug home the nine-pound hunk of pork even though I'm not so crazy about ham, because I had a plan. First, though, we had to make it through the week. I made baked farfalle pasta with cauliflower and diced ham. Ham and eggs. Ham with grits and kale. Laurie and Iris took ham sandwiches to work and school, respectively.

Today, Saturday, I commandeered the remainder of the ham and the bone and made a rich ham stock. After a couple hours of simmering, the meat practically shredded itself, and the broth was perfectly rich, smoky, and salty. I cooked a bag of split peas in the ham stock and added some sautéed vegetables, potatoes, the shredded ham, and a dash of sherry vinegar. I lifted the spoon to my lips and tasted. It was so good I barely noticed that it was ham for dinner, again. Beaming, I set the soup on the table.

"Didn't I tell you I hate soup?" said Iris.

———— ❧ ————

Roasted Trout with Fennel, Onion, and Cilantro
45 minutes
Little Fingers: Let them stuff!

Trout range in size from about 6 to 16 ounces. That's a big range. Buy a second fish if necessary. As for the vegetables, I find I want to eat far more of them than can fit inside a fish, so I serve extra on the side. I also found that I prefer bacon on the side rather than in the stuffing, so by all means crisp up a couple of slices and use the rendered fat for cooking. Bacon as a side dish with dinner is underrated, don't you think?

You may find rainbow or golden rainbow trout at your market; if you have a choice, I recommend the rainbow, since it usually costs less and isn't artificially colored. Either fish will work well in this recipe; they taste the same.

Serves 2 to 3

1 tablespoon bacon grease, lard, or butter
1 large bulb fennel, cored and sliced
1 small onion, sliced
salt and pepper
2 tablespoons minced cilantro
1 large farmed trout (12 to 16 ounces)
lime wedges for serving

1. Preheat the oven to 450°F. Heat the bacon grease in a large skillet over medium heat until shimmering. Add the fennel and onion, sprinkle with salt, and cook until nicely browned and tender, 8 to 10 minutes. Transfer to a bowl, season with pepper and additional salt to taste, and stir in the cilantro.

2. Place the trout on a greased and foil-lined baking sheet. Stuff the belly of the trout generously with the vegetable mixture. Roast 15 to 20 minutes, until just opaque throughout (check the thick part along the back of the fish). Bring the whole fish to the table, peel back the skin, and serve chunks of fish topped with some of the stuffing and a generous squeeze of lime juice.

Beating Eggs

By Pete Wells

From the *New York Times Magazine*

What better dad to take over in the kitchen than *New York Times* food editor Pete Wells? In his "Cooking With Dexter" columns in the *Times* Sunday magazine section, Wells confirms what a surprising experience cooking with and for kids can be.

I confess that I looked askance at the food allergies that seem to plague every classroom these days—where did they all come from?—until doctors told us that my son Dexter had a whole raft of them. He was a year old when we learned he would have to avoid tuna, clams and shrimp. And onions. And garlic. Peanuts, almonds, walnuts and cashews. Sesame and poppy seeds. Egg whites, chickpeas and lentils. Soybeans and anything containing soy, which by itself put about half the supermarket off limits.

The list of banned ingredients was so extensive that I had visions of Dexter becoming some kind of boy in the plastic bubble, living in isolation within a Habitrail network of peanut-free tubes. My wife and I understood almost right away that we wanted to teach Dexter not to eat food that could kill him, without teaching him to be afraid of food. I came to think of this as the birthday-party dilemma: Can a toddler have fun at a birthday party when his parents keep snatching away the cake?

Although certain foods were now deadly enemies, I didn't want our family to treat them that way. From the moment they began to eat from a spoon, I tried to teach both our boys to see food as a

pleasure. As the baby books prescribe, my wife and I would introduce the child to one new ingredient at a time and stick with it for
a few days. Each time I felt like a game-show host, opening a door
to reveal a fabulous prize. You've won a whole week of glamorous—
papaya!

The blotches and bumps started appearing on Dexter's skin at
about 9 months. Tiny ovals rose on his chest when he ate a bowl of
cottage cheese. Eating fish with his fingers, he rubbed his neck,
and minutes later the spot simmered with pink and white hives.

The rashes came on fast and usually went just as quickly. We
stopped feeding him the problem ingredients and didn't worry all
that much until a plate of scrambled eggs gave him a reaction
worse than anything we had seen before. He sneezed, scrubbed at
his nose and coughed. His skin went gray. He slumped against us
listlessly while we furiously dialed for a doctor.

A teaspoon of antihistamine brought Dexter back to normal
within minutes. It took me and my wife a lot longer. We went to
one allergist after another, armed with question upon question. We
showed his babysitters how to give him a shot of epinephrine. In
restaurants we asked for lists of ingredients, and then asked again to
be sure: Could there be sesame seeds in the bread crumbs? Are the
potatoes fried in peanut oil? The servers almost never knew, but
most tried to find out. At least at home, we could know for sure.
And as the main cook in the house, I learned to make do without
some of the things I had always relied on.

The strange thing was how easy it was. Even eggs, which I had
always considered indispensable, turned out in many cases to be
merely optional. Ground meat, for instance, is sticky enough to
cling together and form a lovely meatball without any help from
an egg, particularly if you bake the meatballs instead of frying
them. Custard desserts were out of the question, but not puddings
thickened with cornstarch, or panna cotta, which is set with gelatin. Eggless French toast isn't French toast, but with some minor
fiddling, I was able to make tender pancakes (very popular) and
crisp waffles.

For tips on the minor fiddling, I will always be grateful to my
unlikely allies, the vegans. Even now, it's hard for me to believe
this. I've eaten monkey-brain pâté and fried crickets and moose

salami and, in a sushi bar, some leggy creature via the Tsukiji fish market in Tokyo that looked less like a fish than a centipede. I have also eaten fly eggs. Vegans—and in this they are certainly not alone—won't touch fly eggs. Most of them won't eat honey, because it is made by the sweat of an animal's brow and because taking it might harm the colony of bees that produced it. I regard vegans with wonder, and they would probably regard me with horror. But I want to write this in 40-foot letters in the sky: Vegans have made amazing discoveries in the field of eggless baking.

Thanks to a cookbook called *Vegan Cupcakes Take Over the World*, by Isa Chandra Moskowitz and Terry Hope Romero, our house has been filled with dairy- and egg-free frosted cupcakes. Moskowitz, in an interview with the *New York Times*, said, "Eggs are the big lie in baking." On her Web site, the Post Punk Kitchen, she concedes that eggs give baked goods structure and leavening. "However," she writes, "like a bad boyfriend, they can be replaced, and with pleasing results."

Baking soda and baking powder mixed with a little vinegar can take over the egg's leavening job, except in recipes that rely on beaten egg whites. (I doubt that even the most ingenious vegan baker has figured out angel food cake.) Structure is a harder problem to solve. In the oven, the egg proteins in a batter firm up, holding the cake together. Without those proteins, larger cakes rarely stay in one piece.

I recently talked to Christi Craig of Wauwatosa, Wis., another parent who has been searching for a good egg-free recipe for a classic American birthday cake. Her 7-year-old son, Willie Hutchinson, is allergic to nuts and eggs, and so she has tried water-based recipes that probably date from the Depression and a powdered-egg substitute, which she adds to Betty Crocker mix in place of the three eggs called for on the back of the box. This cake looks and tastes good, she said, but like most eggless cakes, it has a tendency to fall apart. She has become expert at patching over rough spots with icing and, when necessary, plastic action figures.

"I sort of walk a dangerous line," she said. "The cake is pretty enough that if we eat it fast enough, nobody notices."

Eggless cupcakes, because they are smaller, can triumph over their structural weakness.

Moskowitz and Romero might not like to hear it, but I've un-done some of their best work, substituting buttermilk for rice milk, for example. I don't mess with their chocolate cupcakes, though, because they're perfect in their vegan form, moist and sweet and dark with cocoa. One year on my wife's birthday we served them to a friend who has serious problems with lactose, a vegan and Dexter.

The three of them sat and compared their dietary restrictions while licking frosting off their fingers. If Dexter was really in a bubble, at least the company was good. And so were the cupcakes.

Chocolate Cupcakes for Almost Everybody

For the cupcakes:
1 cup soy or rice milk
1 teaspoon vinegar
¾ cup sugar
⅓ cup vegetable oil
1 ½ teaspoons vanilla extract
1 cup flour
⅓ cup cocoa powder
¾ teaspoon baking soda
½ teaspoon baking powder
¼ teaspoon salt
   For the chocolate glaze:
1 cup confectioners' sugar
¼ cup cocoa powder, sifted
3 tablespoons soy or rice milk
Chocolate sprinkles (optional).

1. Preheat the oven to 350° and prepare a dozen muffin cups—either outfit a muffin pan with paper or foil liners, or use a baking sheet and set out 12 paper liners nested inside foil liners, or else use silicone muffin cups.

2. In a large mixing bowl, stir together the soy or rice milk, vinegar, sugar, vegetable oil and vanilla extract. In an-other bowl, stir together the flour, cocoa powder, baking

soda, baking powder and salt. Sift the dry ingredients into the wet ingredients, pausing two or three times to stir, and keep stirring until all the large lumps are gone.

3. Pour the batter into the cupcake liners until they are about two-thirds full. Bake until a toothpick inserted into the center comes out clean, about 20 minutes. Cool on a wire rack.

4. When cool, whisk the chocolate glaze ingredients until smooth and spread the glaze on the cupcakes. If you choose, top with sprinkles. Makes 12 cupcakes. Adapted from *Vegan Cupcakes Take Over the World*, by Isa Chandra Moskowitz and Terry Hope Romero.

Note: They're called Chocolate Cupcakes for Almost Everybody because they contain flour, which won't work for celiacs.

Getting to Know Him

By Francis Lam

From *Gourmet*

A CIA-trained chef with a truly gifted prose style, Francis Lam
seems to be New York's current foodie It Guy, judging from
the number of times his gourmet.com posts are quoted on
other people's blog sites. Perhaps, this essay suggests, he can
thank the foodie genes he inherited.

My grandfather died in a place that doesn't exist. He
died in a place in my memory, a Hong Kong that was,
for a boy from the New Jersey suburbs, a pinball machine of
noises, colors, and flavors. I loved my childhood summers there. I
remember walking through honey-thick humidity to my favorite
noodle shops, where the steaming pots and the steamy air gave resonance to the wontons, dumplings whose name literally means
"swallowing clouds." I remember my grandfather taking me to the
landmark restaurant Fook Lam Moon, where waiters would greet
him by name, where there was never a menu but instead conversation and a negotiation about freshness, where he would squeeze
my arm and ask what I wanted to eat.

When people ask me how I got so into food, I think of those
summers. I think of my grandfather, about how he came up so
poor he couldn't afford to have his children live with him, but
when he finally made his fortune, he dedicated it to eating and
sharing food. My parents used to put me on his bony knee and tell
him about my good grades in school, but it was at the table where
I most felt his pride, as he watched my small, clumsy hands aiming

chopsticks at the particularly prized morsels, the things he could once only dream of being able to provide. "This one," he would declare, "knows how to eat." It sounded like nothing could be more important.

He died almost 15 years ago, well before he could see his hungriest grandson turn his appetite into something approaching a respectable career. So, these many years later, I find myself in Hong Kong and mainland China, going to places I remember him taking me to, going to places I only remember hearing about, looking to find something about him, about his love of food that came down to me. Great-Uncle Nine, the last of my grandfather's brothers, offered to be a guide. He holds a place of respect in my family, not just because of his seniority, but also because he has an almost supernatural palate. "I've seen him eat a piece of fish and tell how long it was out of the water," my father whispered to me while glancing surreptitiously at him, tiny and unassuming, at the other end of the table. "He can tell if a chicken's ever been in a refrigerator."

Great-Uncle Nine and his wife carry their own bottle of soy sauce around town. I learned this while having dim sum with them at the Renaissance Harbour View Hotel, when she pulled out scissors from her purse to trim rice-noodle rolls that hadn't been cut to the appropriate size. "How can you enjoy them if they crowd your mouth?" Great-Uncle Nine asked as he uncapped his sauce. The night before, he had asked our waiter to scoop our rice from a particular place in the pot. This is who I'm descended from.

His amazing sensitivity and memory for flavors mean that, in our world of compromise, Great-Uncle Nine frowns through most of his meals and treats the declining quality of chicken as an existential crisis. But one morning during my visit, even he had occasion to smile at a dish of pepper-crusted smoked beef tongue. We spun the lazy Susan around at an alarming speed, throwing the kick-ass scent of Texas barbecue into the otherwise refined air of the room. My mother—20 years and counting of vegetarianism under her belt—turned to me and said, "Son, get a piece of that and wave it under my nose." This is who raised me.

Despite the elation brought on by a truly good smoked tongue, Great-Uncle Nine frowned when I suggested we go to Fook Lam Moon. "Your grandfather isn't here," he said. "They don't know us there anymore." But I protested that a good restaurant should be a good restaurant no matter who you are, and he relented.

Although it has undergone a sleek, angular makeover, I instantly recognized the elevator banks where hostesses used to lead us, radioing upstairs that Mr. Lam was here. I remembered how tall they seemed, how beautiful in their silk, elegant and gracious as they held the doors open, tipping their heads slightly.

A woman behind a host stand pointed to the elevators and told us which button to press. Upstairs, we walked past shelves of extraordinary wines labeled with the names of regulars, a roll call of the Hong Kong elite. We ordered some of the classics by memory, and I was amazed at the crackling, paper-thin skinned suckling pig: sweet fat dripping down pencil-width ribs. But when the chicken came out abused by the fryer and the lotus-infused rice tasted of little other than rice, I couldn't help but wear the disappointed face Great-Uncle Nine was too polite to make. I watched servers dote over a nearby table of men in suits and wondered: Was it the place that had changed or our place in it? Was the culture of this city still fixated on food, or had I inherited an obsession that was now merely personal?

"Maybe you should see an old street market, to see how things used to be," my father suggested, in part to be helpful, and in part, I think, just to cheer me up. I had always thought of my grandfather as being old, and even before he passed I regretted not spending enough time with him, not getting to know him and the world he lived in. Now, trying to do that a decade and a half too late, I realize that my father is an old man, too. I love walking around this city with him, having him guide me. I love how he knows the place and when to turn, curbing my tendency to find and lead. I feel like a kid, led by a grown-up. I feel like his son. I feel like the name my parents have called me my entire life, "Jai Jai," which means "little boy."

He might have felt it, too. As we walked down Hennessy Road, he spotted a tram station and turned to me as if by an instinct he hadn't exercised in decades, asking, "Wanna take the trolley car? We can sit upstairs so you can see out the window." As if he, too, misremembered his son as a wide-eyed three-year-old.

Graham Street's name in Cantonese is Ga Hahm, which sounds a lot like "Make it saltier," and it's a raucous old-line street market, the pavement sliced with water from the fishmongers and covered in bruised and trampled-on vegetables.

My father and I stood next to a rickety stall that looked as if it were made of magazine covers. Under them, a woman sold baskets and baskets of eggs from Thailand, Holland, America, Beijing, Germany. We watched a fishmonger across the way clean eels with a cleaver as big and thick as a novel. He pinned them down with a pair of awls at either end, and I heard the crackle of eel bones breaking as he slid his blade through. I heard the deep thud when he jammed his knife into his heavy board, standing it up at the ready for his next eel.

"Hello! Hello!" the egg lady called. "What are you doing?"

"Watching," I said.

"Well, watch somewhere else. We're trying to do business here."

In the middle of the market, there is an ancient store, the Wing Woo, in a building 130 years old and looking like it. Bags of noodles hang from the ceiling, bumping into bare lightbulbs when the wind blows. Jars of herbs share space with a feather duster and tilting bags of mushrooms—it's the kind of place where everything leans into everything else. Wooden planks identify wavy piles of rice like grave markers, and bottles of ancient Worcestershire sauce are behind glass cabinets, nearly obscured by cans of creamed corn. The owners weigh each purchase carefully in a rusty iron balance scale, their ingots strewn haphazardly across their work area.

As I walked around the market, I marveled at how something so resolutely unmodern could coexist with gleaming skyscrapers here in Central, the Wall Street of Hong Kong. Then I remembered an iconic tourist poster of those skyscrapers standing behind an ancient Chinese junk floating in the harbor: This city is a meeting place of the very old and the very new. It is so small, so packed together, that even in Central people have to live, and people have to shop for food. Beneath glass and steel, there still has to be an earthy underbelly. I held this thought for weeks, buoyed by it. Later, I would hear that the market is slated for demolition. Spectacular tensions between the old and the new tend to have a way of resolving themselves, I guess.

Maybe I was just afflicted with a bout of romantic nostalgia for a place I never really knew. But when Great-Uncle Nine led us into mainland China, even I didn't know how to romanticize our family's ancestral village. When my great-grandfather left to find work a century ago, it was a tiny village tilling lean soil that was never good for much more than a little bit of rice and a few sweet potatoes. It's still an absolute nowhere, but now a nowhere that is home to over 100,000 and a shoe factory that makes its own clouds. On the way, passing through the city of Guangzhou, Great-Uncle Nine talked about being there when the Nationalist army beat a retreat from Mao's Communists, running for their lives and threatening to gun down anyone in their way. We drove by a once grand hotel, where he had seen a piece of shrapnel the size of a man shatter the street, just a few feet from the crowded lobby. I grew solemn, imagining the terror, when he said, "And over there, there used to be this place that had the most delicious squab."

A day later, we were in Zhishan. The sky was a stern gray. The streets felt like they were made of dust. I saw a chicken break out of its cage, running from its owner across a parking lot.

We went to the five-story lookout tower my great-grandfather helped build, with gun turrets at the corners to protect the village from bandits. The tower was to double as our family home, but he never found it in himself to move back. It has been empty, but for a few photographs on the walls, for all this time. Its caretakers greeted us with warmth and tangerines. We walked, our shoes clacking on the hard floors, echoing through the boxy rooms. A bed here, a pair of ancient ebony chairs there; a small shrine to those passed away—portraits of my great-grandfather, his wife, his concubine; a photo of my grandfather, tinier than I ever remembered.

On the roof of the tower, I looked out to the land. There were mountains, hills really, covered with abnormally ordered trees. They were stripped bare, someone told me, and replanted to prevent fires. I tried to imagine the taller buildings—apartments, factories—gone, leaving the squat clay-shingled homes. I tried to place myself here, in this village, in this house without ghosts. I couldn't. Maybe it's because my family doesn't actually have people here, only a haphazard legacy of forgotten photographs. "I don't know what to do with this," I thought.

I do know what to do, though, with the bag of rice I brought home from there, the rice of my people. At the border, going back into Hong Kong, I was stopped by an incredulous customs officer; I guess it made for an alarming X-ray. "You're carrying twenty-five pounds of rice?" she asked. "I went to my old village. . . ." I began to explain. "Oh," she said. She waved me through.

An Uncalculating Science

By Molly Wizenberg

From *A Homemade Life*

Seattle writer Molly Wizenberg may have landed her book
contract due to the success of her award-winning blog
orangette.com, but as you read this funny, lively, tender
account of the making of a food writer, it's clear her family
history lies behind it all.

Every night, when he came home from work, my father
went to the kitchen. First, to set the mood, he'd take off
his suit jacket and pour himself a Scotch. Then he'd while away a
few minutes at the counter, his belly pressed against the drawer
pulls, leafing through the day's mail. Then, fully readied, he'd open
the refrigerator and, easing into action, began the final stage of the
day, dinner. That was where he relaxed: in the kitchen, in the space
between the refrigerator and the stove. Sometimes he would scour
the cookbook shelf, looking for ideas, but mainly he would move
by feel and by taste—stewing, sautéing, melding this and that, and
much to my consternation, hardly ever keeping note of what he'd
done. I can only think of a handful of recipes that he ever wrote
down in their entirety, his potato salad being one of them. (I'm
pretty sure he knew it was his best shot at immortality.) His experiments were many, and most of them were fruitful, but his was an
uncalculating science. His cooking was personal, improvised, and
maddeningly ephemeral.

Burg was never a late sleeper. Most weekend mornings, he
would get up early to cruise the garage sales in his khakis and top-
siders. He had a good eye for secondhand shopping, and with few

exceptions (like the kitchen scale that zeroed at 700 grams and still sits, unused, in my closet) he usually did us proud. Over the years, he brought home old leather suitcases embossed with loopy initials, oil paintings in gilt frames, coffee grinders, and silver candy dishes. He even found a few vintage lapel pins shaped like ladybugs or flowers or delicate little spiders, which always made my mother swoon. Then, at mid-morning, he sat down with me, and we ate breakfast.

Sometimes he made omelets, and sometimes he scrambled eggs. But most of the time, our breakfasts tended toward the sort of thing that could be doused in maple syrup, such as pancakes or French toast. From an early age, I was schooled in the doctrine of pure maple syrup. As a native Canadian and former East Coaster, my father would have nothing else. His chosen brand came in a round-bellied plastic jug the color of Silly Putty and had a permanent home in the door of our refrigerator, right next to the jar of horseradish. It would loll from side to side whenever we opened the door, dropping crusty bits of dried syrup onto the shelf. I loved unscrewing the cap, the way the crystallized sugar made a raspy crackle under the grooved plastic lid.

My father's pancakes were very good, and I'll tell you more about them in a minute, but as is the case for most things cooked in lots of hot fat, it was his French toast that I couldn't get enough of. He would put a cast-iron skillet on the stove and, just to its left, on the tiled counter, a Pyrex brownie pan. Then he'd take up his station in front of them, cracking the eggs into the Pyrex pan and whisking them lightly with milk. Working methodically, he would drag slices of stale bread through the square, pale yellow puddle, soaking them like fat sponges, and then he'd slide them, bubbling and hissing, into the pan. I could smell it from my bedroom at the other end of the house, the smell of custard meeting hot fat. At the table, I'd douse them in syrup and swallow in gulps, almost burning my tongue. His French toast was exceptional, and I'll tell you why: it was cooked in oil, not butter.

It sounds strange, I know. Most people make a face when I tell them, so don't feel bad. I'm used to it. But really, it was tremendous. My father had done his share of comparisons, and for a stellar outcome, he swore by oil. Even in the last weeks of his life, lying in a hospital bed and hooked up to a morphine drip, he was counseling me and my sister on the merits of oil over butter. The hot oil, he explained, seals the surface of the bread, forming a thick, crisp outer crust. Meanwhile, the center melts into a soft, creamy custard, not unlike the texture of a proper bread pudding. The man was clearly onto something, because I've never had a better French toast. *Never.* I don't throw those words around lightly.

For a long time, I wasn't sure I could replicate it. But I figured it was worth a shot. Going the rest of my life without it wasn't a palatable option. So I consulted a few recipes, bought myself a bottle of neutral-tasting oil, and set to work.

The key, and I learned this the hard way, is that you can't pussyfoot around when it comes to the amount of oil. This is no time to worry about calories. It's time to upend the bottle and *pour.* A glug will not do. I don't understand those French toast recipes that call for only a tablespoon or two of fat. How on earth can you get a nice, crispy crust if you don't have lots of hot, bubbling oil? You cannot. Let's not argue about this.

The second point to note is that you need somewhat squishy bread, and it needs to be slightly stale. When it comes to bread for my dinner table, I like rustic, chewy types with thick, craggy crusts, but for French toast, you want something a little softer and more mundane. That way, it easily soaks up the custard, giving you a lovely, moist center.

I can say this all now, but it wasn't easy, I'll tell you that much. I had to eat my way through some pretty crappy French toast to get back to my father's. But I'm happy to report that I finally got it. Or as close as I can get, anyway, given that he never had a recipe to start with.

It was an April morning, I think, when I finally got it right. My father was born in April, so it felt auspicious. It was unseasonably cool that morning, but the sun was out—a rarity in Seattle so early in the season—and I remember thinking that its yellowy light made the new leaves look like tiny stained-glass windows. It reminded me of a poem that my father once wrote on the back of an index card. I found it in his bathroom drawer about a year after he died, when we were going through his old clothes and cufflinks. I think it was intended for my mother, although she let me keep it. I don't think Burg would mind my sharing it, but if he does, I trust he'll find some way to let me know. Or then again, since I've said awfully nice things about his cooking, maybe he'll let me enjoy my French toast in peace.

Sunrise
(A Too-Long Haiku)

The sun bursts
Out of the eastern night
And flames the sky
With joy—
Your smile.

Burg's French Toast

I had to make a lot of phone calls to get this French toast right. My mother, my sister, and my uncle Arnie all had a hand in helping me to develop this recipe. What follows is a result of our pooled memories and my own trial and error.

My mother swears that Burg always made his French toast with day-old "French bread," or its Oklahoma City grocery store equivalent, an oblong loaf of squishy bread with a thin, crisp crust. You're welcome to use any bread you like, so long as it has a soft, light crumb and isn't too dense. Some baguettes work well. I've also used challah, and I think it's nice, although my sister doesn't like it. Whatever you use, make sure that it's a day or two old.

As for the oil, when I say to "coat the bottom of the skillet," I mean to completely coat it. Don't just pour in a little bit and let it run around until it covers the pan. You want a good amount of oil here. You won't be sorry. As my sister says, oil is a "converting force" in French toast cookery. Once you've tried it, you won't go back.

3 large eggs
1 cup whole milk

1 tablespoon sugar

1 teaspoon vanilla extract

¼ teaspoon salt

Pinch of freshly ground nutmeg

Canola or other flavorless oil, for frying

6 to 8 slices day-old bread (see headnote), cut on the diago-
nal, about ¾-inch thick

Pure maple syrup, for serving

Break the eggs into a wide, shallow bowl or, as my dad did, an 8-inch square Pyrex dish. Whisk the eggs to break up the yolks. Add the milk, sugar, vanilla, salt, and nutmeg and whisk to blend.

Place a heavy, large skillet—preferably cast iron—over medium-high heat, and pour in enough oil to completely coat the bottom of the skillet. Let the oil heat until you can feel warmth radiating from it when you hold your hand close over the pan. To test the heat, dip the tip of a finger into the egg mixture—*not* the oil!—and flick a drop into the oil. If it sizzles, it's ready.

Meanwhile, when the oil is almost hot enough, put 2 to 3 slices of bread into the egg mixture, allowing them to rest for 30 seconds to 1 minute per side. They should feel heavy and thoroughly saturated, but they shouldn't be falling apart. Carefully, using tongs, place the slices in the skillet. They should sizzle upon contact, and the oil should bubble busily around the edges. Watch carefully: with hot oil like this, the slices can burn more quickly than you would think. Cook until the underside of each slice is golden brown, 1 to 2 min-utes. Carefully flip and cook until the second side is golden, another 1 to 2 minutes. Remove to a plate lined with a paper towel, and allow to sit for a minute or two before serving.

Repeat with the remaining bread. If, at any point, the bread starts to burn before it has a chance to brown nicely, turn the heat back a little. You want to keep it nice and hot, but not smoking.

Serve hot with maple syrup.

Yield: 6 to 8 slices, serves 2 to 3

THE LAST MEAL

By Todd Kliman

From washingtonian.com

Though he's one of D.C.'s most admired food writers—a former
award-winning columnist for *City Paper*, now food and wine editor
of the glossy monthly the *Washingtonian* and columnist for NPR's
Monkey See Web site—even Todd Kliman was surprised by the
enormous response to this very personal essay.

One of my most enduring memories is of riding through
the southern Maryland countryside on Saturday afternoons with my mother and father, my father at the wheel, all of us
in hot pursuit of the smell of barbecue. My father loved ribs, and
thought nothing of getting in the car and driving an hour and a
half to Charles County to find them. The name of the places have
faded from memory, but not the images: the thick, aromatic smoke
curling above the ramshackle white houses, the three of us at a picnic table, licking our fingers or wiping them on the slices of white
bread that came with an order, the flies buzzing about our heads.

My father loved these kinds of afternoons. Loved the quest.
Lighting out for a destination, not knowing what you'd find, hoping for the best. And even if it was lousy, which sometimes it was,
coming home with a good story.

Most of the friends I grew up with did not venture beyond meat
and potatoes, spaghetti and macaroni-and-cheese, but that was not
my experience. We ate everything. Thai and Spanish and French
and German and Japanese and Korean and Vietnamese and Indian

and Mexican and Greek. My father loved the stuffed grape leaves at Ikaros, in Baltimore, and so I wanted to love them, too. He was the one who turned me on to pupusas. He introduced me to bulgogi and crepes, to hot-and-sour soup and the pleasures of hot pot.

So long as a restaurant had character, had soul, he loved it. Dives, taverns, pubs, it didn't matter; good was good. His mother scolded him, repeatedly, for taking a ten-year-old to a bar, but my father never listened. I spent many a raucous Saturday night in the late, lamented Henckel's—hard by the railroad tracks and probably once a bordello—chowing down on a Chenckelburger as my father and mother worked their way through the foot-high ham sandwiches and knocked back bottles of beer.

The other dive he loved was The Irish Pub, in Baltimore. In the summers of '77 and '78, I could have gone to camp, but I chose to stay home. Instead of archery and swimming, I spent a few days every week in my father's large, light-filled studio, drawing quietly by myself in a corner as he worked on his towering canvasses. Every other week, we went to the Irish Pub for lunch for the magnificent cheeseburgers, thick and oozing juice.

You don't realize the imprint these things make on you, don't realize that you are merely picking up a long thread that has been left for you, until you gain some distance on your past.

When I was in graduate school in the early '90s, I stumbled upon a pool hall and bar whose owner devised a special menu every Friday afternoon to feature the cooking of his grandmother. $6.95 got you a thick slice of grilled meatloaf—you could see slices of garlic and bits of thyme in the meat—skin-on mashed potatoes, gravy and beans. I went back to campus and told my friends, who all said: That dump? And laughed. That night I called my father, who I knew would understand. He said: "Sounds terrific! When are we gonna go?"

I came to writing about food after having written about seemingly everything else—sports, media, subcultures, business, travel, politics, books. And initially, when someone would ask me how I got into food writing, I would answer that I'd sort of stumbled into it. But at some point I knew that simply wasn't true. I had been preparing since I was a little boy.

My father got a kick out of my being a food critic, and I loved taking him out to eat with me. We went everywhere. It was a new chapter in our eating adventures.

He made no distinctions in his mind between a refined restaurant and a casual, unpretentious spot, and paid no heed to reputation or buzz. As an artist, he craved his solitude, which he needed to think and create, and he could be irascible if he didn't have long blocks in the day to work on his paintings and read and refuel the well, as Hemingway put it. But then he longed for contact. He loved the energy of a good restaurant, the sense of possibility in the air. Strangers coming together, blowing off steam, finding community, if only for a couple of hours. A good restaurant restored you, lifted you up, sent you on your way a new man. Often, a host or hostess would show us to a table somewhat out of the way, presuming that a man in his 70s would be looking for a quiet spot. But that wasn't my father, who until several years ago jumped in the car at a moment's notice to drive twelve hours to lecture about his work or about art history at a college or gallery. He preferred to sit at the bar. Somehow, food was always better at the bar. The world looked better at the bar.

When he became sick, I was bewildered. It couldn't be. Daddy? He had the energy of a 40-year-old. I had thought he was indestructible.

He couldn't go out the way he used to, or as often as he used to, but food was still a salve. And still a part of our bond. The day we met with the surgeon to discuss the plan for his cancer treatment, I went out and got a deli tray. Bagels, lox, whitefish. It had been a long and anxious couple of weeks, and most meals he just picked at his plate. But that night, he ate with the old relish.

Chemo and radiation conspired to destroy what was left of his appetite. But somehow, he always found room whenever I brought him a restaurant meal. I often thought that I could save him through food. Every day it was something different, some new meal to look forward to. One night when he was at National Rehab Hospital last April, following his surgery and an infection that sent him into the ICU for weeks, I snuck in shrimp 'n' grits from Vidalia, corn muffins, lemon chess pie. It had been a long day of therapy, probably not the best time to have taken him such refined cooking. He didn't eat much, a few bites of this, a couple bites of that. But that was okay. It was enough to see him nodding his head in appreciation, the deep contentment that crossed his face.

He got stronger, came out, learned to walk again. One day in May he told me he was ready. He wanted to go out again, wanted to accompany me on my rounds.

We covered the area. Virginia, Maryland and D.C. High end and low end. On trips into the gallery in Alexandria where he was artist-in-residence this past year, Artery 717, he dug into fried cod and chips at Eamonn's and lunched on the egg-and-bacon salad at Restaurant Eve (in the bar). He discovered Ethiopian and loved it. He slurped back bowls and bowls of *pho*. And of course, there was barbecue. Lots of barbecue.

He was in and out of the hospital with one problem or another through the summer and fall, but he always came out. And almost as soon as he was home and settled in, he was ready to go to another restaurant.

One day in December, I swung by the house to pick him up to take him to lunch. He was sitting on the hospital bed with his coat on when I walked in the door. "He's been sitting in his coat *for three hours*," my mom said.

I figured we would hit a place close by, something simple. He was checking into the hospital the next day to have another surgery.

We got into the car, and he said: "Let's go somewhere."

"You sure? Are you up for it?"

"I've been looking forward to this all day," he said. "Anywhere, anywhere you want. Virginia, wherever. Anywhere you need to go. I've got all day."

I took him to Present, in Falls Church, a Vietnamese restaurant I had been to before and wanted to write about. It might not have been the sort of place he was drawn to, it didn't have the noise and crackle he loved, but its serenity was comforting, its sense of order. And the menu with its admonishment to live in the moment—in the present—was oddly fitting, with the next day looming so large.

He was stronger than he'd been. He'd gained thirty pounds since the chemo and radiation—most of it, my mother believed, from restaurant food. He didn't eat much of her cooking anymore, but he ate when he was out, or when restaurant food was around. I told him he'd become the equivalent of a social drinker—a social eater.

We took our time, and we talked and talked. He was worried about the surgery. He said he didn't know if he would make it this time. Our anxiety seemed to lift, a little, as we worked our way through the meal. He drank two Vietnamese coffees and took a few bites from every bowl and plate that was on the table. When we left, two and a half hours later, the place was empty.

In the car, I asked him if he wanted to hit another place.

"You're kidding," he said, giving me a long, appraising look. And then, the old adventurer: "Sure, why not?"

On second thought, I decided that it was probably best to get back. My mom was waiting for him. Another time.

For days, he talked about the meal and the coffee. "Terrific, just terrific." He even talked about it in the hospital, in the weeks after his surgery. All his nurses learned just how good the coffee was, how dark and rich, how good a time he'd had.

That afternoon turned out to be our last excursion. He was in the hospital for 61 days. He never did come out, there was no "another time."

I lost more than my father, my best friend, and my mentor when he passed away two weeks ago. I lost my restaurant partner. The adventure won't ever be the same.

THE EGGS AND I

By Francine Prose

From *Saveur*

With a novelist's instinct for vesting emotion in the mundane
details of daily life, Francine Prose—author of *Goldengrove*,
Household Saints, *Blue Angel*, and many others—poignantly
describes a season of chicken-raising, when grief and healing
lay eggshell-deep below life's routines.

Breakfast was salvation. That summer, a stranger might
have thought that we were making a sacrament, or a
fetish, out of breakfast; the eggs still warm from the henhouse, the
toasted homemade bread, the rough-cut bacon, the occasional
squash blossom picked from the garden, stuffed with mozzarella,
and deep-fried. But anyone who knew my husband and me would
have understood that those perfect eggs over easy were life pre-
servers in disguise. Breakfast was making it possible to get through
the rest of the day.

It was the summer of 2005. My mother had died in May. She
was elderly, and her illness was brief, but we were blindsided by
grief. As everyone knows, there's nothing you can do to prepare
for such a loss, but I think that my husband, Howie, and I sensed,
early on, that our fragile psyches would either shatter or endure on
the tensile strength of small (mostly edible) pleasures. That spring,
we doubled the size of the vegetable garden at our house in the
Hudson Valley, and a few weeks after my mother's death we got the
chickens.

Their arrival—and, later, their departure—had much to do with
Michael and Laura, the house's caretakers, who keep the pipes

from freezing in the winter and mow the lawn when we're not around in the summer. An avid reader of *Mother Earth News*, Michael persuaded us that poultry husbandry was simpler and less demanding than we might have imagined. It was Michael who installed the coops in an empty shack, which he proceeded to cover with so many layers of scrap metal that the wiliest fox or coyote (at night, we could hear both giggling and howling nearby) would have needed a blow torch to get in. And it was Michael who found the old woman who sold us the chickens—year-old Rhode Island Reds, five dollars apiece, plump and healthy and gorgeous and ready to start laying.

Our ten chickens made their entrance in unglamorous cardboard boxes. Unpacked and released into their new home, they adapted so quickly that it was as if they'd always lived here. How pretty they were with their glossy, russet feathers, catching and beaming back the sun as they scurried across the green lawn! And who would have imagined that they were so intelligent! The birds almost instantly found their roosts and started pecking at the corn that we tossed at their feet. We watched anxiously, proudly, like the parents of newborns, as they settled into their comfy, straw-lined metal cubbies. Within an hour, one of them began to make restless, clucking noises that, even to a novice, seemed to hint at the imminent arrival of an egg.

"You go get it," Howie told me, as if, being female, I'd be better suited to deal with matters of parturition. I hesitantly nudged the hen aside and groped beneath her warm feathers. My God, there it was. Of course, I knew that's what chickens did, and yet, as I cradled the egg in my palm, I couldn't have been any more surprised if I'd produced it myself. Encouraged by their friend's example, several other hens followed suit, and by the end of the morning we had enough eggs for breakfast.

I remember how shockingly bright the yolks seemed, the dazzling marigold orange that made me wonder, Hey, what were those pale, bleached globs that passed themselves off as egg yolks? But it was the taste that surprised me the most: the sweet, concentrated intensity of flavor; the pure, unadulterated eggness. The difference between a store-bought variety and what our hens had brought forth was akin to the chasm between a garden-ripened tomato and those greenish rocks that you used to see in the super-market before agribusiness discovered a better way to fake the ap-pearance of ripeness. What I remember the most clearly was the sudden recognition that this was the first meal I'd felt like eating, let alone enjoyed, in months.

Simply frying a just-laid egg was an experience completely dif-ferent from anything I'd known before. No matter how distract-edly or awkwardly I turned my eggs over easy, the yolks held their shape, perfect orange islands rising from the cratered lunar land-scape of the crisp-bottomed whites. At some point early in the season, I read an article that said that free-range eggs were lower in cholesterol than their mass-produced counterparts. I didn't check the research; I didn't wait to read the statistics. I took it as license to eat as many eggs as I wanted, without anxiety or guilt. From then on, there were sponge cakes, eggy homemade pastas, frittatas, clafoutis, flans, and wobbly, delicious puddings. No matter how many times I'd been warned about the possibly harmful ef-fects of overindulgence in omelettes, to eat eggs that summer was to choose life over death. Our hearts had been broken, and the notion of heart-healthy had come to seem beside the point. The closest I came to pure happiness during those difficult months was when I was eating a breakfast that Howie cooked, one that I'll never forget: two fried eggs draped atop paella left over from the night before, fried until it too had formed a delectably dark crust.

THE BEST THING about the evenings was the way the chickens somehow knew that it was time to wrap it up and how they scrab-bled in an uneven line toward the nice, locked-down henhouse, where they would be safe for the night.

I felt gratitude toward our chickens. I wanted them to be happy. That was why, at the beginning, we took "free range" too literally. It was amazing how quickly the hens discovered the flower beds, how they enjoyed digging up and scattering the flower bulbs. Just before our entire farm began to look like a barnyard, Michael built the chickens a large enclosure that they could reduce to dust, in which they could then happily frolic. Eventually, a neighbor help-fully pointed out that a chicken's disposition and productivity had less to do with real estate than—as is so often the case throughout the animal kingdom—with loneliness and sex.

We needed a rooster. The search for one brought us to an odd local institution: a shelter dedicated to the rescue of farm animals who would otherwise have been eaten. The shelter's standards for adoption were so selective and strict that, we were warned, a home visit might be required before we could have the roosters. The director, an idealistic young woman (her chest crisscrossed with angry welts inflicted by a furious rabbit) took us on a tour that featured the largest hogs I'd ever seen, including one that had been saved from a pig race in Colorado, a contest in which the winner received the prize of being killed and roasted. I didn't ask how the hog had gotten here from the Rockies, nor did I ask about all the humans in need of rescue, perhaps with plates of roast pork. I kept quiet. I wanted the roosters.

And, oh, how desirable they were, strutting around the poultry yard, switching their ebony tail feathers banded with butterfly wing blue, their puffy chests covered by plumage that ranged from bright yellow to deep brown. I say roosters because there were two. "Two mellow brothers from Woodstock" was how the director described them. They had to be adopted together. Were we willing? Yes, we were.

We took them home in cages and set them free, and within a matter of minutes the two mellow brothers had gang-raped all ten of our hens. For those who have not watched chicken sex—well, it's not a pretty sight. Rooster love is nasty, brutish, and short and often involves the rooster's stepping on the chicken's head. I watched in horrified fascination, and when it was over I wondered at the utterly strange things that have the power to distract us even briefly from grief.

BREAKFAST BY BREAKFAST, we got through the summer, inching back toward what I suppose you could call normal life. I talked about the chickens a lot. It seemed that chickens and books were the only subjects I could safely discuss without the fear that tears would well up in my eyes.

Whatever we might have thought of the roosters' courtship style, the chickens seemed to like it. They got fat and gave us so many eggs that we were giving them away to friends, which, I can tell you, is a wonderful thing to be able to do. The roosters developed a dominance pattern. The alpha-mellow brother ruled the roost, as they say, and kept all the hens to himself, while the less powerful brother vented his frustration by (ineffectually, thank heaven) attacking our daughter-in-law and a friend's son. The beta rooster started to scare me.

Fall came. We returned to the city and went up to the country on weekends. When we drove into the driveway on our first return trip, we rushed to say hi to the chickens before we walked into the house. Over a few weeks, one of the chickens and one of the roosters had escaped from the fencing and been killed—one by a fox or a coyote, one by a neighbor's dog.

In October, Michael got a puppy. And in November he called to say that the dog had proved smarter than the foxes and the coyotes. Michael was truly sorry. All the chickens were dead. I cried, but in my heart of hearts I was a little relieved. I'd been worried about how the chickens might do if the winter proved severe.

A summer passed, then another. We still talk about getting chickens, eating those fresh eggs again. But Michael has a more demanding job, beyond taking care of us, and neither Howie nor I wanted to devote the time or energy that animal husbandry, however undemanding, demands.

But I can still see them crossing the lawn; how shiny and attractive they were, how pleasant it was to watch them. And I can remember exactly how the morning sun lasered across the kitchen and sought out two blazing-orange yolks surrounded by buttery coronas of white, in the center of a blue plate. I'm more thankful than I can say for that sweet gesture of condolence. Those chickens gave me their everything, and I haven't forgotten.

Now, when a friend is suffering, there's advice that I long to give but never do. I suppose I'm afraid of sounding flippant or facile, of hurting the already wounded. But, dear reader, let me give it to you. You can take it if you want. When things are really, really bad, if possible, raise chickens.

Recipe Index

PERMISSIONS ACKNOWLEDGMENTS

ABOUT THE EDITOR

HOLLY HUGHES is a writer, the former executive editor of Fodor's Travel Publications, and author of *Frommer's 500 Places to Take the Kids Before They Grow Up*, *Frommer's 500 Places to See Before They Disappear*, and *Frommer's 500 Places for Food and Wine Lovers*.

SUBMISSIONS FOR
BEST FOOD WRITING 2010

Submissions and nominations for *Best Food Writing 2010* should be forwarded no later than May 15, 2009, to Holly Hughes at *Best Food Writing 2010*, c/o Da Capo Press, 11 Cambridge Center, Cambridge MA 02142, or e-mailed to best.food@perseusbooks.com. We regret that, due to volume, we cannot acknowledge receipt of all submissions.